Between Stillness and Motion

Between Stillness and Motion

Film, Photography, Algorithms

Edited by Eivind Røssaak

AMSTERDAM UNIVERSITY PRESS

The publication of this book is made possible by a grant from the Norwegian Research Council.

Front cover illustration: Tobias Rehberger, ON OTTO, film still (Kim Basinger watching THE LADY FROM SHANGHAI), 2007. Courtesy Fondazione Prada, Milan
Back cover illustration: Still from Gregg Biermann's SPHERICAL COORDINATES (2005)

Cover design: Kok Korpershoek, Amsterdam
Lay-out: JAPES, Amsterdam

ISBN   978 90 8964 212 7 (paperback)
ISBN   978 90 8964 213 4 (hardcover)
e-ISBN   978 90 4851 209 6
NUR   674

Contents

The Algorithmic Turn

Archives in Between

Acknowledgements

This book would not have been possible without the help of many generous colleagues and supportive institutions. My sincere thanks go to my former colleagues in the cross-disciplinary research project *Media Aesthetics* at the University of Oslo and the University of Copenhagen: Liv Hausken, Ina Blom, Arild Fetveit, and Susanne Østby Sæther. The idea for this book was born and developed during this project. This research project was financed by the Norwegian Research Council and generously hosted by the Department of Media and Communication at the University of Oslo. Thanks also to the National Library of Norway for support in the book's final stages. Most importantly, thanks to the contributors for taking part in the joint book seminar at Lysebu Conference Center overlooking the woods of Oslo in 2008, where these ideas were consolidated and developed during lectures, presentations, conversations and idle talks into the night. Thank you also to the Society of Cinema and Media Studies for hosting several of the papers at their conferences over the past decade. Talks and conversations with colleagues and students at these conferences and at our respective universities and institutions also helped foster these ideas. Thanks also to Christian Refsum, Nevena Ivanova, Jihoon Felix Kim, Jon Inge Faldalen, D.N. Rodowick, W.J.T. Mitchell, Mary Ann Doane and Alexander Galloway for inspiration and idle talks, and finally, to Thomas Elsaesser for making this publishing project possible. Thanks also to our tireless copy editor, wordsmith Kiersten Leigh Johnson.

Eivind Røssaak
Oslo, Berlin and New York, March/April 2011

Introduction

The Still/Moving Field: An Introduction

Eivind Røssaak

This collection of essays seeks to introduce an affirmative critique of and fascination for the different uses of stillness and motion in a wide variety of expressions – pre-cinematic, cinematic, post-cinematic and new media. The debate on stillness and motion is as old as art history, but within cinema studies, it became the subject of widespread debate during the 1970s. At its root, it was informed by apparatus theory and the idea of negating movement through enlightenment. Its axiom was that cinematic movement is an illusion, that movement is an "ideological effect of the cinematic apparatus."[1] Any artistic deconstruction of motion through ruptures or the revelation of a series of stills was rapidly integrated into this critical program. The still image was the hidden or even repressed basis behind the industrial illusion of cinematic motion.

Today, we are experiencing a broad range of cinematic turns within the art scene as well as a technological revolution through the use of computer-generated imagery, which means that the entire critical program, based as it was on the materiality of celluloid, has lost some of its initial urgency.[2] The use of the interplay between stillness and motion must be recontextualized. Fresh concepts are needed to see these works in a broader, more complex media aesthetic environment. We want to investigate the possibility of a thicker description, which allows contributors to discover and open up the field through close analysis of specific works and media practices. Contemporary media rely on a complex connection between the forces and intensities of time and speed relations, which affect the body of the spectator or user. The body is not just the carrier of a personal history, but a storage site and an intensified receptive surface in a media-saturated society. Thus, the body belongs to a history of media and mediations. A crucial part of this embodied media history involves the encounters with audiovisual material such as in Tobias Rehberger's work ON OTTO, discussed in Ina Blom's article. Mediations and bodies participate in a larger collective and technical environment, which instantiates and re-imagines the history of media and affects.

From Optical Toys to Computer Imaging

In a strange way, the history of images between the still and the moving returns to the very origins of cinema; in fact, even earlier. The viewing pleasure of pre-cinematic optical toys such as the thaumatrope, the stroboscopic disc and the phenakistiscope stems from the paradoxical difference between what they look like before and after the toy is activated. It is a mind-blowing ride from stasis to kinesis and back. Early film exhibitors also addressed this experience. They were concerned with demonstrating the abilities of the new medium of the *ciné-matographe*, as the Lumière Brothers called their multipurpose machine. Time and again, they would astonish their audiences with their special presentation technique. Initially, the brothers Lumière presented the moving image as a projected still, before the projectionist brought the image to life by cranking up the machine.

One hundred years later, one of the most striking features in contemporary cinematic practices in movie theaters, art galleries, and new media platforms is the frequent use of slow motion and other techniques of delay. It is as if the moving image has become increasingly refashioned in the direction of demonstrating its abilities to remain motionless, or to move in ways that are barely visible. Several moving image artworks, particularly the ones in galleries and museums, seem to excel in featuring indiscernible differences between motion and stillness, in stops, still frames, freeze effects, slow-motion effects, and even stuttering. According to art historian Boris Groys, the contemporary cinema of delay and slow motion – from THE MATRIX to 24 HOUR PSYCHO – negotiates with its other – immobility – as a way of understanding its relationship to both earlier forms of representation and to the mediascape of the contemporary consumer. As Groys writes,

> In the course of its long history of antagonism between the media, film has earned the right to act as the icon of secularizing modernism. Inversely, by being transferred into the traditional realms of art, film itself has, in turn, increasingly become the subject of iconoclastic gestures: by means of new technology such as video, computer, and DVD, the motion of film has been halted midstream and dissected.[3]

In this way, cinema comes to reflect upon its destiny in a new media environment. The contemporary examples are many: from Bill Viola to Douglas Gordon, Sam Taylor-Wood, Sharon Lockhart and others. While some artists prefer the latest media techniques like digital artist Jim Campbell, others hark back to earlier techniques or combine new and old techniques like in the avant-garde filmmaker Ken Jacobs' most recent works.

We have also seen a growing awareness and conscious reflexivity regarding mediation and new technology in pop videos as well as in commercial cinema. Directors like Michel Gondry operate in both fields. The fame of a blockbuster movie like THE MATRIX (Andy and Larry Wachowski, 1999) rests to a large extent on its striking use of special effects such as the so-called bullet-time effect. This was a new, never-before-seen combination of slow motion and frozen movement effects that was immediately copied in countless other cinematic practices around the turn of the 21st century. These experiments are now often mimicked in vernacular video and disseminated on platforms like YouTube. The Spanish artist Sergio Prego devoted a series of low-budget videos to strange versions of the bullet-time effect involving jumps and splashes of large chunks of thick paint. It has become clear that the effect actually stems from the artist Tim McMillan's frozen-time experiments from 1980, and even further, back to Eadweard Muybridge's photographic experiments from the 1870s. Like a micro-genre in cinema, certain still/moving effects such as the bullet-time effect seem to have travelled through all of the different registers of cinematic practice from the big screen to YouTube, and from art galleries to computer games developed by a new generation of software artists producing a variety of generative or interactive images, like in Mario Klingemann's work.

The aftermath of the 100th anniversary of cinema and the challenges from new media have led to a reconsideration of what the moving image is and can be, revealing the contingency of a certain order of the moving image we have called cinema. This order is now passé. The moving image is no longer simply something to be observed during a 90-minute screening in a darkened movie theatre. Perhaps classical or institutional cinema will end up being the parenthesis and not the norm when it comes to studying the life and history of the moving image.[4] The ubiquity of the moving image in contemporary art and communications has reopened the key question – what is a moving image? – in new ways.

Assembling the Field: The Three Phases

The questioning of the moving image is no longer just the activity of film scholars alone. It spans several disciplines from media, film, theatre, dance and art history to anthropology and into architecture, information science, technology and biology. This collection of essays tries to assemble the investigation of the moving image around the emergence of the cross-disciplinary field we tentatively call the still/moving field. This is a vital arena for inquiry regarding the moving image after the end of cinema as we used to know it. Titles from the past decade such as: *Stillness and Time: Photography and the Moving Image; Between Film and Screen: Modernism's Photo Synthesis; Death 24x a Second: Stillness and the Moving Image; Still Moving: Between Cinema and Photography; Le cinéma de l'immobilité, L'Entre-Image; Le temps exposé: Le Cinéma de la salle au musée; Freeze Frames: Zum Verhältnis von Fotografie und Film; The Still/Moving Image: Cinema and the Arts; Viva Fotofilm: Bewegt/Unbewegt, Cinema before Film; The Cinematic* and *Stillness in a Mobile World,* bear witness to the emergence of a still/moving field.[5]

For the sake of a tentative overview, I would argue that we can organize the still/moving field in three partially chronological phases of mutually dependent questioning: a turn to the *in-between*, a turn to history, and a turn to algorithms. The turn to the in-between was, not surprisingly, first taken up in France. It stems from Raymond Bellour's long engagement with what he calls "l'entre-images", an ambiguous French neologism with multiple meanings: the between-the-images, the in-between-images, or the images in between, and it deals, in many ways, with the aesthetic and ontological tensions and passages between photography and film, stillness and motion.[6] A key reference point in the debate is Roland Barthes's *Camera Lucida: Note sur la photographie* (1980), where he radically distinguishes between photography and cinema. In one essay, Barthes even comes close to asserting that the essence of cinema is found in the still.[7] A few years later, Gilles Deleuze wrote his seminal philosophical study *Cinéma I-II* (1983 and 1985), in which he opposes the semiological gaze (Christian Metz' theory in particular) and anything that tends to immobilize film, like calling film a language or asserting that cinematic movement is the result of an illusion, etc. To him, movement and time become the all-determining factors for understanding cinema. Raymond Bellour's position is important for understanding the genesis of this field. In one of his most important articles on the still/moving image, he places himself between Barthes and Deleuze, and between Freud and Bergson; ultimately, between the still and the moving, to explore the blind spots of these two positions. Bellour writes that

> There is one category of time not considered by Gilles Deleuze in his dynamic taxonomy of images: the interruption of movement, the often unique, fugitive, yet perhaps decisive instant when cinema seems to be fighting against its very principle, if this is the movement-image. [...] what kinds of instants does the interruption of movement imply?[8]

To Bellour, the interruption of movement emphasizes the fact that a film "cannot be reduced to the overly natural time of illusion, indexing a time-space at the juncture of the visible and the invisible".[9] Ultimately, immobility may produce a *movement* of emotion or the intellect not available in the movement-image. These *movements* of immobility are explored further by George Baker, Christa Blümlinger and Liv Hausken in the present collection.

I would also place important contributions by Serge Daney and Laura Mulvey in this turn to the in-between. Their contributions are of a more political character. They investigated how the still or uses of stillness in cinema also address issues of psycho-social management and control. Laura Mulvey, in her germinal article on "Visual Pleasure and Narrative Cinema" (1975), asks why the representation of women in cinema very often involves moments of stillness and pause in the narrative. Women become an indispensable element of spectacle; "her visual presence tends to work against the development of a story line, to freeze the flow of action in moments of erotic contemplation." The woman as an "alien presence" has no other value than "to-be-looked-at-ness," Mulvey argues.[10] Daney was also concerned with how cinema organizes the visual through the freeze. As the language of modernist films was appropriated by television, he observed that techniques of delay and the freeze-framing of an object would rapidly become the visual language of commercials and consumer industries.[11] Now, a new generation of Hollywood directors like the Wachowski Brothers (THE MATRIX, 1999), McG (CHARLIE'S ANGELS, 2000) and Baz Luhrmann would soon reappropriate the language of advertising back into cinema to create a new kind of cinematic reflexivity on visual culture through rapid changes and cuts between fixity and movement.

The turn toward the in-between opened up an important aesthetic and political line of questioning with regard to the moving image, but it didn't produce much new knowledge as far as early film history is concerned. Philosophers such as Gilles Deleuze viewed early cinema simply as a primitive cinema, unable to create the complexities of modern time-images. This would change with the emergence of what has been called the New Film Historians. During the 1970s and 1980s, New Film Historians such as Noël Burch, Tom Gunning, André Gaudreault, Thomas Elsaesser, Charles Musser and filmmakers like Ken Jacobs would discover the riches of early film in multiple ways, and Kemp Niver's work to make available the large paper print collection at the Library of Congress would instigate much new research. Burch and Gunning have concluded that early film must be regarded as a system that functions according to a different logic of presentation than the modes and rules arriving later with the so-called classical narrative cinema.[12] The turn toward history also led to important new research into the complexities of pre-cinema. Today, the work of Eadweard Muybridge and Etienne-Jules Marey is no longer simply viewed as primitive photography leading up to cinema, but as two complex and distinct approaches to the analysis of motion. While Marey produced most of his sequential images on a single plate using a photographic gun, Muybridge used a battery of cameras, each of which was separated from its neighbor by a variable distance, depending on the subject. One could perhaps say that Marey develops the fixed-plate chronophotography into a registration of movements *in time,* each image separated by equidistant intervals, while using a single fixed lens. Muybridge develops the style into a registration of movements from different places *in space.*[13] In striking ways, Muybridge's style is taken up again in later digital capturing techniques such as the bullet-time effect in THE MATRIX (1999). This research into pre-cinema and early cinema has instigated new ways of looking into the relationship between stillness and motion.[14] Tom Gunning's, Mark B.N. Hansen's and Trond Lundemo's articles in the present collection relate to this research. If Mulvey could be placed within the turn toward the in-between, I would place Mary Ann Doane's study of cinematic time and Linda Williams' study of stilled and moving bodies in the turn toward history. Even if Williams addresses many of the concerns that Mulvey raises, the difference between them lies most obviously in Williams' keen awareness of how both film theory (such as psychoanalysis) *and* cinematic techniques from Muybridge's period to those employed today are "historically determined – and determining – mechanisms of power and pleasure."[15]

The turn toward the algorithm is the last paradigm that I will consider in this reconfiguration of the still/moving field. New technologies and new artistic strategies produce a new interrogation of the image. The turn toward the algorithm could, as Laura Marks and others would argue, as easily be called a turn toward information, code, the digital, the interface or the software.[16] Researchers are not yet in agreement with regard to exactly where the key change is to be found, but what all these terms have in common is a critique of the image, in the sense that much of critical attention has been directed toward the instability and malleability of the image. The image is no longer a given, but an instantiation of code to be algorithmically manipulated, processed and disseminated in endless new ways. D.N. Rodowick argues in his work *The Virtual Life of Film,* that the reason for this, is that while the relationship between input and output is continuous with regard to the analogue image, the relationship is discontinuous with regard to the digital image. While Eivind Røssaak starts his discussion in this volume at this juxtaposition, Mark B.N. Hansen focuses on the role of the interface in contradistinction to a strong contemporary tradition. Jay David Bolter and Richard Grusin stated in their now classic work *Remediation* that new media tend to remediate older media like the page, the book, film or photography, and Lev Manovich argued in his *The Language of New Media* that with the computer "cinema is now becoming *the* cultural interface, a toolbox for all cultural communication, overtaking the printed word."[17] This line of argument tends to lose what is singular, different, and, indeed, "new" with new media, according to Hansen; new media develop a visual interface onto new ways of engaging with the world, with what he calls "movement variations." Hansen addresses in particular how new media interfaces can foster a transduction between the human and the inhuman in ways not conceivable with cinema.[18] While both Manovich and Hansen address the interface as a new and flexible gateway to old or new experiences either in terms of visuality or of embodiment, Thomas Elsaesser thinks of interfaces "not primarily as visual, and not so much as subject/object, inside/out, becomings or involving movement, but instead instantiating invisible passages, bridges or zones, transit points or security areas continuously upsetting the dichotomies of inside/outside, center/edge, image/frame etc." He quotes Alexander Galloway who writes: "Let me point out that the word 'interface' has been unfortunately infected by a colloquial usage designating screens, keyboards, controllers, and so on; I use the term instead in the specific computer-scientific sense of an algorithmically and linguistically determined bridge of inputs and outputs between two different code libraries."[19] Galloway criticizes fundamentally the *what-you-see-is-what-you-get* logic (WYSI-WYG-logic) of the interface. "The difficulty of the WYSIWYG logic is that it is undeniably a lie [...]. The interface lies about what it is doing in order to deliver a more perfect experiential truth. Software knows it is true that it is false [...], it is necessary to demonstrate that the transparency of the new and the opacity of the old are not natural qualities of media, but are the results of socially and historically specific processes," Galloway writes.[20] The interface is the result of syntactic techniques of encoding that exist behind the interface to create specific effects. The interface is seen as a "control allegory"; it "asks a question and, in so doing suggests an answer."[21] Systems theory and algorithms become key factors in understanding this new regime of control and manipulation. In other words, the algorithmic turn implies both a critique of the visual layer of our culture and a new way of understanding communication and aesthetics altogether. Mark B.N. Hansen, Thomas Elsaesser, Arild Fetveit, Trond Lundemo, Ina Blom and Eivind Røssaak demonstrate different ways of navigating through this landscape in the present collection.

The Topics

Aesthetic astonishment and reflexivity have always nurtured the still/moving field. The increased attention toward ambiguity and playfulness at stake in the construction of the contemporary moving image, in the commercial cinema theatres, in art galleries and on the Web, often demonstrate a self-conscious research into the histories, uses and lives of images in an expanded media field. Part of this reflexivity appears in a renewed interest in older, even pre-cinematic techniques, and their media archaeological relationship to new media and image technologies. This collection of articles traces these foldings and implosions of the moving image theoretically and through examples. If Barthes began his research into film from the still, this collection of articles commences with motion. Motion, here, is not considered an illusion based on a series of still images. Indeed, the collection starts out with motion as a fact within the arts even before cinema, in the form of philosophical toys. Another common feature among the contributions is the keen interest in figuring out how forms of motion and movement variation relate to certain affects and bodily emotions, and, as in Blümlinger's, Blom's and Lundemo's contributions, in particular, to certain forms of power.

The book is divided into five sections, each dealing with the topic of stillness and motion from a specific angle. The first section, "Philosophies of Motion", reinvestigates the question of whether images are actually in motion at all. Tom Gunning's article, "The Play Between Still and Moving Images: Nineteenth-Century 'Philosophical Toys' and their Discourse" explores how the persistence of vision thesis promoted the idea that perception deals primordially with still images and represses the phenomenon of moving vision, which persists in the description of the moving image as an "illusion". By revisiting the scientific discourse on the processes of vision and the historical documents that first set out to present and promote the new philosophical toys in the nineteenth century such as the thaumatrope, the stroboscopic disc, the phenakistiscope, the anorthoscope and the zoetrope, Gunning proposes a new understanding of motion informed by phenomenology.

Mark B.N. Hansen continues his investigation into how new media engages the body in new ways in his essay, "Digital Technics Beyond the 'Last Machine': Thinking Digital Media with Hollis Frampton". In his essay, "For a Metahistory of Film", filmmaker Hollis Frampton proposes moving beyond the divide between photography and cinema. Frampton embraced the wisdom of sculptor August Rodin who, in reference to Muybridge, argued that "It is photograph [sic] which is truthful, and the artist who lies, for in reality time does stop". What lies behind Frampton's embrace of Rodin's position here is, however, not what we might first think, for in Frampton's case, what is patently not at issue is some claim for the superiority of one medium over another, in our case, of photography over cinema. Rather, what is at stake is a distinction between two types of time: what Frampton calls historical and ecstatic time, respectively. He also links temporal ecstasies, and, hence, temporal caesura, to subjectivity. Frampton is busy thinking of cinema as the "Last Machine", as an "infinite cinema", a virtual or conceptual cinema that registers all appearances of the world, taken from all possible vantage points, regardless of its artifactual embodiment. According to Hansen, Frampton's aesthetic is appropriate for a media age that is constituted on top of digital *technics*, and more specifically, for a situation in which media forms are outputs that, in a crucial sense, are technically discontinuous from technical materiality. Hansen proposes exploring the aesthetic potentialities of digital technics in the wake of Frampton's conception of infinite cinema.

While the previous section addresses the inherent ability of images to take on various types of motion, the next section, "The Use of Freeze and Slide Motion", highlights film's affinity with arrest and the still image. Christa Blümlinger investigates the use of freeze-frame, or the visual standstill, in R.W. Fassbinder's films. When Garrett Stewart defined the figure of the freeze-frame as a reproduced, projected individual image that entails the suspension of the sequence and the negation of the filmic image, he considers this form of interruption – with an eye on the narrative cinema – as having the potential of a critical inquiry and the possibility of 'filmic reflexivity' within a narration. To Blümlinger, this cannot always be taken for granted. Each case has to be analyzed concretely. While the freeze-frame in the classical cinema is quite rare, it's only because the classical cinema developed other modes of stasis and fascination. Serge Daney argues that advertising, video clips, and the films based on these forms today mobilize an excess of visual standstills that become a form of exchange between visual regimes. Blümlinger shows how various stylistic figures found in Fassbinder's films have, despite the seriality of some productions, led some critics to place his work in modern auteurist cinema. But the figure of the standstill in Fassbinder's work has seldom been noted until now, probably because it often appears marginally – in a literal sense. For Fassbinder, the freeze-frame was a specific form of visual standstill that can be found as a figure of brief cessation or sudden interruption usually at the beginning or end of his films. To Blümlinger, Fassbinder's standstill by no means just represents a kind of banalized repetition of a modern stylistic figure in the wake of the New Wave, but rather is tied to a certain idea of film and a kind of media theory.

Liv Hausken's "The Temporality of the Narrative Slide-Motion Film" elaborates some of the challenges posed when one explores a slide-motion film. Visually, a slide-motion film like AÑO UÑA consists of photographic stills, mainly sequences of freeze-frames. Auditively, it is like any live action film, with music, diegetic sound, sound effects, and, unlike Chris Marker's well-known LA JETÉE, AÑO UÑA even contains dialogue. The tension between the past and the present, the absent and the arriving, is, nevertheless, quite different from the film expression of LA JETÉE, not least because of the architecture of the diegetic space. Through an analysis of the spatiotemporal complexity of the narrative slide-motion film, Hausken tries to show how these films seem to demonstrate the materiality of the moving image as well as question nearly all of the basic film analytic terms.

"The Cinematic Turn in the Arts" section is devoted to three investigations of artistic strategies connected to the cinematic turn within the art scene. In "Stop/ Motion", Thomas Elsaesser initially gives a broad overview of some of the most discussed artists and works in this trend, before moving on to discuss the more complex issues facing both cinema and the museum when they marry. "One of the most powerful forces at work in bringing museum and moving image into a new relation with each other is the programmatic reflexivity of the museum and the self-reference of the modern art-work", Elsaesser writes. Entering a museum is like crossing a special kind of threshold, of seeing objects not only in their material specificity and physical presence, but also in understanding this 'there-ness' as a special kind of statement, as both a question and a provocation. This 'produced presence' of modernist art is both echoed and subverted by moving image installations, often in the form of new modes of performativity and self-display that tend to involve the body of the artist.

In After "Photography's Expanded Field", George Baker revisits his very in-fluential essay, "Photography's Expanded Field", to extrapolate on the forms and possibilities opened up by the expansion of the medium of photography and its relationship to motions and emotions as forms of subjectivity. He speci-fically investigates the motivations for why so many contemporary artists posi-tion their practice between mediums, or engage in the cinematic opening of the still photograph. Another way of stating this radicalization would be to say that Baker's concern today is less with the 'objective' or structural mapping per-formed in his earlier essay; the interpenetration of forms, the expansion of med-iums like the photograph also has a "subjective" logic, and thus Baker turns to the desiring politics of the expansion of photography.

In "On ON OTTO: Moving Images and the New Collectivity", Ina Blom inves-tigates the German visual artist Tobias Rehberger's ambitious 'film' project ON OTTO, which is not really a motion picture, but a project that involves all of the production steps and competences of a normal 'Hollywood' movie, including roles for, among others, Kim Basinger, Danny DeVito, Willem Dafoe, Justin Henry and music composed by Ennio Morricone. Blom considers this project as part of a series of works in the field of contemporary art that explore media apparatuses as complex systems intimately intertwined with the practices of life and labor. Blom rethinks or recontextualizes the questions of stillness, cin-ematic motion and collective emotion through the multiple cinematic materials in the project ON OTTO, which are displayed, not primarily on screens, but in an architectural/sculptural environment that addresses social structures in a new way.

The fourth section, "The Algorithmic Turn", revisits some of the topics from the first section and explores how the logic of the computer generates a new audiovisual culture. While the first section discusses the issues in a more phenomenological and philosophical sense, this section explores a series of contemporary pop videos and "software cinema". In "Mutable Temporality In and Beyond the Music Video: An Aesthetic Post-Production", Arild Fetveit delineates a new post-production aesthetic. He sees the aesthetic strategy of the sampling of pre-existing material across different media as prevalent in a range of articulations across the worlds of both art and media. New forms of temporality have also evolved with extended uses of slow motion and curious forms of mutable temporalities, where the movements of bodies are controlled not only during the recording, but also in the later re-working of the footage. What emerges from these developments, according to Fetveit, is a new post-production aesthetic, where post-human embodiment can sometimes be observed.

Eivind Røssaak, in his "Algorithmic Culture: Beyond the Photo/film Divide", investigates how the still/moving issue has been transformed from a matter concerning media specificities to one that has become part of a larger culture of interactivity and exchange. He opposes the nostalgia for authenticity and indexicality that is so prevalent in traditional film studies and contends that digital images are no longer one image, but a multiplicity, beyond the photo/film divide and always open to new forms. This alters some of the typical uses of stillness and motion within new media experiments. Rather than relying on the notion of remediation, Røssaak develops a notion of the moving image as a processual and sensitive system governed by algorithms and machines attuned to the nervous system of a collective memory. Røssaak presents a series of examples to explore the new dimension of the multiple image. His examples come from the history of photography, the software cinema of Ken Jacobs and Gregg Biermann and from newer interactive Web media such as Mario Klingemann's work.

The final section, "Archives in Between" includes Trond Lundemo's discussion of Albert Kahn's archive, *Les Archives de la planète*, which has significant ramifications for comprehending the relationship between film and photography and contemporary digitalization. Albert Kahn created *Les Archives de la planète* between 1912 and 1932 using color photography, film and (to a lesser extent) stereoscopy. This means that the archive, both conceptually and physically, depends on connections and divisions between still and moving images. These intersections between the still and the moving depict a constituting heterogeneity of the archive subsequent to the introduction of time-based media. "Movement is also at the core of the entrance of the anonymous and the mass into visibility", Lundemo asserts. Kahn wanted to make an "inventory of the surface of the globe inhabited and developed by man as it presents itself at the start of the 20th century in order to fix once and for all the practices, the aspects and the modes of human activity, whose fatal disappearance is only a question of time." With few exceptions, the film shots in *Les Archives de la planète* were not edited for exploitation and remained as raw "rushes" to be revived at a later time. The archive, according to Lundemo, was based on Kahn's anticipation that various modes of human activity were about to undergo a "fatal disappearance". These images describe places one cannot visit in the future, and are as such emblematic of modern mankind's experience. The survival of these images now depends on the convergence of various media as a result of their digitization. Lundemo discusses in great detail both the problems and the possibilities of this digital encoding of our photographic and filmic past.

Notes

1. Jean-Louis Baudry, "Ideological Effects of the Basic Cinematographic Apparatus" [1970]. *Film Quarterly*. Vol. 28. No. 2. Winter. 1974-1975, 39-47.
2. The "cinematic turn" was perhaps first elaborated by Raymond Bellour in his catalogue article, "La double Hélice" for the exhibition *Passages de l'image*, curated by R. Bellour, C. David, C. Van Assche. See the catalogue *Passages de l'image*, ed. R. Bellour, C. David, C. Van Assche (Paris: Editions du Centre Pompidou, 1989). The article is available in English as "The Double Helix" in *Electronic Culture: Technology and Visual Representation*, ed. T. Drucker (New York: Aperture, 1996).
3. Boris Groys,"Iconoclasm as an Artistic Device: Iconoclastic Strategies in Film", trans. M. Partridge. In *Iconoclash: Beyond the Image Wars in Science, Religion, and Art*. Eds. Bruno Latour and Peter Wibel. (Cambridge, MA: MIT Press, 2002), p. 282.
4. Siegfried Zielinski, in his *Audiovisions: Cinema and Television as entr'acts in history* (Amsterdam: Amsterdam University Press, 1999 [German orig. 1989]), has called the institutional cinema an "intermezzo" or "entr'acte" in history.
5. See *Stillness and Time: Photography and the Moving Image*, David Green and Joanna Lowry (eds.) (Brighton: Photoworks, 2006), *Still Moving: Between Cinema and Photography* Karen Beckman and Jean Ma (eds.) (Durham: Duke University Press, 2008), Garrett Stewart: *Between Film and Screen: Modernism's Photo Synthesis* (Chicago: University of Chicago Press, 1999), Laura Mulvey: *Death 24x a Second: Stillness and the Moving Image* (London: Reaktion Books, 2006), Ludovic Cortade: *Le cinéma de l'immobilité: style, politique, reception* (Paris: Publications de la Sorbonne, 2008), Raymond Bellour: *L'Entre-Images: Photo, Cinéma, Video* (Paris: Éditions de la Différence, 1990) and *L'Entre-Images 2: Mots, Images* (Paris: P. O. L. Trafic, 1999), Dominique Païni: *Le temps exposé: Le Cinéma de la salle au musée* (Paris: Cahiers du Cinema, 2002); *Freeze Frames: Zum Verhältnis von Fotografie und Film* (eds.) Stefanie Diekmann and Winfried Gerling (Bielefeld: Transcript, 2010), Eivind Røssaak: *The Still/Moving Image: Cinema and the Arts* (Saarbrücken: Lambert Academic Publishing, 2010), *Viva Fotofilm: Bewegt/unbewegt* (eds.) Gusztáv Hámos, Katja Pratschke and Thomas Tode (Marburg: Schüren Verlag, 2009), François Albera and Maria Tortajada: *Cinema before Film: Media Epistemology in the Modern Era* (Amsterdam: Amsterdam University Press, 2010), David Campany, Ed., *The Cinematic* (Cambridge, MA, London: MIT

Press Whitechapel, 2007) and *Stillness in a Mobile World,* eds. David Bissell and Gillian Fuller (London: Routledge, 2011).

6. "'L'entre-images' is an expression that I have invented to summarize all the types of passages between photo, film, video and even digital images (just appearing at the time)." It is untranslatable as such in English. (Raymond Bellour, e-mail to the author, April, 2011).

7. Roland Barthes, "The Third Meaning", *Image, Music, Text,* trans. Stephen Heath, (New York: Hill and Wang, 1977).

8. Raymond Bellour, "The Film Stilled" [orig. "L'interruption, l'instant", 1987], *Camera Obscura* 24/1991, p. 99, 105. Bellour's pioneering work on stillness and motion in its many disguises and disparate contexts is collected in the two volumes *L'Entre-Images 1-2* (1990-1999) and reviewed by Dana Polan in *Discourse* 16.2 (Winter 1993-94), p. 196-200.

9. Raymond Bellour, "The Film Stilled", *Camera Obscura* 24/1991, p. 108.

10. Laura Mulvey, "Visual Pleasure and Narrative Cinema" [1975] in Braudy and Cohen (eds.), *Film Theory and Criticism* (Oxford: Oxford University Press, 1999), p. 837.

11. Serge Daney, "La dernière image" in *Passages de l'image*, R. Bellour, C. David, C. Van Assche (eds.) (Paris: Editions du Centre Pompidou, 1989), 57–59; on Daney and the question of *arrêt-sur-image* see Raymond Bellour, "L'effet Daney ou l'arrêt de vie et de mort," *Trafic* 37 (Spring 2001), 75-86.

12. Noël Burch's research goes back to his work "Porter, ou l'ambivalance", *Screen* 19-4 (Winter 1978-79). Tom Gunning's view is prominent in "An Aesthetic of Astonishment: Early Film and the (In)credulous Spectator," *Art and Text* 34 (Autumn 1989). The New Film History research is presented more fully in Thomas Elsaesser (ed.), *Early Cinema: Space, Frame, Narrative* (London: BFI, 1990) and Wanda Strauven (ed.), *The Cinema of Attraction Reloaded* (Amsterdam: Amsterdam University Press, 2007).

13. The many-faceted differences between Marey and Muybridge are discussed more extensively in Martha Braun, *Picturing Time. The Works of Etienne-Jules Marey (1830-1904)* (Chicago: The University of Chicago Press 1992), Phillip Prodger (ed.), *Time Stands Still: Muybridge and the Instantaneous Photography Movement* (New York and Stanford: Oxford University Press, 2003) and Mary Ann Doane, *The Emergence of Cinematic Time: Modernity, Contingency, The Archive* (Cambridge, MA: Harvard University Press, 2002).

14. Many of the footnoted references in this introduction are examples of this.

15. Linda Williams, *Hardcore: Power, Pleasure, and the "Frenzy of the Visible"* (Berkeley: University of California Press, 1989/1999 expanded version), p. 46.

16. See Laura Marks, "Enfolding and Unfolding: An Aesthetics for the Information Age." *Vectors Journal.* Volume 2. Issue 2, Winter 2007. Available at http://vectors. usc.edu/projects/index.php?project=72 (last accessed March 31, 2011).

17. Jay David Bolter and Richard Grusin, *Remediation: Understanding New Media* (Cambridge, MA: MIT Press, 1999) and Lev Manovich, *The Language of New Media* (Cambridge, MA: MIT Press, 2001), p. 85-86.

18. See Hansen's article in the current collection as well as his *New Philosophy for New Media* (Cambridge, MA: MIT Press, 2004) and *Bodies in Code: Interfaces with Digital Media* (London: Routledge, 2006).

19. Thomas Elsaesser, e-mail to the author, March 2011. The citation from Alexander
     Galloway's article "Notes on 'Gaming'" (Oct 1, 2007) can be found at
     http://rhizome.org/profiles/alexandergalloway/ (last accessed May 3, 2011).
20. Alexander Galloway, "What You See Is What You Get?" In *The Archive in Motion:
     New Conceptions of the Archive in Contemporary Thought and New Media Practices,* ed.
     Eivind Røssaak (Oslo: Studies from the National Library of Norway, 2010), 168.
21. Alexander Galloway, "The Unworkable Interface". *New Literary History.* Volume 39,
     Number 4, Autumn 2008, pp. 935.

Philosophies of Motion

The Play between Still and Moving Images: Nineteenth-Century "Philosophical Toys" and Their Discourse

Tom Gunning

Cinema is an art of the moving image, yet materially it could be said simply to be made up from a series of still images. This apparent paradox between still and moving images has been noted by nearly all accounts of cinema, but resolving this exchange between stillness and motion, or rather the transformation of one into the other, still eludes both empirical scientific explanation and, I feel, reflects deeply rooted ideological prejudices. The moving image, I claim, constitutes a sort of a scandal, which has been consistently resolved by being described as an illusion, something in other words that does not "really" exist. I want to explore the complexities of the introduction of the moving image in the nineteenth century and the limitations that come from seeing simply as an illusion.

Persistence of Vision: Vision and Its Fallacies

Jonathan Crary has claimed that nineteenth-century visual devices focused on the question of the body and the senses, emphasizing defining and measuring the processes of the body and the senses and thereby disciplining them. Thus the nineteenth century approached vision in a new mode: "Vision, rather than a privileged form of knowing, becomes itself an object of knowledge, of observation. From the beginning of the nineteenth century a science of vision will tend to mean increasingly an interrogation of the physiological make-up of the human subject, rather than the mechanics of light and optical transmission."[1] Optical illusions do not simply obscure the truth about the world, but rather offer new information about the process of perceiving and the perceiver's body.[2]

Focusing on human perception redefined the complex problem of seeing things that are "not there." Discovering the nature of visual illusion revealed the essential processes of vision, just as knowledge of disease reveals the processes of the health. The most common form of seeing something which was "not there" may be the afterimage, which at the turn of the nineteenth century became the subject of intense investigation. Close attention to this subjective

phenomenon exemplified the new attitude towards perception that Crary describes. The way afterimages were described and the role they played within
the optical devices known as philosophical toys, which produced moving
images, vividly reveals the assumptions generated and the tensions raised by
the moving image in this new intellectual and technological context.

Contemporary perceptual psychologist R.L. Gregory defines afterimages (of
which there are both positive and negative types) as "the continuing firing of
the optic nerve after the stimulation".[3] In other words, after an object has been
removed from the field of vision an image of it lingers, due, in Gregory's explanation, to a physical process within the retina, especially if the object were
bright or the gaze fixated. By means of an afterimage we paradoxically see an
object even in its absence. This phenomenon had been observed for centuries,
including discussions by Aristotle, Ptolemy, Ibn al Haytham and Leonardo da
Vinci.[4] The afterimage forms the most dramatic example of what are often
called "subjective visual phenomenon", i.e. seeing images that result from a
bodily response rather than from a "sampling" of the world. Studying and demonstrating this phenomenon led to the first proliferation of optical philosophical toys. As Crary puts it, "beginning in the mid-1820s, the experimental study
of afterimages led to the invention of a number of related optical devices and
techniques."[5] These devices announced the invention of modern motion pictures and popularized the concept of the persistence of vision as the means of
creating an illusion of apparent motion.

"The persistence of vision" exemplifies the nineteenth century's understanding of visual illusions as primarily a physiological phenomenon, which can be
demonstrated, triggered and even measured through mechanical and optical
devices. Few concepts have been evoked so often in relation to visual devices
and especially moving images, and yet so disputed as this one. As an explanation of the phenomenon of apparent motion it has now basically been discarded, but still must be dealt with as a revealing historical and cultural legacy
(and one that displays its own phantom persistence, as perceptual psychologists
like Joseph and Barbra Anderson have lamented).[6] As Mary Ann Doane has put
it "The theory of persistence of vision may be "wrong", but the question remains – why was it so firmly ensconced and what function did it serve in the
19th century?"[7] The attitude toward vision maintained by the persistence of
vision thesis, reveals the interface nineteenth century scientists thought they
had discovered (and in many senses had *manufactured*) between human perception and the machine. The attraction of the theory for the nineteenth century, I
believe lies largely in its essentially mechanical view of the human sensorium
(and its persistence in some accounts of cinema to this date indicates how much
a mechanical view of perception and cognition still underlies the assumptions
most people maintain about vision). Persistence of vision and the optical de-

vices I discuss here form a circular logic in which the devices are the cause of visual illusions as well as demonstrating their explanation. Besides spawning images of motion, these devices forged a new dependent relation between the still and the moving image, as each enacted the trick of a transition from a static image to a moving image. However, we might claim the real trick lies in making the moving images appear as nothing more than a peculiarly tricky modification of the still image, an epiphenomenon founded in the inert and reliable still image. That the theory of persistence of vision has been debunked therefore takes on more significance than simply a passing moment in the explanatory fashions of science. Persistent afterimages offered a theory of perception which parsed movement into static phases and still images, an attempt thereby not only to discipline the moving image, but to dissolve its movement into its opposite.

So what is this theory in which movement is paradoxically explained through persistence? The theory is founded on the fact that motion picture devices (whether the first nineteenth-century devices such as the phenakistiscope or zoetrope or the later motion picture films) all employ a continuous series of still drawings or photographs depicting separate phases of an action on some sort of material support. A device moves these still images through some sort of viewer at a sufficient speed to create what is often called "apparent motion". A dancer dances, a horse gallops, a man walks. How does this happen? In 1912 one of the earliest books published on the nature of cinema, Frederic Talbot's *Moving Pictures: How They Are Made and Worked* provides an especially vivid description:

> Suppose, for instance, that a series of pictures depicting a man walking along the street, are being shown on the screen. In the first picture the man is shown with his left foot in the air. This remains in sight for 1/32 of a second, and then disappears suddenly. Though the picture has vanished from the eye, the brain still persists in seeing the left foot slightly raised. One thirty second part of a second later the next picture shows the man with his left foot on the ground. The shops, houses, and other stationary objects in the second image occupy the positions shown in the first picture, and consequently the dying impression of these objects is revived, while the brain receives the impression that the man has changed the position of his foot in relation to the stationary objects, and the left foot which was raised melts into the left foot upon the ground. The eye imagines that it sees the left foot descend.[8]

The first book written about film by an experimental psychologist, *The Photoplay a Psychological Study*, was published in 1916 by Hugo Munsterberg and offered a summary – as well as an early rejection – of the persistence of vision theory in psychological terms:

> Every picture of a particular position left in the eye an afterimage until the next picture with the slightly changed position of the jumping animal or the marching men

was in sight, and the afterimage of this again lasted until the third came. The after-images were responsible for the fact that no interruption was noticeable, while the movement itself resulted simply from the passing of one position into another. What else is the perception of movement but the seeing of a long series of different positions? If instead of looking through the Zoetrope we watch a real trotting horse on a real street, we see its whole body in ever-new progressing positions and its legs in all phases of motion; and this continuous series is our perception of the movement itself.[9]

Munsterberg wryly comments on the theory: "This seems very simple. Yet it was slowly discovered that the explanation is far too simple…"

Munsterberg put the crux of the critique (which has basically stood to today, although many film scholars seem unaware of it) succinctly as, "The perception of movement is an independent experience which cannot be reduced to a simple seeing of a series of different positions."[10] Munsterberg claims that a "higher mental act" is superadded to the physiological process, which he admits does not fully explain the phenomenon.[11] While contemporary theories of perception do not deny the phenomenon of an afterimage and the apparent motion that the older theory sought to explain, they agree that simply retaining a series of after-images in different positions cannot automatically yield a moving image (the effect would more likely be that of multiple superimpositions). Contemporary theories have broken the motion into multiple interrelating factors, whose complexities still allow some degree of controversy and uncertainty, even if the inadequacy of the old theory cannot be disputed. As the Andersons show, the phenomenon of persistence of vision as the explanation of the continuous moving image can be broken into two issues:

> Why is the image continuous, and why does it move? In other words, why do the separate frames appear continuous rather than as the intermittent flashes of light which we know them to be? And why do the figures on the screen appear to move about in smooth motion when we know they are in fact still pictures?[12]

Not long after the emergence of cinema, perceptual psychology already supplied alternative explanations to the persistence of vision thesis, as Munsterberg was aware. In 1912 Max Wertheimer took up the issue of apparent motion and his critique of the persistence of vision theory inaugurated the beginning of Gestalt psychology by questioning the mechanistic assumptions of previous perceptual psychology. Wertheimer attributed apparent motion to three factors, summarized by the Andersons as: (1) beta movement (the object at A seen as moving across the intervening space to position B), (2) partial movement (each object seen moving a short distance), and (3) phi movement (objectless or pure motion).[13] Writing more recently R.L. Gregory's classic account of visual per-

ception *Eye and Brain* simplifies the situation and states that the continuous action as seen in a motion picture film "relies upon two rather distinct visual facts.
The first is persistence of vision, and the second the so-called *phi phenomenon*."[14]
Most perceptual psychologists today agree that multiple factors contribute to
apparent motion.

Playing with Vision: The Thaumatrope

Picking up and playing with a nineteenth-century optical device allows anyone
to re-experience the transformation of a still image into…something else. Beyond demonstrating the phenomenon of the afterimage or apparent movement
the fascination these images draw from us endures. A true phenomenology of
that experience may be sharpened through attention to successive theories of
vision, but it also exceeds the context of the history of science. The moving image breaks out of its intended context when its playfulness triumphs over its
philosophy.

The Thaumatrope, one of the earliest optical philosophical toys, has a somewhat indirect relation to apparent motion, but demonstrates the flicker fusion
aspect of persistence of vision quite dramatically, through its ability to fuse a
continuous image from two rapidly alternated separate images. As Crary says
of the Thaumatrope, "Similar phenomenon had been observed in earlier centuries merely by spinning a coin and seeing both sides at the same time, but this
was the first time the phenomenon was given a scientific explanation *and* a device was produced to be sold as a popular entertainment. The simplicity of this
'philosophical toy' made unequivocally clear both the fabricated and the hallu-
cinatory nature of its image and the rupture between perception and its object."[15]

The purveyor and promoter of the Thaumatrope, John Ayrton Paris was a
distinguished medical doctor and scientific author who had used his philosophical toy to demonstrate the principle of persistence of vision to the Royal Society in 1824. But he aggressively promoted the device's role as an educational
toy and wrote a rather long novelistic account of how toys and games could
teach young people the nature of the universe and their own perceptions. This
1827 book (so popular it went through several editions and revisions) embeds
these devices into a very revealing discourse of popular nineteenth century
science. Its title says it all: *Philosophy in Sport Made Science in Earnest: An attempt
to illustrate the first principles of natural philosophy by the aid of popular toys and
sports.* The chapter he devotes to the Thaumatrope opens with a clear argument
for the educational use of illusions: questioning human senses and demonstrat-

ing their unreliability. According to Paris, the trick of the Thaumatrope lies not just in the hand, but lurks concealed in the eye itself, whose nature is revealed by the device. Paris' narrator, Mr. Seymour, declares to his young charge, "I will now show you that the eye also has its source of fallacy." His adult interlocutor, the local vicar, exclaims "If you proceed in this manner, you will make us into Cartesians." Paris provides a useful footnote to explain the term:

> The Cartesians maintained that the senses were the great sources of deception; that everything with which they present us ought to be suspected as false, or at least dubious, until our reason has confirmed the report.[16]

Mr. Seymour translates the toy's name to mean "*Wonderturner*, or a toy which performs wonders by turning round." The Thaumatrope's wonder is "founded upon the well-known optical principle, that an impression made on the retina of the eye lasts for a short interval after the object that produced it has been withdrawn."[17] The twirling of the card causes the images on each side to appear before the eye as if present at the same instant, which Seymour describes as, "a very striking and magical effect."

As with most philosophical toys, the lessons of the Thaumatrope depended on the manipulator not only being in control of the device, but also being able to examine its elements both in motion and stillness. Anyone could see that each side of the disk presented only a part of the composite image which spinning produced. Thus the illusion could both be produced and deconstructed by the child who operated the device. The classic Thaumatrope composite images (e.g. a bird + a cage; a vase + flowers; a horse + a rider; a bald man (or woman) and a wig) did not present a moving image at all, but rather a sort of superimposition, merging two separate pictures into a new unity.

The Thaumatrope displays the fascination produced by an optically produced image. Paris claims the composite image derives from a "fallacy" of the eye. Most discussions of persistence of vision claim it results from a "defect" or "weakness" of the eye. Herein presumably lies at least one basis for the production of motion being described as a trick or deception (Talbot says "the camera is a more perfect trickster than the most accomplished prestidigitator"[18]). The spinning disc is faster than the eye. The illusion presumably derives from the lingering, persistent afterimage, by which we see something after it has, in fact, vanished from our visual field, or, in the case of the Thaumatrope's composite image, we see an image which does not strictly correspond to anything in reality (there is no "bird in a cage", only a bird on one side of a card and a cage on the other). This image is the product, Paris seems to claim, of a collusion between the device and our eye, or, alternatively the tricky device has taken advantage of the weakness of our eye (C.W. Ceram in fact refers to the "laggard sense of sight" in describing Plateau's experiments with afterimages,[19] and Talbot intones about motion pictures, "The illusion is wholly due to one glaring deficiency of the human eye, of which the utmost advantage has been taken") in order to make us believe we see something that does not, in fact, exist.[20]

I have always found such description of this ability to blend two images into a single one as a imperfection of the eye curious and extremely Cartesian, in the sense of driving a wedge between what we know and what we see – and decidedly valuing what we *know* over what we *see*. Following Paris's cue, we might view the Thaumatrope as a machine for producing young Cartesians, as much as illusions. But to understand this new form of image, I think we must let the movement speak rather than concentrate exclusively on the explanation. When I twirl a Thaumatrope, although I do see a composite image, I do not mistake it for the equivalent of the images imprinted on either side of the disk. The image has an unfamiliar quality. It is less material than the printed images, and, as Paris stresses, less opaque; I can in effect see through it. I am inclined to think of it as visual rather than tactile, something I can see but not touch. And yet I am very aware of its production (and my manual role in producing it). Mary Ann Doane, one of the few film scholars who attempts to describe the image produced by optical devices, captures its odd nature which she indicates aligned it with the possibility of deception and trickery: "The image of movement itself was nowhere but in the perception of the viewer – immaterial, abstract, and thus open to practice of manipulation and deception. The toys could not work without this fundamental dependence upon an evanescent, intangible image."[21] Most likely this is best described as a "virtual image" an image whose existence consists in its appearance and effects rather than its materiality, and which, in relation to optics, the OED defines as an "image resulting from the effect of reflection or refraction upon rays of light" (thus David Brewster used the term in 1831 to describe the effect of an image appearing behind the mirror caused by a convex mirror). As a trick, this virtual image surprises me, not only because I know it isn't "really there," but because I participate in its appearance. As simple as the device is, the Thaumatrope cannot function without someone serving as simultaneous viewer and manipulator. The image appears as the result of this interaction. As Doane states about early optical devices, "The tangibility of the apparatus and the materiality of the images operated as a form of resistance to this abstraction, assuring the viewer that the image of movement could be produced at will, through the labor of the body, and could, indeed, be owned as a commodity."[22] The viewer of the Thaumatrope was both the astonished spectator and the producer of the image. Mannoni reproduces a Thaumatrope with a painter before a blank canvas on the one side and a small portrait of a lady on the other. Twirling the disc, the resulting composite image places the lady on the canvas, as if stressing the device's role in creating, not just a composite, but a composite *image*.[23]

But if we are aware of the act of twirling the Thaumatrope as a form of production, we are also aware that it produces only an ephemeral image that vanishes as soon as the turning stops. While the implication of Paris's Cartesian discourse is that the Thaumatrope should make us aware of the feeble and deceptive aspect of our senses, I wonder if the imagery of the discs, their often irreverent sense of humor and fantasy encourages such sober disillusionment. I want to stress the ludic and aesthetic dimension of the toy, the delight that comes from playing with oneself and one's perception. Why, in fact, shouldn't this ability to see the superimposed image be viewed as a faculty, an ability, rather than a defect? I experience the production of this virtual image as extending my conception of vision rather than experiencing some sort of failure to maintain the distinction between the two images. After all, this is a toy, a device to give pleasure, not cause frustration. We certainly feel as we twist the thread of the Thaumatrope and watch the image it produces that we are escaping the ordinary, that we are seeing in a different manner; we glimpse a virtual world. Although the superimposed image may not necessarily produce an image *of* motion, it is an image *in motion* and therein lies its uniqueness. What it does not resemble is the fixed and static image that constitutes the norm of pictorial expression (a norm, I believe, we could claim that the art of picture-making also constantly challenges and re-conceives). To claim that the Thaumatrope-produced image does not exist or exists simply as an illusion, reveals a prejudice towards perception as a static process, veracity as something viewable only from a fixed and stable perspective, vision understood as a still picture. I am claiming that the moving image fascinates partly because of its constant impulse to exceed what is already known and already grasped, in favor of mobile possibilities.

Wheels of Life: Flickering Moving Images

The optical devices that succeeded the Thaumatrope produced not just superimposed virtual images, but images that moved, using revolving wheels or drums with slots or indentations through which the viewer peered. The aperture provided by the viewing slot not only turns what would otherwise be a continuous blur into a stable visible image, but also inscribes the viewer into the apparatus, setting a place and means for observation and controlling it with precision. The breakdown of a continuous movement into a series of flashes or flickers – basically the creation of shutter effect – was essential for the production of motion in nearly all cinematic devices to come. As Austrian scientist Simon Stampfer explained its function in his stroboscopic disc in 1833, "the light falling on the change of the images is interrupted, and the eye receives only a momentary visual impression of each separate image when it is in the proper position."[24] The production of motion was founded upon a breakdown of vision into flashes, flickers of instantaneous vision produced by a rapidly revolving shutter. The complexity of effects triggered by this simple device is worth extensive contemplation. Stampfer indicates the role of the aperture and shutter in aligning image and viewer and exposing the still images to a brief view in such a way that the transition between images is occluded. Like a mechanical conjuror, the shutter hid the moment of change (when one image replaced another) from view.

Paris's book for young scientists explains the apparent movement produced by these devices in terms of a theory of motion which claims that perceiving motion is less something *seen* than something *deduced*: "Now it is evident, that before the eye can ascertain a body to be in motion, it must observe it in two successive portions of time, in order to compare its change of place." He supports this statement with a quote from Lord Brougham (Lord Chancellor and member of the Royal Society), "Our knowledge of motion is a deduction of reasoning, not a perception of sense; it is derived from the comparison of two position; the idea of a change of place is the result of that comparison attained by a short process of reasoning."[25] This claim seems somewhat different from the more physiologically based persistence of vision theory, but it reveals a central prejudice about the actual perception of motion: that motion must be the product of a mental (or physical) processing of still images. This persistence of the still image as the true substance of the moving image is the specter that haunts the nineteenth-century understanding of the moving image.

While the explanations of vision offered by Lord Brougham resolve motion back into still images, the toys more commonly ran the other way, as is seen in the Phenakistiscope, invented by Belgian scientist Joseph Plateau (and basically identical in principle and manufacture to the Stroboscope invented and presented about the same time by Simon Stampfer).[26] Curiously, Plateau first produced a device whose turning wheel and aperture and shutter mechanism produced a still image rather than a moving one. In the Anorthoscope (described by Mannoni) a distorted anamorphic drawing rotated and viewed through a revolving slotted disc produced a "perfectly steady and recognizable image."[27] Although produced for sale in 1836, the Anorthoscope was a commercial failure, while Plateau's next revolving wheel toy, set off what Mannoni has called a "Phenakistiscope craze."[28] It could be claimed that this device provided the first unambiguous example of a optical moving image. The name of the device, derived from the Greek *phenax* – cheater or deceiver – marked the view it offered as deceptive. Here is Plateau's physical description of the device:

The apparatus …essentially consists of a cardboard disc pierced along its circumference with a certain number of small openings and carrying painted figures on one of its sides. When the disc is rotated about its center facing a mirror, and looking with one eye opposite the opening… the figures are animated and execute movements.[29]

The viewer holds the device by a handle in one hand while peering through the slots and sets the wheel turning, usually spinning it with a single finger of her other hand. The slots punctuate the vision of images on the moving disc as Stampfer described, converting the passing figures into a flickering series of individual images (or rather producing a single moving image) rather than a continuous blur.

Apparently the idea of a moving figure came to Plateau only after his experiments with the "illusion" of a still image produced by the Anorthoscope. He had also demonstrated the apparent stillness of a rapidly revolving device with a repeated identically drawn figure. As the wheel revolved with some sixteen figures of a standing man drawn on its periphery, the figure appears within the viewing slots as a single static image. Mannoni theorizes that the example of the Thaumatrope may then have inspired Plateau to the next crucial move. Now the figures drawn on the periphery portrayed a single figure engaged in the successive stages of a simple repetitive motion: a dance, sawing wood, opening one's mouth in a grimace, juggling balls, or, perhaps most mesmerizingly, a series of abstract geometrical gyrations and transformations. As William B. Carpenter, vice president of the Royal Society, pointed out in 1868, the Phenakistiscope substituted "for the repetition of similar impressions…a series of gradationally varied impressions, produced by drawings of the same figure in different positions."[30] Although the succession of poses yields a single progressive action, the revolving wheel makes it a potentially endless cycle, with no clear conclusion, other than that caused by the operator/viewer's boredom or manual fatigue. The movement portrayed here is posed between brevity and endlessness, an instant of action or an eternity of Sisyphean repetition, the first appearance of the cinematic loop that evades the linearity of action through its circular technology. The most famous of Plateau's phenakistiscope disc shows a male dancer performing a pirouette.[31] The dancer performs a 360-degree turn.

Like most of his contemporaries, Plateau believed the device demonstrated the natural outcome of optical afterimages, as for the first time explicitly subsumed under persistence of vision:

If several objects that differ sequentially in terms of form are represented one after another to the eye in very brief intervals and sufficiently close together, the impression they produce on the retina will blend together without confusion and one will believe that a single object is gradually changing form and position.[32]

One could see this pirouetting dancer as the origin of the optical moving image (in other words, as a continuous moving image produced by an optical device). Like the Thaumatrope, the Phenakistiscope or Stampfer's Stroboscope create a virtual image, an optical phenomenon that is not identical to any of the images that make it up. Rather than an image with a single material base it is a perceptual image produced by motion, and thus virtual. In this sense it could be called a "trick" produced as it is by a device that must be operated. But the same process of revolving disc and slotted shuttered viewing could produce an equally "tricked" *still* image, as in Plateau's Anorthoscope (or the more famous Faraday Wheel). Motion is necessary for the trick, but the trick does not have to yield a moving image.

But the effect of the motion produced remains powerful, and Paris describes "the great astonishment they felt, at observing the figures in constant motion, and exhibiting the most grotesque attitudes." In spite of these uncanny and grotesque effects, Paris, however, (or his narrator) uses the device to explain our normal perception of motion:

> Each figure is seen through the aperture and as it passes and is succeeded in rapid succession by another and another, differing from the former in attitude, the eye is cheated into the belief of its being the same object successively changing the position of its body. Consider what takes place in an image on the retina when we actually witness a man in motion; for instance, a man jumping over a gate, in the first moment he appears on the ground, in the next his legs are a few winches above it, in the third they are nearly on a level with the rail, in the fourth he is above it, and then in the successive moments he is seen descending as he had previously risen. A precisely similar effect is produced on the retina, by the successive substitution of figures in corresponding attitudes as through the orifices of the revolving disc; each figure remaining on the retina long enough to allow its successor to take its place without an interval that would destroy the illusion.[33]

The true sleight of hand employed here is that the devices that produce motion from a series of still images are now being used to explain – not the process of the toy itself – but normal human perception. If the toy creates an illusion of motion, one wonders if the precisely similar process of the toy and what happens "when we actually witness" motion indicates that all perception of motion should also be considered an illusion, and if not why not? Like Lord Brougham's description of movement as a process of reasoning and comparing, Paris's explanation of actually witnessing movement starts from the assumption that in perception the still image is primary, that movement consists of a mental deduction based on comparing static positions. What we see happening in Brougham's explanation and Paris's lesson drawn from the Phenakistiscope – and this is one reason the discourse about the invention of cinema involves more than simply a technical history – is human perception being modeled on a mechanical explanation of a mechanical device (rather than exploring the new device in terms of human perception).

The Phenakistiscope generated a number of offspring, all of which similarly animated drawn successive figures in loops of repetitive motion when viewed through revolving devices. The most popular was the Zoetrope, in which, as Carpenter described it, "We look through slits in the side of a vertical revolving drum at the interior of the opposite side of the drum…and when one of the long strips covered with figures is placed in the lower part of the drum, and is viewed through the slits in its near side, the effect is exactly the same as that produced by looking through the slits near the margin of the disks of the Phenakistiscope."[34]

The Moving Image: More than an Illusion

It is worth pausing at this threshold in the nature of imagery that the Phenakistiscope and its successors crossed. Since the beginning of culture, movement has played a role within art works through the physical movement of actors and dancers, puppets and automatons, or shadows and pictorial figures. But with these mechanical devices we actually see moving images produced optically. I maintain this marks a revolutionary moment in the history of the image – one we have not fully appreciated or explored. To describe the perception achieved by these devices without recourse to the mechanical description of how they operate remains a challenge, precisely because their effect overturns our dominant concept of representation as a picture. We are more comfortable describing how the devices work than how they affect us as viewers.

Let me be clear. These devices do not represent motion; they produce it. They do not give us a picture of motion (such as a comic strip panel of Ignatz Mouse's brick sailing through the air with lines indicating its trajectory); they *make pictures move*. For perceptual reasons, which we still understand only in part, we actually *see* movement, provided the apparatus is properly made and operated. Earlier devices represent, or allude to, movement through multiples pictures. Magic lantern slides, protean or transforming pictures (pictures showing different images depending on a change in light) and even Thaumatropes could represent different phases of an action, although in a limited number (usually two). A trick lantern slide showing a dancer in two successive poses could be manipulated rapidly and smoothly and give an impression of motion through this alternation. But a viewer is always aware of the individual static phases and the gap between them. The Phenakistiscope generated a new sort of image, an image that moved.

The reader might observe that my task in describing this threshold might be easier if I simply described what the Phenakistiscope produces as an "illusion" of motion. But this is a thorny term and I don't want to descend into philosophical conundrums. From one viewpoint I would agree we are dealing with something like an illusion, in that the successive drawings of Plateau's dancer never move – *except in a Phenakistiscope*. But I am not willing to say that when the wheel is spun and I look through the aperture I do not see a figure of a dancer moving. My position is obviously phenomenological; that is, I maintain that perceptions need not be dissolved into their physiological process (I am not against doing this – if we are studying physiology rather than moving images). But my task here is to describe our perception as we experience it. The riddle of the perception of the moving image lies in the fact that no one can explain it purely physiologically and the psychological explanations are still debated. In other words, we have a true challenge to explanation here. Yet the phenomenological description, while still difficult, is, I think, possible. We see motion, and yet it is somehow truly different from a physical dancer or puppet. We see a moving image, two dimensional in appearance. As an image, it has something of the virtuality of the composite picture in the Thaumatrope, provided, as I believe we do, we sense the flicker fusion occurring.

A moving image delights us with its novelty, because most images do not move; but also for its familiarity, since it recalls for us the way we perceive the world, *which is primarily moving*. Recent investigators of perception claim the greatest distortion in our understanding of visual perception comes from assuming it is founded on static images, pictures, to which somehow movement is superadded. As the ecological and phenomenologically-minded perceptual psychologists (such as J.J. Gibson and Alva Noe) have demonstrated, movement provides the norm for visual perception, because our eyes are moving, our bodies are moving and the world around us moves as well, in concert and independently of us. The static retina image is a myth created in the perceptual laboratory. I believe our investigation of the discourse surrounding the early moving image devices shows that the mechanistic worldview of the nineteenth century was determined to see human perception in terms of machines. Thus the education offered by philosophical toys included not only the disciplining of the body that Crary finds embedded in these devices, but a worldview in which the viewer identified his (and others!) perception with the operation of a machine. This is an education with social and political consequences. Sometimes the greatest trick lies in claiming something is only a trick and that one can unmask it easily.

However, I would maintain that reexamining the experience of the moving image, even in these devices, need not be limited to this lesson. While I resist describing the moving image as an illusion, I think one might still see it as a trick, a trope, a turn, a transformation that surprises, partly because we do indeed see it, not simply mistake it. The moving image is an illusion only if we assume our eyes are defective. If we think of seeing as a multifaceted way of exploring the world (and indeed of delighting in it), then a trick need no more be an illusion than is a difficult gymnastic or acrobatic turn or a feat of juggling. While the educational logic of "Philosophy in Sport made Science in Earnest" labors to transform astonishment and delight into earnest discipline, it also exceeds its purpose. The dancer pirouettes endlessly and if its visual fascination may serve the end of seduction into taking one's place willingly within the apparatus (or before the screen, or at the keyboard), this need not be the only pleasure produced (nor need pleasure only lead to complicity).

This apparatus, while it subjects our vision and behavior to a specific regimen necessary for the transformation into a moving image to take place, also remains very much in our hands and within our sight. The productive gestures are highly visible rather than concealed; we operate the Phenakistiscope and Zoetrope with the flick of our hands or fingers. We see the whole apparatus and it parts and can observe the still images before we set them into action. These philosophical toys display what Crary calls "the undisguised nature of their operational structure," their evident "mechanical production" based in "the functional interaction of body and machine."[35] They lack the concealing of the operational mechanism that Theodore Adorno would identify with the Phantasmagoria, and which become part of the regimen of the classical cinema.[36] Mary Ann Doane states it explicitly: "The optical toy is anti-phantasmagoric in this respect – it does not hide the work of its operation but instead flaunts it." [37]

The moving image entered the nineteenth century in peculiar circumstances. First, it displayed a dialectical relation between still and moving images. But the educational discourse surrounding philosophical toys remained fixed upon the primacy of the still image, and describing the "illusion of motion" as the product of the rapid presentation of still images before a "defective" eye. This reduction of motion to an illusion served philosophical ends. William Carpenter in his 1867 history of "the Zoetrope and its Antecedents" claimed that the study of these devices allowed young people to cultivate a "scientific habit of thought" founded on a comparison "between the *apparent* and the *real*."[38] Even more radically, it was claimed such devices taught young people that the process of seeing motion somehow depended on atomistic still images, and then "cheating" the eye into seeing things that were not actually there. In this scenario, maintained by many to this day, the eye is deficient and weak, while the machine is powerful.

As Mary Ann Doane emphasized (and Crary indicated) optical devices present the machine as a toy, unthreatening and inviting. Part of its attraction lies in the manipulation of the apparatus itself, which one holds in one's hand, as much as in the evanescent image it produces, which Doane characterizes as their tactility, manipulability and materiality. These optical toys, as she elegantly puts it, mark a moment when the viewer "seemed to hold movement in his or her hands."[39] Yet, even acknowledging the nostalgia that such a simple control of the device evokes, the production of the moving virtual image remains a crucial threshold in the modern transformation of the image I am tracing. As Doane describes it, "a hesitation in the transition from still to moving image underscores the wondrous nature of its effect, its alliance with the toy that takes on life."[40] While the trick of motion undoubtedly partakes of the uncanny effect of the animating of the inanimate, the stuff of childhood fables and myth for millennia, it takes on new meanings in the modern era. No longer restricted to the myths of archaic culture or the fairytales of the nursery, we now dwell within a environment enlivened by moving images, even though the new dimensions implicit in this modern revolution in image has now been rendered banal by its omnipresence. It is our duty as theorists to rediscover and pay attention to it.

My survey of several nineteenth-century devices for the production of moving images has tried to break away from simply drawing up a linear series of the devices that "led" to the movies. While not denying that narrative, in this chapter I tried to show the deeply dialectical relation between still and moving images which these devices reveal, especially when approached phenomenologically, rather than simply technically. Most centrally, I am arguing that the absolute novelty of the moving image – so delightfully evident in all these devices – posed a sources of anxiety (or at least confusion) for its early explicators, who used their explanation to reduce the moving image to an "illusion" founded in the "reality" of still images and the fallacy of human perception. A strong prejudice against recognizing the mobile nature of visual perception is revealed by this discourse, a prejudice that the cinema and media studies must still labor to overturn.

The best introductory textbook on Cinema, David Bordwell and Kristin Thompson's *Film Art: An Introduction* still promotes this view, claiming in its opening pages: "Moving-image media such as film and video couldn't exist if human vision were perfect."[41] One wonders how to imagine this "perfect" vision in which all motion would presumably cease and dissolve into a succession of still images. Although Bordwell and Thompson simply invoke this perfect vision as a rhetorical heuristic it reflects the distrust, and indeed pedagogical discredit of the senses that much of film studies has adopted from the nineteenth century. Although Bordwell particularly offered a trenchant criticism of the description of film spectatorship known as apparatus theory, which saw cinema and especially the "illusion of motion" as part of the ideological swindle of the basic cinematic apparatus, that suspicion of the moving image seems to persist.

My investigation of the moving image offers another take on the theory (and history) of the apparatus. Although being vigilant about the nature and method of ideological deception remains a duty of the theory of media, assuming an Enlightenment critique of perception seems to me a distraction rather than a foundation for a political praxis. I share Jonathan Crary's attempt to provide apparatus theory with historical, technological and phenomenological specificity. However if the optical devices serve as a mode of disciplining subjects and workers and citizens, I find the realm of the moving image provides equal opportunities of criticism and analysis. And I do not believe that delight necessarily cancels those possibilities out. The proliferation of devices of the moving image demands a critical history of their uses and experiences. But if a utopian celebration of new media can blunt the edge of criticism (and produce an amnesia about what we have learned from previous practices of visual images), puritan suspicions of the senses and their playfulness seems to be an equally deadly route to take. There may yet be uses for philosophical toys.

Notes

1.   Jonathan Crary, *Techniques of the Observer: On Vision and Modernity in the Nineteenth Century* (Cambridge: MIT Press, 1990) p. 70.
2.   Ibid., p. 97.
3.   R.L. Gregory, *Eye and Brain:The Psychology of Seeing* (London: World University Library, 1997) p. 49.
4.   Nicholas J. Wade, ed., *A Natural History of Vision* (Cambridge: MIT Press 1998), pp. 159-166.
5.   Crary, p. 104.
6.   Joseph & Barbara Fisher Anderson: 'The Myth of Persistence of Vision', *Journal of the University Film Association* 4 (Fall 1978): 3-8.
7.   Mary Ann Doane, "Movement and Scale: Vom Daumenkino zur Filmprojektion," in Apparaturen bewegter Bilder, Kulture und Technik, vol. 2, ed. Daniel Gethmann (Munster: LIT, 2006), pp. 123-137. German translation of "Movement and Scale: From the Flip-book to the Cinema." I have used a manuscript kindly supplied by the author of the original English version and use the page numbers from that manuscript.

8. Frederick Talbot, *Moving Pictures: How They are Made and Worked* (London: J.B. Lippincott Co, 1912), p. 6

9. Hugo Munsterberg, *The Photoplay: A Psychological Study* (New York: Appleton and Company, 1916) p. 60.

10. Ibid., p. 61.

11. Ibid., p. 69.

12. Barbara and Joseph Anderson, Anderson, p. 3.

13. Ibid., p. 4.

14. Gregory, p. 109.

15. Crary, p. 106.

16. John Ayrton Paris, *Philosophy in Sport Made Science in Earnest. An attempt to illustrate the first principles of natural philosophy by the aid of popular toys and sports.* London: John Murray, 1849, fifth edition) p. 337. This reference to Cartesians does not appear in the book's first edition. Unless otherwise noted all quotes are from this later edition, although I have also consulted the first edition as well.

17. Ibid., p. 339.

18. Talbot, p. 2.

19. C.W. Ceram, *Archeology of the Cinema* (London: Thames and Hudson, 1965) p. 18.

20. Talbot, p. 2.

21. Doane, pp. 11-12.

22. Doane, p. 12.

23. Laurent Mannoni, *The Great Art of Light and Shadow: Archeology of the Cinema* (Exeter: University of Exeter Press, 2000) pp. 206-207.

24. Wade, p. 209.

25. Paris, p. 357.

26. Wade, p. 207.

27. Mannoni, p. 211. See also Stephen Herbert, *A History of Pre-Cinema* (London: Routledge, 2002) pp. 303-321.

28. Ibid., p. 219.

29. Wade, p. 208.

30. Herbert, p. 295.

31. Jacques Deslandes reproduces a drawn version, which he identifies as 'the first Phenakistiscope drawn by Plateau". Deslandes, *Histoire comparitif du cinema* Vol. 1 (Paris: Casterman, 1966), p. 36.

32. Plateau, quoted in Wade, p. 209.

33. Paris, p. 359.

34. Herbert, pp. 297-298.

35. Crary, p. 132.

36. Theodore Adorno, *In Search of Wagner* (London: NLB, 1981), pp. 85-96.

37. Doane, p.11.

38. Herbert, p. 301.

39. Doane, p. 23.

40. Ibid., p. 24.

41. Bordwell, David and K. Thompson. *Film Art: An Introduction.* Ninth Edition. (New York: Mc Graw Hill), 2010, p. 8.

Digital Technics Beyond the "Last Machine": Thinking Digital Media with Hollis Frampton

Mark B.N. Hansen

A Digital Frampton?

In his pioneering introjection of Hollis Frampton into debates about digital media, Peter Lunenfeld situates experimental film – for which Frampton serves as an exemplar – as a ground condition for much of what, circa 2000, comprised new media art production. Suggesting that experimental cinema in its heyday, from the 1950s to the 1970s, managed to achieve "the status of *gesamtkunstmedium*", Lunenfeld argues that it "can serve as a model for computer-inflected art. I believe," he states, "that the most interesting new media works aspire to the condition of the experimental cinema without quite realizing it".[1]

Lunenfeld's claim can be understood as a specification of Lev Manovich's more general and wide-ranging argument concerning the cinema's role as cultural dominant. In *The Language of New Media* (1999), Manovich positioned cinema as "*the* cultural interface, a toolbox for all cultural communication, overtaking the printed word."[2] In this scenario, again circa 2000, new media plays the role of cinema's rejuvenator: "Cinema, the major cultural form of the twentieth century, has found new life as the toolbox of the computer user. Cinematic means of perception, of connecting space and time, of representing human memory, thinking, and emotion have become a way of work and a way of life for millions in the computer age. Cinema's aesthetic strategies have become basic organizational principles of computer software. ... In short, what was cinema is now the human-computer interface."[3] Just as Lunenfeld's argument for the particular cinematic aspirations of new media art situates it squarely within the cinematic genealogy traced out by Manovich, so too does his strategy run the risk of compromising what is singular or different – indeed, what is "new" – about new media.[4]

For this reason, I suggest that we reverse the directionality of the correlation between experimental film and new media, substituting for Lunenfeld's claim the notion that *experimental film aspired,* as it were in advance of its actuality, *to the condition of new media*. To substantiate such a claim, one could invoke the lifelong interest a filmmaker like Hollis Frampton displayed in different media platforms and in the juxtaposition and interpenetration of different media; or one could cite the various discussions Frampton devoted to the digital image and the work he did as part of the Media Arts Lab at SUNY, Buffalo. I want here to take a different, more circuitous, but I think ultimately more profound and compelling path from Frampton to new media, but also from new media back to (and beyond) Frampton. The crux of this exploration concerns the nexus of technology, time, and movement, and Frampton's role here is to anticipate the contemporary repositioning of cinema *within* a larger media ecology – one that extends both *beyond* film into the post-cinematic as well as *before* film into the prehistory of the cinematic – but whose single and dominant principle is movement. On this account, cinema becomes reconfigured as a particular framing of universal movement, or movement-variation, that is determined by its specific temporal scale; as one of framing among others, it undergoes a relativization and becomes open to transformation by other media forms that, like digital media, may be capable of broaching its formerly defining homologies with the temporal syntheses of consciousness.

With his various meditations – both theoretical and artistic – on the contingency of cinema's technical specifications and the rich temporal virtuality that these specifications foreclose, Frampton could be said to explode cinema both from within and from without. In a sense, he operates equally as a filmmaker, indeed a filmmaker of the most experimental sort, who seeks to question, challenge and extend the boundaries of the medium of film, *and* as a new media practitioner *avant la lettre*, who embraces (if only, for the most part, in theory) the technical possibilities of computational media *that precisely exceed the scope of cinematic representation*. While I want to reserve my in-depth engagement of Frampton's work and thought for a later section, let me simply mention a couple of his more stimulating ideas that cross the divide between these two vocations.

First, there is his intriguing claim, in that most intriguing of texts, "For a Metahistory of Film", that "cinema is the Last Machine" and that cinema is "probably the last art that will reach the mind through the senses".[5] This claim is made somewhat less opaque, to my mind at least, by his specification of the precise endpoint of the Age of Machines: while it is "customary", Frampton claims, to date this moment to the advent of video, this dating is "imprecise", and, indeed, not nearly early enough. In place of video's advent, Frampton suggests the appearance of "radar", which, he notes, "replaced the mechanical reconnaissance aircraft with a static anonymous black box".[6] What this specification helps to clarify is the correlation between cinematic representation and human sense perception that serves to qualify cinema as a "mechanical art", one that could teach and remind us "(after what then seemed a bearable delay) how things looked, how things worked, how to do things ... and, of course (by example), how to feel and think."[7] With radar – and subsequently, with a proliferating host of media innovations (culminating in today's computers) that involve a similar end run around human sense perception – this correlation, and this mimetic-pedagogic function of cinema, finds itself suspended. That, I suggest, is what Frampton means when he claims that cinema is the last art that will reach the mind through the senses.

Another closely related and equally intriguing claim involves Frampton's questioning of the temporal technicity of cinema. Noting that cinema is a "Greek word that means 'movie,'" Frampton divorces cinema from the artifactuality of its institutional apparatus, which is to say, the fixed projection of moving images at a rate of 24 fps: "The illusion of movement is certainly an accustomed adjunct of the film image, but that illusion rests upon the assumption that the rate of change between successive frames may vary only within rather narrow limits. There is nothing in the structural logic of the filmstrip that can justify such an assumption."[8] Given its close association with Frampton's metahistorical concept of the "infinite film" (a film that would appear to comprise all the images potentially generated by the world throughout its entire history), we might perhaps best understand this claim as an attempt to liberate movement or variation – the interval between any two states, which is precisely how I propose we understand cinematic movement – not simply from its historical subordination to still images (which informs our received notion of cinema as a sensory illusion created by the animation of photograms) but from the overcoding such movement-variation undergoes via its historical elective affinity with the cinema, understood narrowly as a technically-specified, institutionally stabilized regime of representation. In other words, what I believe to be at stake in Frampton's seemingly outrageous claim for the radical temporal flexibility of cinema is nothing less than a shift in focus concerning the operation of movement and its relation to time: a fundamental shift from movement as an artifact of cinema narrowly considered to movement-variation as the basic component of all worldly relationality. By calling his art "simply" "film" – film that would encompass all potential passages between frames or "images" ranging from those most alike to those most different[9] – Frampton aims to expose the minimal logic of connection and distance that informs variation as such. If we read his account of the infinite film in relation to Bergson's conception of a "universe of images" – a conception according to which images comprise the materiality of the world – we can appreciate the fundamental and multi-scalar imbrication of movement and time it involves: what there is is continual "virtual" variation between images that can and must be actualized in concrete movements operating across a host of timescales.

We can now understand just how limiting and indeed how misguided were the terms on which an earlier generation of critics (one to which both Lunenfeld and Manovich belong) sought to couple Frampton and the digital. For it is not just insufficient but it is downright mistaken to claim, as does Lunenfeld, that Frampton's MAGELLAN project anticipated the cultural form of database and loop that, following Manovich's analysis, comprise the defining tropes for contemporary digital media. Lunenfeld writes:

> In the early 1970s, Frampton posited "the infinite film": a forever unfinished cinematic system incorporating all modes of filmmaking, all examples of those modes, and one that could grow and change as its medium matured. Frampton's "infinite film" is a Platonic database for our spectacular culture. It is the Alexandrine dream ... distilled from the librarians who were promised by the Ptolemiac kings of Egypt that they would have the opportunity to catalogue every book of their era.[10]

What is wrong or misguided about this claim is not the general correlation it posits between Frampton's work and the defining aesthetic properties of new media objects and networks; no, what is wrong here is Lunenfeld's complete neglect of the temporal dynamics of selection, his purely spatial treatment of the infinite film. MAGELLAN operates on the cusp of what can be considered to be cinema: it challenges the temporal artifactuality of institutionalized cinema (by, for example, forgoing the cinematic synchronization of consciousness, as it does in spreading out the one minute films comprising the "Straits of Magellan" section across the span of a year) at the same time as it instantiates alternate, non-(pre- or post-) cinematic temporalities (by way, for example, of its sheer magnitude and imposed conditions of viewing, which function [or would have functioned] to make viewing MAGELLAN *as a film*, that is in its entirety in a single session, simply impossible). As such, it exemplifies how Frampton anticipates the condition of new media: how his cinematic aesthetic was in fact rooted in a media temporal modulation of movement.

Movement and the Impression of Reality

In a talk at the 2010 Society for Cinema and Media Studies conference in Los Angeles, Tom Gunning made a plea for cinema scholars to question one of the longest-standing – and least-interrogated – assumptions of our discipline: the notion that cinema (understood in its institutionalized form as still images projected at a constant frame rate of 24 fps or close to it) is the product of a fundamental sensory illusion, that cinema results from technology tricking our senses.[11] To give a sense of just how widespread this assumption is, Gunning singled out how cinema is characterized by Bordwell and Thompson in their *Film Art*, the most popular and, arguably, the best introductory textbook that is responsible for reproducing the ideology of cinema for new generations of students. On the book's first pages, Bordwell and Thompson write: "Watching a film differs from viewing a painting, a stage performance, or even a slide show. A film presents us with *images* in *illusory* motion."[12] That the authors choose to emphasize the term "illusory" along with the crucial term "images" suffices to make the point at hand here.

This point – or rather, the positive claim that comes out of it, namely that the perception of movement in cinema is *not a mere sensory illusion, but has a basis in phenomenological experience* – animates much of Gunning's recent work on cinema both in relation to certain strands of film theory and in the context of the transformations, both of cinematic practice and its theorization, brought about by the introduction of new media technologies. If I understand Gunning's deep argument correctly, the ultimate payoff of this line of thinking – beyond a restoration of a certain tradition in film theory, running from Münsterberg to Metz, that places movement at the core of cinema's operation – is the securing of a commonality linking cinema backwards to pre-cinematic devices as well as forwards to new media. Accordingly, in place of the divisive debates around the digital that have ranged from the highly theoretical – whether new media can function indexically[13] – to the concretely practical – whether digital film cameras and projection systems can adequately "mediate" the materiality of the filmic image,[14] what Gunning's argument seeks to install is a return of sorts to the phenomenological immediacy of image media, which is to say, to the phenomenological impact of movement (or, more precisely, of movement-images), that is at issue *in all moving image media*, and not just in celluloid (or analog) cinema.

In adapting Gunning's argument for my purposes here, I want to suggest that what Gunning claims about the phenomenological "reality" of movement in relation to cinematic and post- (and pre-) cinematic movement-images can (and must) be expanded and generalized to the movement of all worldly material processes, or to what I propose to call *movement-variation*. Effectively, this expansion-generalization calls to the fore the process of temporalization associated with selection and the production of concrete intervals; more specifically, it implicates time rather than space as the crucial materialization through which movement attains phenomenological reality, in any and every case. Accordingly, if institutionalized cinema, in artifactualizing selection within a particular temporal scope, comprises one instance of such temporal materialization, it by no means comprises the only – or even, the most exemplary – such instance. For this reason, our thinking concerning movement must go beyond the cinematic movement-image and indeed, must seek to clarify how cinema, as one concrete

regime of movement-images among others, itself instantiates, specifies, and ar-
tifactualizes a more general operation of movement-variation. For cinema's specific power – the power to move us phenomenologically, to generate (sensory)
impressions of reality – derives from the more general power of movement-variation, the power to induce temporalizations that operate at divergent timescales and that, as we shall see below, confound the actual with the virtual in
highly productive and interesting ways. Understood within such a context, new
media offers a way of expanding the range of movement in which we can participate, and is thus – in an irreducible sense – in a relation of continuity and
compatibility with cinema.

In "Moving Away from the Index", Gunning credits Christian Metz – specifically, the presemiotic Metz – with the realization that movement is the "cornerstone of cinema's impression of reality".[15] To substantiate this claim, Gunning
turns to an early, neglected essay of Metz's, namely "On the Impression of Reality in the Cinema", where Metz argues that it is movement – and not iconic or
indexical representation – that confers the "impression of reality" on cinematic
experiences. Not without significance for the theme of this volume, Metz's claim
arises on the basis of a contrast between cinema and (still) photography and
deserves to the quoted at some length:

> we may ask ourselves why the impression of reality is so much more vivid in a film
> than it is in a photograph…. An answer immediately suggests itself: It is *movement*
> (one of the greatest differences, doubtless the greatest, between still photography and
> the movies) that produces the strong impression of reality…. Two things, then, are
> entailed by motion: a higher degree of reality, and the corporality of objects. These
> are not all, however. Indeed, it is reasonable to think that the importance of motion in
> the cinema depends essentially on a third factor, which has never been sufficiently
> analyzed as such…. Motion contributes *indirectly* to the impression of reality by giv-
> ing objects dimension, but it also contributes *directly* to that impression in as much as
> it appears to be real. It is, in fact, a general law of psychology that *movement is always
> perceived as real*….[16]

In seeking to pinpoint exactly why movement has this power to confer reality
on experience, Gunning stresses the role of participation; participation comprises nothing less than the hinge linking the movement-image to the immediate reality claimed for the perception of movement:

> We experience motion on the screen in a different way than we look at still images,
> and this difference explains our participation in the film image, a sense of perceptual
> richness or immediate involvement in the image. … Motion always has a projective
> aspect, a progressive movement in a direction, and therefore invokes possibility and a
> future. Of course, we can project these states into a static image, but with an actually
> moving image we are swept along with the motion itself. Rather than imaging pre-

vious or anterior states, we could say that through a moving image, the process of motion is projected onto us. Undergirded by the kinesthetic effects of cinematic motion, I believe "participation" properly describes the increased sense of involvement with the cinematic image, a sense of presence that could be described as an impression of reality.[17]

Through participation, the movement in the image (the moving-image) seamlessly and directly *becomes* the real perception of movement by its embodied spectators.

By far the most opaque moment in Metz's essay occurs when he invokes the source that makes possible such seamless and direct becoming: namely, the "insubstantiality" of movement. (By "insubstantiality", Metz would seem to mean something like "immateriality".) Movement's insubstantiality literally renders it immune from the doubling that is constitutive of representation; unlike solid objects, which can be captured in representational images that refer to their experiential (most notably, tactile) properties, movement actually suspends the very machinery of representation. Metz extracts the most radical consequences from this situation:

> Movement is insubstantial. We see it, but it cannot be touched, which is why it cannot encompass two degrees of phenomenal reality, the "real" and the copy. Very often we experience the representation of objects as *reproductions* by implicit reference to tactility, the supreme arbiter of "reality" – the "real" being ineluctably confused with the tangible.... The strict distinction between object and copy, however, dissolves on the threshold of motion. Because movement is never material but is *always* visual, *to reproduce its appearance is to duplicate its reality....* In the cinema *the impression of reality is also the reality of the impression*, the real presence of motion.[18]

Three points need to be made here.

First, what Metz is effectively claiming in this passage is that cinema, once movement is restored to the role of its fundamental principle, cannot be considered a representational medium at all: due to the necessity and inescapability of our participation in it, cinematic movement *does not* and *cannot* represent movement; on the contrary, it does nothing but *generate* movement. More bluntly still: cinema is not about the objects it depicts but rather exclusively about our experiencing of them. And that is why the impression of reality – cinematic movement – is also the reality of the impression – the movement it induces in the viewer.

Second, Metz's transitivity claim (impression of reality = reality of impression) comes at a cost: namely, the cost of the materiality of cinema's reality. Metz is straightforward here when he states that movement "is never material but is *always* visual": this conclusion would seem to follow from the particular insubstantiality of the cinematic image (but couldn't we question Metz's assumption that the visual need be non-material?), and it is a price that Metz certainly seems willing to pays without a second thought.

Third, when Gunning glosses Metz's transitivity claim as marking a difference between "reality" and "realism", he would appear to be engaging in an effort aimed at reconciling these two points, or rather, more precisely, at affirming the first while nonetheless preserving the materiality that movement accrues by way of its belonging to the broader depresencing of the world. Thus, on Gunning's interpretation, cinematic movement would still be immaterial or insubstantial in relation to theatrical representation,[19] without ceasing to belong to the movement of the world or what I will go on to call "movement-variation". Such a move on Gunning's part, I would suggest, anticipates his more recent position whose ultimate gambit, as his paper included in this volume attests, is to situate moving images within the ontologically broader movement of the world.

From Movement to Movement-Variation

With his notion of duration and the method of intuition necessary to experience it, Bergson makes it possible to extend the operation of movement-impression beyond the rarified domain of cinema and the other arts. According to Bergson, we can only experience movement, without artificially dividing it up, by inserting ourselves into it, by fusing our own duration with its duration. In his own invocation of Bergson, Gunning likens this process to the activity of participation described by Metz:

> Although Metz does not refer directly to Henri Bergson's famous discussion of motion, I believe Bergson developed the most detailed description of the *need to participate in motion* in order to grasp it. Bergson claims, "In order to advance with the moving reality, you must replace yourself within it" (*Creative Evolution*, 308). For Bergson, discontinuous signs, such as language or ideas, cannot grasp the continuous flow of movement, but must conceive of it as a series of successive static instants, or positions. Only motion, one can assume, is able to convey motion. Therefore, to perceive motion, rather than represent it statically in a manner that destroys its essence, *one must participate in the motion itself.*[20]

What is crucial here is the generality of Bergson's claims for movement and participation, and what holds these two together – what insures that movement is necessarily correlated with participation through movement – is duration. From the Bergsonist perspective, cinematic movement (like any concrete movement) is part of a larger domain of movement, what I propose to call movement-variation. Movement-variation can be understood as the correlate of duration in the precise sense that duration's materiality is comprised of incessant, asynchronous and heterogeneous temporal change across divergent scales of being. The world *is* movement-variation.

Accordingly and irregardless of how we understand Bergson's criticism of the "cinematographic illusion",[21] we must situate cinema, the art of the movement-image, within a much vaster domain of movement-variation. In this sense, too, the restoration of the phenomenological basis of the impression of reality – the restoration at issue in Metz and in Gunning – must be understood not as some "reality effect" specific to the cinema, but as an instance of a broader phenomenological claim about movement and sensation. Put another way, if part of Gunning's point is that post-classical film theory goes awry in dismissing the sensory experience of moving images as (psychological) illusion, the resulting affirmation of a certain "genuineness" of the senses must be extended to the sensory experience of movement as such (not just cinematic movement). Indeed, the "reality" of sensory experience in the cinema itself *stems directly from* the broader "genuineness" that characterizes sensory experience as such.

With his concept of "thinking-feeling", Brian Massumi expands Metz's reality of impression well beyond the domain of cinema. Specifically, Massumi seeks to reposition the divide separating representation and participation in relation to the "direct and immediate self-referentiality of perception." In addition to being the perception of an object, Massumi suggests, perception is always doubled back on itself – *it is always also the perception of its own passing*. As the correlate of and source for the doubleness of perception, the object's constitutive "out-of-sync-ness" with itself is implicated within a phenomenology of appearance that, like Gunning's insistence on the "genuineness" of sensation, focuses on the "reality" of perception's immediate participation in the movement-time of objects rather than their representational status. Like Gunning, Massumi is struck by the insistence of movement's reality, which he defines as "what we can't not experience when we're faced with it. Instead of calling it an illusion – this movement we can't actually see but can't not see either – why not just call it abstract? Real and abstract."[22] The "genuineness" that Massumi accords "abstract" experience serves to deepen and also to exfoliate the immediate, reality-conferring power of movement: as a kind of surplus or excess of the object in relation to itself, a folding into the object of its potentiality to be experienced otherwise than it is in its strict actuality, abstract experience embeds embodied living within worldly "depresencing" in a way that confounds any subject-object distinction.[23]

Returning now to the question of cinema, of its specificity as the art of the movement-image, we can better appreciate how it functions as a technology to modulate duration. In selectively transforming worldly movement-variation into movement-images, cinema exemplifies the potential of technology to insinuate itself into the process of framing – into the condensation of worldly depresencing that yields the capacitation of a presencing body.

Temporalizing the "Moving-Still"

In her recent work on movement and image, Erin Manning focuses attention on the practice of Etienne-Jules Marey who, in contrast to fellow chronophotographer Eadweard Muybridge, concentrated on creating, and not simply analyzing and representing, movement:

> To look at Marey's photographs is to feel them. Feeling is an amodal experience that is a passing-between of sense-modes. … Affectively, feeling works on the body, bringing to the fore the experiential force of the quasi chaos of the not-quite seen. This not-quite is the quality of potential we perceive in many of Marey's movement images. *These images do not represent movement, they move-with the movement of the feeling taking form.* They are affective because to see is to feel-with, to participate in the intensive passage from the virtual to actualization. What is amodally felt, perceived-with, is the microperceptual appearing at the threshold of sight, but not actually seen.[24]

Based on this understanding, chronophotography is credited with opening up movement not simply to a retroactive appreciation of its complexity but *to an actual living through, a feeling of or being affected by, that which remains imperceptible within it*. What Marey's chronophotographic images afford is an opportunity for us to *"see-feel"* – recalling Massumi – the very emergence of movement: "What must … be felt", Manning specifies, "are the microperceptions through which the displacement is activated. Many of … these perceptions are non-sensuous because they work at the level of the barely there, below the threshold of sensuous perception. Rather than the sensory perception itself, *we must feel the relation out of which the movement event emerges.*"[25]

In relation to Marey's work and the question of its divergence from cinema, what is of particular interest here is the claim that such *seeing-feeling* arises in conjunction with the perception not of moving images, but rather of still images that – because they enfold movement's virtuality into themselves – are "always already moving". What Manning understands to be Marey's predilection for the still image marks a certain disjunction between his practice and the cinema, at least as the latter was historically institutionalized:[26]

> Marey's focus was on making felt the incipience of movement in its very *taking-form*. Marey was never interested in how poses could be combined to elicit a sense of move-

ment; his main concern was mapping the imperceptible within movement's conti-nuum.... [In his experimentation with gases, Marey] sought to make apparent that which cannot be seen: the movement of air. This radically empirical exploration – *radical because it makes felt the force of the virtual within the actual* – brings to the fore the force of the imperceptible taking-form. With Marey, as with [digital artist Jim] Camp-bell, what stands out is not the cinematographic habit of adding movement to a pose, but a direct encounter with perception in the making. The poses are always already moving.[27]

In seeking to comprehend what is at stake here, we must ask an important ques-tion about images and their relation to movement: why is it necessary – and indeed, *is it necessary* – to oppose the still to the moving image as Manning does? Is there no other way for us to move beyond our culturally-inherited fixa-tion on *displacement*, on the spatialization of time and movement?

It seems to me that the answer to this two-part question is intimately bound up with the principal wager of the second section of this paper, where the re-ceived historical status of cinema was put into question. There, following Tom Gunning, I argue that cinema is more than simply the animation of still images and resulting sensory illusion, that in fact cinema presents a case of the direct sensory "pickup" of movement (or movement-images).[28] If we accept this posi-tion, it becomes impossible to play off the still against the moving image in quite the way that Manning does here: cinema – the art of the movement-image – cannot be reduced to a mere illusion based on the animation of still images, but is the direct presentation of movement to the perceiving mindbody. Rather than being opposed to one another, still and moving images offer different *but complementary* mediums for expressing movement, and in fact Marey's practice illustrates the potential of both types of image to induce the direct experience of movement, *beyond* the logic of displacement.

Technical Distribution

Marey's interest in what we *cannot* perceive informs his own self-distancing from the institution of cinema. Rather than seeking to represent natural move-ment, Marey aims to capture "*extreme speeds*": thus, he slows down "the flight of a bird" or a "bullet from a revolver" and he "accelerates the crawling of a star-fish at the bottom of an aquarium."[29] In short, rather than reproducing *some-thing that we are already able to experience*, Marey focuses on movements that are not simply beyond our perceptual grasp but that open a "cognitive" interface onto the largely imperceptible realm of movement-variation, onto what

Georges Didi-Huberman felicitously calls "the dance of every thing".[30] Nowhere is this anti-cinematic impetus more consequential than in Didi-Huberman's characterization of the "chronophotographic magic" that appears when
the dancer Loïe Fuller gives a "concrete, indubitable, prolongable and trans-
formable existence" to the Mareysian "trail of movement":

> This dynamic touches most closely the Mareysian *trail* in the *delay* and the marvelous
> slowing down produced by the drapery [the veil Fuller wears to perform the *Serpen-
> tine Dance*]: not only does this latter produce the wake [*sillage*] of the bodily gesture,
> but it slows down the accomplishment of the gesture through its own sumptuousness
> [*grandeur*].... Its trace, born of the *speed* of the gesture, retains its memory *for a long
> time* and only *very slowly* gives way to the following trace. Such is its "chronophoto-
> graphic" magic, its way not of rendering visible bodies in movement but of trans-
> forming the *visual milieu* itself into something like a *generalized site of change or varia-
> tion* [*mouvance généralisée*]."[31]

What is at stake in the "magic" of chronophotography is a certain technical distribution of sensation: chronophotography *supplements* human perception by
coupling it to an open machine for recording, analyzing and visualizing the imperceptible "transcendental-sensible" preconditions for perception. Chronophotography does not bring the imperceptible into actual experience, as Manning
would have it, but puts present perception into relation with its own immediate
pastness. What results from this is not a recomposition of the body rooted in the
enfolding of incipiency into actual perception, but a technically distributed cognitive-perceptual system in which the human body is only one element among
others rather than the sole element. As part of such a distributed system, technology does not function *like* the emergent body; rather, it functions according
to its own protocol – in Marey's case, as a proto-digital inscription, analysis and
visualization system – that extends cognitive-perceptual capacities in ways *that
do not get directly embodied*, that do not pass entirely through emergent embodiment but that remain – in some crucial sense – exterior to the human.[32]

No one has more clearly grasped this situation, with reference to Marey, than
historian of photography Joel Snyder, who writes that, in Marey's work:

> there is no question of substituting mechanical instruments for a fallible human med-
> iator and of correcting thereby what might otherwise have been falsified.... *The gra-
> phic data show what otherwise cannot be found in the realm of events and processes detectable
> by human beings* and accordingly, questions concerning the reliability or accuracy of
> machine-generated visualizations cannot be answered by recourse to a human arbi-
> trator, no matter how exquisitely sensitive or impartial. Questions about the accuracy
> of these data can be resolved only by appealing to other, perhaps even more refined
> mechanical instruments.[33]

Marey goes so far as to liken his mechanical instruments to "new senses of astonishing precision", by which he means not technical prostheses of human senses, but properly *machinic* senses capable of sensing what remains to us imperceptible.[34] The point of Marey's work, as Synder repeatedly emphasizes, is not substitution (of machinic senses for human senses): "machines", he notes, "can be constitutive of their own field of investigation", or as Marey repeatedly asserts, they can have their "own domain".[35]

What digital technology adds to this model of technically distributed sensation, when it becomes the technical basis for inscribing, analyzing and visualizing elements of our experience that we can't directly experience, is a capacity *to temporally modulate our encounter with these imperceptible elements*. This capacity is related directly to the capacity of the digital to operate at more fine-grained temporal intervals than previous media technologies, including chronophotography, but this technical singularity of the digital does nothing to change the basic structure of the human-machine coupling as Marey had already envisioned it. Thus, our coupling to digital technologies still involves a coupling of two autonomous systems: on the one hand, a computational media machine that can, for example, inscribe, analyze, and visualize movements at temporal scales that are simply unrecognizable to our natural perception; and, on the other, an embodied human perceiver whose experience can be re-composed as a result of the feeding back of what was imperceptible in perception into new future-oriented present perception. Put another way, digital technology brings a marked increase in the temporal granularity at which our experience can be parsed, which is to say, a magnification of the scale of inscription, but it also brings an unprecedented flexibility to our subsequent interaction with the experience it inscribes and analyzes as data. Rather than being bound by the form of the still photograph or the cinematic moving image, the sensory output of the computational media machine can range across a much wider temporal scale, and can even animate and complexify the apparently frozen or fixed time-frames of these earlier visualization platforms.

In the process of performing the *very same two operations of Marey's chronophotography* – inscription, analysis and visualization, on the one hand, and pictorial depiction, on the other – the computational media machine brings together the quantitative and the qualitative, or better, deploys the results of its quantitative processing to effectuate qualitative effects. And, again like Marey's chronophotographic machines, the computational media machine performs these two operations consecutively and asynchronously, or, in other words, while maintaining some minimal incompressible interval between the first perceptual experience that yields the inscription and analysis of the imperceptible and a second perception that folds this into the ongoing experience of the perceiver. In sum, in digital media no less than in Marey's chronophotography, what is imperceptible to experience can be brought into the reference frame of experience, *but always only after the fact*, in a perception subsequent to the perception emerging *from this imperceptible experience* and that, because of the ineliminable temporal interval, is itself categorically unable to *perceive* its own imperceptible virtual fringe, its "transcendental-sensible" condition of real emergence.

Frampton between Stillness and Movement

Among the many entertaining and inventive asides that populate the writings of Hollis Frampton, two stand out as particularly pertinent to the media specificity of photography and cinema. The first involves a story illustrating what I propose to call the *principle of cinematic equivalence* (or Frampton's law of narrative). It occurs at the beginning of an article called "A Pentagram for Conjuring the Narrative", and recounts a friend's recurrent nightmare "in which he lives through two entire lives":

> In the first, he is born a brilliant and beautiful heiress to an immense fortune. Her loving and eccentric father arranges that his daughter's birth shall be filmed, together with her every conscious moment thereafter, in color and sound. Eventually he leaves in trust a capital sum, the income from which guarantees that the record shall continue, during all her waking hours, for the rest of her life. Her own inheritance is made contingent upon agreement to this invasion of her privacy, to which she is, in any case, accustomed from earliest infancy. As a woman, my friend lives a long, active and passionate life. [Frampton describes various events of her life.] ... In short, she so crowds her days with experience of every kind that she never once pauses to view the films of her own expanding past. In extreme old age – having survived her own children – she makes a will, leaving her fortune to the first child to be born, following the instant of her own death, in the same city ... on the single condition that such child shall spend its whole life watching the accumulated films of her own. ... In his dream, my friend experiences her death; and then, after a brief intermission, he discovers, to his outraged astonishment, that he is about to be reincarnated as her heir. He emerges from the womb to confront the filmed image of *her* birth. He receives a thorough but quaintly obsolete education from the films of *her* school days. As a chubby, asthmatic little boy, he learns (without ever leaving his chair) to dance, sit a horse, and play the viola. During his adolescence, wealthy young men fumble through the confusion of *her* clothing to caress his own unimaginable breasts.... In middle age, his health begins to fail, and with it, imperceptibly, the memory of his previous life, so that he grows increasingly dependent upon the films to know what to do next.... Finally, he has watched the last reel of film. That same night, after the

show, he dies, quietly in his sleep, unaware that he has completed his task ... whereupon my friend wakens abruptly, to discover himself alive, at home, in his own bed.[36]

A perfect counterpoint to this tale of cinematic equivalence – let us call it the *principle of photographic compression* – the second story involves the intimate experience of a massive temporal disjunction:

> Several years ago, a man by the astonishing name of Breedlove became, for the second time in his life, the holder of the world land speed record.... For two runs over a marked course one mile long ... this Breedlove averaged a little over 600 miles per hour....Had the ride been uneventful, we may expect that he would have had nothing at all to say about it; the efficient driving of an automobile at any speed neither requires nor permits much in the way of conscious deliberation. But, as it turned out, something did happen. At the end of his second run, at a speed of about 620 miles per hour, as he was attempting to slow down, a brake mechanism exploded, and in the space of about one-and-one-half miles both drogue chutes failed to operate, and the car went entirely out of control, sheared off a number of handy telephone poles, topped a small rise, turned upside down, flew through the air, and landed in a salt pond. Incredibly, Breedlove was unhurt. He was interviewed immediately after the wreck. I have heard the tape. It lasts an hour and 35 minutes, during which time Breedlove delivers a connected account of what he thought and did during a period of some 8.7 seconds. His narrative amounts to about 9,500 words.... In the course of the interview, Breedlove everywhere gives evidence of condensing, of curtailing; not wishing to bore anyone, he is doing his polite best to make a long story short. Compared to the historic interval he refers to, his ecstatic utterance represents, according to my calculation, a temporal expansion in the ratio of some 655 to one.[37]

Let us treat these two anecdotes as two poles of a temporal continuum, or more exactly, of a continuum between two models for technically artifactualizing time. At one pole stands cinema in its traditional image, where the time of cinema (if not indeed the time of life) rigorously corresponds to the time of consciousness in a one-to-one manner. At the other pole stands photography, following the cliché that a picture is worth, in this case, 9,500 words (roughly a thousand words per second), and where the infinitesimal microtemporality of photography condenses the time of experience by unimaginable – and absolutely imperceptible – factors.

The juxtaposition and resulting interpenetration of these two models – and of these two allegorical anecdotes – establishes (at least) two things: 1) that cinema need not, and typically does not, fulfill the principle of cinematic equivalence; rather, to the extent it is constituted on the basis of techniques for disjoining event time and spectatorial time, cinema can be said to converge with photography, to introject or subsume the latter's power of temporal contraction and dilation; 2) that cinema and photography cannot be, in the last instance, opposed, as they typically have been, for the simple and precise reason that both comprise technical artifactualizations *of the very same temporal phenomenon, of the very same time.* Bearing in mind these two points will help us understand Hollis Frampton's very strange, and very prodigious conception of the "infinite film" – and to understand it not simply in its initial formulation, but as it evolves during the final decade of his art practice and as it continues to evolve in relation to the changes ushered in by new media technologies.

Frampton introduces the infinite film as the cornerstone of what he calls the metahistory of film, in the famous article that bears this phrase in its title. In order to sidestep the supposedly "vexed question" of the relationship between cinema and still photography and to elude the received wisdom that "cinema somehow 'accelerates' still photographs into motion", Frampton shifts gears entirely, offering a metahistory of cinema that suspends the empirical record according to which "photography predates the photographic cinema". Hence the conception of the "infinite cinema":

> A polymorphous camera has always turned, and will turn forever, its lens focussed upon all the appearances of the world. Before the invention of still photography, the frames of the infinite cinema were blank, black leader; then a few images began to appear upon the endless ribbon of film. Since the birth of the photographic cinema, all the frames are filled with images.[38]

On this metahistorical account, far from being the source of cinema, its "originary instance",[39] photography comprises a particular phase in the (logical) evolution of cinema: the phase in which cinema's leader becomes filled with images. Following this premise, the relation between photography and cinema is entirely liberated of all the baggage associated with any historical account. We no longer need to ask how cinema emerged from photography or entertain the notion that cinema is just the animation of still images – something that one day simply happened to befall photography: "History", notes Frampton, "views the marriage of cinema and the photograph as one of convenience; metahistory must look upon it as one of necessity."[40] Even more importantly, we become free to reconceptualize the relationship of still to moving image according to a logic of inclusion or immanence rather than one of media specificity: "There is nothing in the structural logic of the cinema film strip that precludes sequestering any single image. A still photograph is simply an isolated frame taken out of the infinite cinema."[41]

Rethinking the correlation of still and moving images following this logic of inclusion allows us to introject the temporal heterogeneity of photography into the mechanized temporal flux of cinema. Following such an introjection, the traditional picture of cinema as the simple animation of still images becomes untenable for the specific reason that it does violence *to the temporal dynamism specific to photography*, and not just to the primacy of the movement constitutive of cinema. When the photograph (or still image) is taken, as it typically has been by post classical film theorists and historians, as the elementary unit out of which cinema is constructed, it undergoes a fundamental reification: specifically, it is wrested from the processual context from out of which it emerges in order to be objectified as a static and purely empirical entity, a fixed, fully actualized building block for the something else that is cinema. What is lost in the process is the capacity that photography affords – a capacity virtually "contained" in every photograph – to modulate movement (movement-images) at temporal scales that are both extra-perceptual and extra-cinematic. It is precisely this capacity, I would also like to suggest, that informs the theoretical concept of the time-image and that differentiates a Frampton-inspired rethinking of this latter from its Deleuzian "original." Thus, rather than arising in the space *between-two* images (where the images are *per force* treated as static and fully actualized), the direct power of time animates the photograph itself, and indeed, the photograph *as itself a movement-image*, a framing of movement-variation at a micro-temporal scale that is beneath the threshold of both human *and* cinematic perception. The rather counterintuitive conclusion here is that the photograph, no less than cinema *and in its own right*, is a movement-image, and also, that whatever opportunity we might get to "perceive" time directly, to perceive "time-images", involves some interface with infinitesimal movement-variation, which is to say, with the sub-perceptual micro-temporal domain – and virtuality – proper to photography.

Precisely such an introjection of photographic micro-temporality into cinema seems to inform Frampton's theoretical ruminations on movement and stillness as well as much of his cinematic practice. Immediately after defining cinema, in "Incision in History/Segments of Eternity", as "an art that is to be fully and radically isomorphic with the kinesis and stasis – ... with the dynamic 'structure' – of consciousness", Frampton presents a *noema* of photography diametrically opposed to Barthes's famous "*ça a été*:

> On the other hand, if still photography has seemed, since its beginnings, vastly pregnant with the imminence of a revelation that never quite transpires, and if it has never coherently defined a task for itself, we might make free to infer that it mimes, as does cinema, its own condition: we might imagine, in a word, that photography is "about" precisely those recognitions, formations, percipiences, suspensions, persistences, hesitations within the mind that precede, if they do not utterly foreshadow, that discovery, and *peripeteia* and springing-into-motion, and inspiration that is articulate consciousness.[42]

Far from capturing the conjunction of reality and pastness ("that was") that leads Barthes to his well-known melancholic meditations on death and mortality, photography in Frampton's conception operates on the "just-before" of consciousness, the entire microtemporal domain of processes that remain absolutely imperceptible to perceptual consciousness but that nonetheless inform its emergence and indeed make it possible.

In this conception, the "photograph" (or still image) comprises one privileged element (and moment) in a larger photographic process, which is to say, in a process that does not reify the photograph as an exclusive, self-contained artifact (as Barthes does), but that encompasses elements of pre- as well as post-production – the *preacceleration* of movement-perception as well as serial, minimally differentiated takes and variant developings of a single negative. Such an "expanded" field plays a central role in Frampton's revisionary history of photography's never-quite-explicit reckoning with time. Consider, for example, the privilege Frampton accords Edward Weston, who "simply centered his figure, outside [humanly experienced] time and within the nominal spatial ground of the photographic artifact, celebrating, with unexcelled carnality, the differentiation of the moment of perception from all those moments of impercipience during which the resting brain processes only two billion binary bits of information per second."[43] Or consider, the role of the "Quintessential Sample" in the practice of Henri Cartier-Bresson, who, notes Frampton, "speaks of decisive moments, in tones that seem to suggest that the making of art is a process of tasteful selection". When he subsequently recounts his own encounter with Cartier-Bresson's contact sheets, Frampton describes the process of this selection: "36 images of a dying horse were as alike as intelligence could make them, and I am constrained to believe that the 'decisive moment,' if such a thing occurred, happened when the photographer decided which of the three dozen pictures he would print and publish".[44]

Where cinema remains focused on its "appalling ambition" to mime the flux of consciousness, photography offers the potential for – though not the actual experience of, or at least any kind of sustained actualization of – perception beyond perception. Photography, that is, opens vistas onto an imperceptible that, following Frampton's musings, would seem to liberate "our mind" from "our body", or more exactly, to awaken "another mind" attuned not to conscious contents but precisely to the indiscernible nuances that occupy and render dynamic the space between discrete, identifiable stages of movement. On Frampton's account, this potential emerges with the rapid-exposure camera which is able to displace the "single epiphany" of the individual, privileged photograph in favor of the seriality of "36 consecutive images." A certain *New York Times Magazine* cover featuring the serial image of a former American President perfectly illustrates this displacement:

About two-thirds of [the 36 images] exhibited the President's face as a familiar icon of benignant, immobile blandness. But the remaining dozen, more or less uniformly distributed, were pictures of a face that was not quite the same nor yet entirely different, whose expression suggested, during instants newly visible, the extremes of terror and of rage, suicidal despair, the forgetfulness of sleep, or the vacuity of utter confusion.

Commenting on the significance of the displacement, Frampton imagines the birth of a non- or sub-conscious agent operating at cross-purposes to consciousness and capable of directly grasping the micro-perceptual: "It seems to me, almost, that another mind grasped and manipulated the features, reaching out with a kind of berserk certitude through temporal fissures whose durations could be measured in thousands of a second."[45]

If photography came to realize such a potentiality as the culmination of its historical mission, that has everything to do with its own shift from a concern with exploring the visual detail of representable space to a focus on exposing and making proleptically actual the microtemporalities hidden within time. As Frampton depicts it, this culmination coincides with, and is intensified by, techniques of frame-by-frame analysis and subsequent development of technical capacities for analyzing film – or, to be more precise, for slowing down, reversing, and delinearizing the filmic flux. Photographic exploration *of film* furnishes the richest instance of our access to the properly imperceptible domain of microtemporal sensibility, and Frampton's reference to anthropologist Ray Birdwhistell's use of filmic analysis reveals precisely how such access can impact future perception by being fed back into, and thus indirectly influencing, the flux of experience. Birdwhistell, who founded kinesics as a field of inquiry and research, used film to capture the interaction of a mother and infant in a household that had already produced two schizophrenic children; through meticulous, frame-by-frame analysis, Birdwhistell was able to identify one moment in which the mother appeared to give the child contradictory signals. In his recapping of this mediated research, Frampton appears to be struck by the massive temporal disjunction between the time of inscription and the time of analysis: "Birdwhistell states that rigorous examination of such films requires, on the average, about one hundred hours per running second of real time.... If there is a monster in hiding here, it has cunningly concealed itself within time, emerging, in Birdwhistell's film on four frames ... that is, for *only one-sixth of a second*."[46]

Modulating Movement-Perception

Generalized from this specific deployment, the temporal disjunction opened up by the photographic exploration of film forms the impetus for Frampton's own concrete experimentations with the temporal flexibility of cinema. The formal principle at work in these temporal excavations is, as Annette Michelson incisively discerns, the logic of the Dedekind cut. Named for German mathematician Richard Dedekind, the Dedekind cut (formulated in 1831, the year before Fox-Talbot's first photographs):

> is a partition of the rational numbers into two non-empty parts A and B, such that all elements of A are less than all elements of B and A contains no greatest element. The cut itself is, conceptually, the "gap" defined between A and B. In other words, A contains every rational number less than the cut, and B contains every rational number greater than the cut. The cut itself is in neither set.[47]

For our purposes, which is to say, insofar as it concerns Frampton's introjection of photographic (micro-)temporality into film, Dedekind's cut introduces a certain scale flexibility into the concept of the instant. The significance of this flexibility can be discerned by contrasting it with Deleuze's concept of the "any-instant-whatever", which cinema inherits from early modern science and which understands instants to be identical to and equidistant from one another.[48] If the any-instant-whatever names the cinematic construction of the instant, the Dedekind cut – understood as an operation to divide past and future and thus as coincident with the "now"[49] – designates a variable, counter-cinematic, properly photographic instant. This variable instant marks a *caesura that can occur anywhere within a continuity*, and not simply at privileged regular intervals (the spatial equivalent of rational numbers). Indeed, it belongs to a conceptualization of continuity in which continuity is prior to division. As the basis for a media practice, the Dedekind cut thus affords the possibility for an intensive logic of division, one that does not oppose continuity and discontinuity; specifically, it affords the possibility to operate on an intensive timeline and suggests a correlation between virtuality and scale-specificity such that what emerges at more coarse-grained temporal scales relates to what transpires, simultaneously but beyond perception, at finer-grained scales, as actualization to virtuality. On such an intensive timeline, the standardized time of cinematic movement would be doubled by a variable, intensive time of photographic (micro-) movement.

To get even more concrete: the logic of the Dedekind cut informs the ontology of Frampton's infinite film; indeed, on one understanding, Frampton's film simply *is* the postulation of an infinite continuum that can be divided and delimited – actualized – through variant media interfaces and at variant timescales, only one of which is cinema in its dominant, consciousness-miming form. The logic of the Dedekind cut also informs Frampton's critical media practice insofar as this practice involves the introjection of photographic (micro-)temporality into cinematic time. Accordingly, if the MAGELLAN project comprises the larger context for Frampton's theorization of the infinite film, his media practice finds its primal scene somewhat earlier in his career as filmmaker, namely in CRITICAL MASS, the 1971 film made directly in the wake of – and as I shall suggest in response to – his second most critically acclaimed film, *(nostalgia)*. Indeed, if *(nostalgia)* marks Frampton's conversion from (still) photographer to filmmaker, as has been suggested by more than one of Frampton's commentators, CRITICAL MASS may mark his further conversion from filmmaker to media modulator. CRITICAL MASS, in other words, inaugurates Frampton's own anticipation of new media art practice as part of what I termed, at the beginning of this article, experimental film's aspiration to the condition of new media.

While *(nostalgia)* and CRITICAL MASS both address the elective affinity linking photography and memory, they could not differ more in how they do so nor in their respective visions of what is at stake in this affinity. Most striking in this regard is their divergence of temporal scale: whereas *(nostalgia)* embraces the temporal flux of mainstream cinema (24 fps) in order to highlight, and perhaps also to question, the power of photography to recall and to mourn the past, CRITICAL MASS literally introjects the static instantaneity of photography into the cinematic flux.

(nostalgia) comprises thirteen sections (thirteen 100-foot reels of film), each of which includes an image sequence featuring a photograph displayed on a stove burner for about 20 seconds before it begins to burn up and is accompanied by a voice-over description that, as it becomes slowly apparent, does not correspond to the presently depicted photograph, but to the very next one. The effect of the asynchronous presentation of description and image is to activate the viewer's faculty of recollection such that the appearance of each image subsequent to the first one revivifies the now past description, though not without imparting a nagging feeling of lost detail and some sense of disjunction between sensory modes of cognition.

By contrast, CRITICAL MASS depicts a heated domestic argument between a man and a woman standing in front of a blank white wall, and is edited to produce visual and aural stuttering as well as progressively mounting desynchronization of image and sound. While the editing algorithm varies across the film's duration, the most commonly used pattern is, as Frampton describes it "two steps forward and one back", a pattern he calls "phasing";[50] for example, the line "It was a very spontaneous thing" is depicted as a series of back-and-forth phases: "It was ... It was a ... was a very ... a very spont ... very spontaneous ... taneous thing."[51]

Compared to *(nostalgia)*, the scope of "memory" in Critical mass is vastly condensed and enclosed upon itself: thus, rather than a past event or description, the memory of the content of former experiences, what is remembered here is quite literally *the sequence of frames* or "photograms" (following the terminology of Garrett Stewart) immediately preceding the now of perception. Precisely because of its back-and-forth play with the linear flux of cinema, Critical Mass foregrounds the texture of what philosopher Jean-Michel Salanskis, commenting on Husserl, has called "adherent" time (or adherent temporal intentionality). Differentiated from "referential" (temporal) intentionality, which remembers or "recollects" at the time-scale of lived experiences (contents of consciousness), adherent intentionality *retains* the just-past (and *protends* the just-to-come) at a time-scale that lies beneath the threshold of representation. Even more starkly: whereas referential intentionality intends the time of the experience of a consciousness experiencing objects in the world, adherent intentionality intends nothing but the passage of time itself. Accordingly, if referential intentionality supports the time of consciousness as lived experience, adherent intentionality produces the time of life, the basal continuity that underlies and energizes all events in time, including the events of consciousness that constitute lived experience. In normal circumstances, the experience of adherent intentionality remains outside of the scope of awareness; it is more or less akin to the "preacceleration" or incipiency that Manning positions as the virtuality of perception.[52]

Yet because it interferes with this normally nonconscious production of adherent intentionality, Critical Mass brings the structure of retentionality (and protentionality) into the scope of viewer awareness, though certainly not without continuing to stimulate the viewer's ongoing production of temporal adherence. More specifically, Critical Mass introduces a disjunction into the process of temporal intentionality that has the effect of separating what is normally intertwined and putatively inseparable: namely, adherent intentionality and the external "content" that is its necessary manifold and stimulus.

With Critical Mass, then, Frampton would seem to add a new element – a third stage – to the ongoing contemporary critical project of revealing the technical basis of time-consciousness. If Husserl's foundational work in phenomenology emphasized the necessity for time-consciousness to externalize its operation via a "temporal object" (paradigmatically, the melody), and if Bernard Stiegler has recently demonstrated that such an object must be a technical object with temporalizing power of its own (paradigmatically, the real-time televisual flux of global cinema), Frampton underscores the productive dimension of the correlation between the technical synthesis of consciousness and the adherent intentionality of the living. As Frampton configures it, this productive dimension emerges out of the interference that is always, as it were, virtually present when technical syntheses are superimposed upon living ones. In stark contrast to the technical temporal objects Stiegler proffers as surrogates for our collective temporalization in the world today, CRITICAL MASS introduces a tension between the two fluxes that are at issue in the operation of any technical temporal object, no matter how concealed from view: on the one hand, the flux of cinematic images (or photograms) and, on the other, the flux of the living (adherent intentionality). More specifically still, Frampton's unsettling film desynchronizes the flux of our spectatorial time and the flux of the image machine that is supposedly driving it; the result is a certain liberation of our adherent intentionality as the force of time's forward movement.

Insofar as it modulates our encounter with the imperceptible, micro-temporal domain of pre-experiential incipiency, CRITICAL MASS participates in the development of a new, media-centered stage in the technical contamination of phenomenological time-consciousness: rather than a laboratory for excavating the temporal structure of consciousness as it generates lived experiences in the world at large (Stiegler's contribution), the technical temporal object that is CRITICAL MASS explores the temporal experience of its own viewing, or more exactly, it temporally excavates its own constitution in and through the viewer's lived experiencing of it. To put this contrast more starkly: unlike the cinematic temporal objects Stiegler discusses (exemplarily Fellini's INTERVISTA), CRITICAL MASS doesn't use cinema as a means to explore the temporal dynamics of something else (i.e., time-consciousness), but engages a concrete series of cinematic images (the images on two 100 feet reels of film) as itself the experiential structure to be explored.

With this difference in mind, we can understand the profound implications of Frampton's pedagogical claims for his film: "One of the things that goes on in CRITICAL MASS", he tells Scott MacDonald, "is a process of training the spectator to watch the film. The work teaches the spectator how to read the work."[53] In so doing, I want to suggest, what the work in fact teaches the spectator is how she produces adherence – how, by processing the flux of concrete images (photograms), she generates not just the sensory experience of the film, but also the continuous time of her own living. What makes CRITICAL MASS capable of revealing the operation of adherent intentionality is precisely what makes it an experimental film and also, not surprisingly, what explains its anticipation of digital media art: it is precisely because CRITICAL MASS complicates the temporal paradigm of cinema – the coincidence between the flux of images and the flux of spectatorial consciousness – that it can focus attention on adherence. For what Frampton's editing algorithms effectively do (and this applies equally to both the two steps forward and one back that organizes the photograms as well as the gradually mounting desynchronization of the sound track from the images)[54] is create a crisis within retention: in watching the film, the spectator is confronted with situations where what is retained (the just-past of the present of experiencing consciousness) does not in fact coincide with the just-past of the current image or set of photograms, – but rather *with its just-to-come*. Frampton's film literally forces its spectators to retain, and to do so repeatedly, what – at the level of the image and soundtrack – remains still to come. In this way, it not only destroys the temporal coincidence central to cinema's "appalling ambition" to mime the flux of consciousness, but also liberates adherent intentionality from its subordination to the production of a fictional reality effect. In viewing CRITICAL MASS, in short, we do not lend our adherent intentionality to the time of the cinema, that is, to the time of images as the representational content of a fictional or at least remembered experience. On the contrary, we place – or rather, are compelled to place – our power to generate temporal adherence in the service of *photogrammatic* flux, and learn through the startling disjunction between our feeling of our own forward-moving continuity and our perception of a halting, stuttering narrative progress that this power stems not from the media temporal object but from our own living embodiment of worldly "depresencing".

Notes

1. Peter Lunenfeld, "Hollis Frampton: The Perfect Machine" in *Snap to Grid* (Cambridge, MA: MIT Press, 2000), 120-21.
2. Lev Manovich, *The Language of New Media* (Cambridge, MA: MIT Press, 1999), 85-86.
3. Manovich, 86.
4. I have criticized Manovich for this in *New Philosophy for New Media* (Cambridge, MA: MIT Press, 2004), chap. 1.
5. Frampton, "For a Metahistory of Film: Commonplace Notes and Hypotheses" in *On the Camera Arts and Consecutive Matters: The Writings of Hollis Frampton*, B. Jenkins (ed.) (Cambridge, MA: MIT Press, 2009), 136.
6. Ibid., 136.
7. Ibid., 135.
8. Ibid.,137.
9. "The infinite film contains an infinity of passages wherein no frame resembles any other in the slightest degree, and a further infinity of passages wherein successive frames are nearly identical as intelligence can make them", ibid., 137.
10. Lunenfeld, 133.
11. Gunning, presentation at the Roundtable on Cinema and Art History, SCMS, Los Angeles, March 20, 2010, as heard by the author. Se also Gunning's article in the present collection.
12. David Bordwell and Kristin Thompson, *Film Art: An Introduction*, 4th ed. (New York: McGraw-Hill, Inc., 1993), 3.

13. For an example of this line of questioning, see D.N. Rodowick, *The Virtual Life of Film* (Cambridge, MA: Harvard University Press, 2007); Rodowick claims that digital cameras cannot capture duration, which is to say the temporal reality of human experience, but can only inscribe the cycling of the computer as it performs the various algorithms it utilizes to generate images.

14. For an example of this line of questioning, see Babette Mangolte, "A Matter of Time: Analog Versus Digital" in *Camera Lucida, Camera Obscura: Essays for Annette Michelson* (Amsterdam: Amsterdam University Press, 2003).

15. Tom Gunning, "Moving Away from the Index: Cinema and the Impression of Reality", *Differences: A Journal of Feminist Cultural Studies* 18.1 (2007): 29-52, here 40.

16. Christian Metz, "On the Impression of Reality in the Cinema" in *Film Language: A Semiotics of the Cinema*, transl. M. Taylor (Chicago: University of Chicago Press, 1974), 7-8, emphasis added.

17. Gunning, 42-43.

18. Metz, 8-9, emphasis added.

19. The original context for Metz's concept of cinema's "insubstantiality" is the comparison of cinema with the theater, a contrast introduced by Arnheim. Based on Arnheim's view, the theater differs from the cinema in that it takes place in real time and space (whereas films gives us "images only"), and it gives us an experience of "reality itself" rather than an "illusion of reality." While Metz rejects the binary terms of Arnheim's contrast, its basic framework still seems to haunt his conception of "insubstantiality" or at least the unquestioned assumption that what is visual is nonmaterial.

20. Gunning, 42, emphasis added.

21. Deleuze, of course, famously argues that Bergson misunderstood the cinema in *Creative Evolution*, but that his analysis of movement in *Matter and Memory* – which informs the Deleuzian concept of the movement-image – comprises the fundamentals of a solid understanding of cinema's operation. Gunning offers a more specific criticism of Bergson's error in *Creative Evolution* and suggests that Deleuze only reinforces this error: "Great confusion (which I feel Deleuze increases rather than dispels) comes if we do not realize that the analytical aspect of the cinematograph that Bergson took as his model for this tendency to conceive of motion in terms of static instants derives from the *filmstrip* in which motion is analyzed into a succession of frames, not the *projected image* on the screen in which synthetic motion is recreated" (Gunning, 42).

22. Massumi, 3.

23. I borrow the term "depresencing" [*Entgegenwärtigung*] from Eugen Fink, Husserl's last student who worked on the late manuscripts on time (the so-called *C-Manuscripts*) in the early 1930s. Fink coins the term "depresencing" to name the world's ongoing temporalization, the world's continuous moving out of the present into the past (and hence opening up the reality of a future) that, Fink argues, is itself the *condition* for time-consciousness to continue to presence (and to experience its presencing as a thick nowness, that includes a retentional and protentional supplement). See Fink, *Studien zur Phänomenologie, 1930-1939* (The Hague: Nijhoff, 1966).

24. Manning, 94-5, emphasis added.

25. Ibid., 74, emphasis added.

26. Manning does suggest – in the mode of counterfactual speculation – that Marey's work might have opened up a fundamentally different trajectory of cinema than the trajectory that was actualized, and that now comprises the empirical history of cinema: "had Marey's experiments with movement been foregrounded within the history of cinema, cinema's early emphasis on theories of semiosis might have been derouted into a more developed exploration of how cinema moves. This might have redirected the study of cinema from its early academic embeddedness within formalist thought toward early twentieth-century expressions of movement such as the invention of modern dance, Futurism's concern with ontogenesis, Bergson's theory of duration. The effect of this convergence of cinema and movement would have been a foregrounding less of narrative strategies within the cinematic than experimentation with how images provoke durational flows that are themselves mobile even before passing through a projector" (8). Notwithstanding its questionable claims regarding cinema's early emphasis on semiosis and formalism (which probably arose with the advent of post-classical film theory), this is an interesting suggestion. Indeed, I would suggest that Metz's privileging of movement – and Gunning's return to it – marks a moment in what we might, in fact, consider to be Marey's cinematic legacy.

27. Erin Manning, "Coloring the Virtual", *Configurations*, 16.3 (Fall 2008): 325-345, here 326, emphasis added.

28. I borrow the concept of a direct sensory "pickup" from psychologist James Gibson, who argues against a theory of the senses as subjective mediators of perceptual experience. Rather than the senses "translating" environmental information into a form that can be experienced by human mindbodies, sense perception for Gibson involves the direct pickup of information from the environment. See J.J. Gibson, *The Ecological Approach to Visual Perception* (New York: Taylor & Francis, 1986), Chap. 14.

29. Georges Didi-Huberman, "La Danse de toute chose" in *Mouvements de l'air: Etienne-Jules Marey, Photographe des fluids*, Didi-Huberman and Laurent Mannoni (eds.) (Editions Gallimard/Reunion des musees nationaux, 2004) p. 268.

30. See Didi-Huberman, 284: "It is as if the graphic method and chronophotography had as their ultimate stake to make us see and understand the *dance of every thing*." He specifies that this ultimate stake operates a subversion of "the explicit intentions formulated by his system."

31. Didi-Huberman, 300.

32. This is my definition of *technogenesis*. See my *Bodies in Code. Interfaces with Digital Media* (New York: Routledge, 2006).

33. Joel Snyder, "Visualization and Visibility" in *Picturing Science, Producing Art*, eds. Caroline A. Jones and Peter Galison (New York: Routledge, 1998), p. 380, last emphasis added.

34. Etienne-Jules Marey, *La Méthode Graphique*, cited in Snyder 380.

35. Snyder, 381; Marey, cited in Snyder, 384.

36. Hollis Frampton, "A Pentagram for Conjuring the Narrative" in *On the Camera Arts and Consecutive Matters*, 140-41.

37. Hollis Frampton, "Incisions in History/Segments of Eternity" in *On the Camera Arts and Consecutive Matters*, 42-3.

38. Frampton, "For a Metahistory of Film", 134.

39. I borrow this term from Christopher Phillips, "Word Pictures: Frampton and Photography," *October* 32 (spring 1985: 62-76, here 62.
40. Frampton, "For a Metahistory of Film," 134.
41. Ibid., 134.
42. Frampton, "Incisions," 45.
43. Ibid., 45.
44. Ibid., 46.
45. Ibid., 47.
46. Ibid., 47.
47. Wikipedia, "Dedekind Cut," http://en.wikipedia.org/wiki/Dedekind_cut, last accessed 5/14/2010.
48. "It is in this sense that the cinema is the system which reproduces movement as a function of any-instant-whatever that is, as a function of equidistant instants, selected so as to create an impression of continuity. Any other system which reproduces movement through an order of exposures [*poses*] projected in such a way that they pass into one another, or are 'transformed,' is foreign to the cinema" (Gilles Deleuze, *Cinema I: the Movement-Image*, transl. H. Tomlinson and B. Habberjam [Minneapolis: University of Minnesota Press, 1986], 5).
49. Following the suggestion of Annette Michelson, who writes in her foreword to the original volume of Frampton's collected essays, *Circles of Confusion*: "It has been pointed out that Dedekind's axiom constitutes a particularly adroit presentation of our representation of time. [cites the Dedekind axiom] … So it is that we intuitively establish, within Time, a past and a future which are mutually exclusive. Together they compose Time stretching into eternity. Within this representation, 'now' constitutes the division which separates past and future; any instant of the past was once 'now,' and any instant of the future will be 'now.' Therefore, any instant may constitute this division" (Michelson, "Time Out of Mind: a foreword" in *Circles of Confusion: Film, Photography, Video: Texts, 1968-1980* [Rochester, NY: Visual Studies Workshop, 1983], 17.
50. See "Hollis Frampton," in Scott MacDonald, *A Critical Cinema: Interviews with Independent Filmmakers* (Berkeley: University of California Press, 1988), 65.
51. Bruce Jenkins, dissertation, 260.
52. This is especially so in the context of recent work bridging Husserlian phenomenology of time-consciousness and neuroscientific explorations of perception. See, for example, Varela, "The Specious Present…" where the lived experience of consciousness literally emerges out of microtemporal neural processes that, in relation to it, remain virtual.
53. MacDonald, 65.
54. Frampton gives some insight into his process in the interview with MacDonald: "The whole film, of course, was shot as two long takes: the original material is two 100-foot rolls. The sound was continuous; the Nagra was simply left on and that's why you hear the squeals of the slate. Except for that very brief opening passage in which it starts out in sync and immediately disintegrates, it's divided very roughly into fourths, with the passage in the dark forcing two pairs apart. At first, they match, and then in the dark, where there is only sound, each segment of sound, instead of going two steps forward and one back, is simply repeated exactly three times. When the imagery reappears, the temporal overlap resumes, but the unit of

sound cutting is slightly larger. Typically it's about six frames (or a quarter of a second) larger than the image unit, which means that once every four seconds they will coincide exactly. They rotate in and out of sync with each other until finally, they lose sync entirely and are out of step first by one repetition of the word 'bull-ship' and then by two repetitions of the word 'bullshit'...." (MacDonald, 65).

The Use of Freeze and Slide Motion

The Figure of Visual Standstill in R.W. Fassbinder's Films

Christa Blümlinger

Currently, questions of film theory regarding phenomena of cinematographic temporalization are discussed in relation to new media. At the same time, however, these discussions also pick up on earlier theoretical models of the relationship between standstill and motion, the prehistory of the cinema, theories of photography and the snapshot, as well as the aesthetics of modernism and the avant-garde.[1] In the 1920s, the classical film theorist and avant-garde filmmaker Jean Epstein was already describing film in general as a machine that perspectivizes space and time: the ultimate "machine to think time". Slow motion and fast-forward as well as the close-up are central figures in his thought. With his concept of the cinematograph as a "robot brain," Epstein points out the fact that the filmic connection of standstill and movement, discontinuity and continuity represented a profound transformation of perception: Epstein conceives of the cinema as a paradox – the inorganic, "mineral" production of the living.[2] The apparent standstill of a film operates precisely on this paradoxical constellation. It is no coincidence that film theory later worked off the key neorealist works of modernist cinema, such as the films of Rossellini: the Bazinian description of film as a "change mummified"[3] also targets the strange nature of movement in the cinema. Recently, Laura Mulvey has explored once more the contradictory materialization of life and death in film using the example of Rossellini's JOURNEY TO ITALY: cinema's *punctum*, according to Mulvey, is precisely realized where the repression of this contradiction fails, thereby making the spectator feel uncertain.[4]

When Garrett Stewart defines the figure of the freeze-frame as a repeated, projected individual image that entails the suspension of succession and the negation as moving picture, he sees in this form of disruption – with an eye on the narrative cinema – the potential of "cinematic reflexivity" within a narration, "that paradoxical case of real motion without real movements that merely takes the condition of cinema to its limit".[5] But we should qualify this point: the dialectics of standstill and movement can only be examined in a concrete filmic form, and should be considered historically. While the freeze-frame in classical cinema is quite rare, that is only because classical cinema developed other modes of stasis and the production of fascination (Mary Ann Doane, for example, points out that the close-up also serves to interrupt narrative flow),[6] Serge

Daney argues that advertising, video clips, and the films based on these forms today mobilize an excess of visual standstills that becomes a form of exchange between visual regimes.[7]

As Gilles Deleuze points out, what we directly perceive as a moving image in the cinema is an "intermediate image as immediate given,"[8] created from single frames. The individual frame of the filmstrip cannot be perceived as an image in the projection unless it is frozen, and thus becomes a visible "freeze-frame". From the perspective of the spectator, Roland Barthes writes about the possibility of the virtual selection of an individual frame that was selected not in relation to a suggested meaning, but in light of the filmstrip. The choice would be made not according to criteria of the moments privileged in the course of the film – or in any narrative – but, as it were, a random card would be taken from the deck in search of an additional significance, one that is at a distance from the realistic authority of the running image, what Roland Barthes calls the "obtuse meaning"[9] in the individual photogram. This meaning emerges fragmentarily and unpredictably, as a kind of utopian virtuality. Deleuze also seems to define the cinema as a system that reproduces movement in relation to a random moment, the "any-instant-whatever," but as a function of "equidistant instants selected so as to create an impression of continuity."[10] Raymond Bellour, commenting on Barthes's and Deleuze's conceptions of the relationship between the instant and duration, raises the question of the nature of the *interruption* of filmic movement: Should it be seen as one privileged instant among many "any-instant-whatever," or rather as a privileged instant that appears singular and unique?[11] Bellour points out that the answer cannot be of a general or formal nature, but that the question needs to be explored historically or singularly in relation to a particular oeuvre or film.

The question that Bellour poses in his consideration of the filmic instant in modern cinema's forms of interruption is that of the snapshot, when it becomes both "the pose and the pause of film",[12] that is, the more general question of the figure of the "photographic" in film (and not just the individual stilled image, the "photogrammatic"). A similar argument for conceiving standstill and movement via the relationship between photography and film can be found in Philippe Dubois, who locates the possibility of conceptualizing photography as it inheres in film at the point of intersection between the two media. He describes the filmic individual image as a "dialectic image, that points to an object that is neither (truly) film, nor (simply) it is a bit more than a photograph (it is its beyond) and a bit less than film (it is its this world)," furthermore as the "embodiment of the idea of an intermediate member of the chain, the fold between photograph and film, the exact point (*punctum*) of passage between the two".[13]

Individual images are only perceptible if we slow down or stop the film. If the film is not run according to its realistic running time, but in a new space-time order linked back to its textuality and its materiality, a form of reflexivity can emerge. Such an analytical gesture applied to the relationship between standstill and movement draws the filmic itself into consideration, a system consisting of mutually determining categories of the visible and the invisible. The film in projection, based on a celluloid strip, usually conceals its material basis from the consciousness of the spectators, achieving what film theory terms the "reality effect." The *arrêt-sur-images* or freeze-frame may point to the materiality of film, the celluloid strip, which is usually denied by what Thierry Kuntzel calls the "projection film".[14]

As far as the historical dimension of the phenomenon is concerned, Serge Daney has proposed one of the most interesting theories of the freeze-frame or *arrêt-sur-image*. In a series of writings,[15] Daney shows, with the freezing of the last shot in Truffaut's LES QUATRE CENTS COUPS, how a figure enters the film body that he terms a "hallucinated form",[16] a figure that represents a modern form of transgression. According to Daney, this figure eventually transforms over the years, often as the final shot in a film, becoming a clichéd, symptomatic standstill that, unlike Truffaut's film, is no longer part of the (cinema) image, but rather, the so-called "visual" (i.e. advertising, logos, or television series). In Daney's terms, I would like to propose that in Fassbinder, the freeze-frame can indeed be placed on the side of the image (that is, the cinema), but paradoxically, it is actually produced in the interest of a critique that aims at certain dimensions of the so-called "visual".

Various stylistic figures observed in Fassbinder's films – the framings that allow for a theatricalization of scenes, objects cut off in the visual foreground that have the function of a scenic ramp, or shifts in focus that accentuate various points of view – have caused critics to place the work, despite the seriality of some productions, in the category of modern auteur cinema. However, the figure of the standstill in Fassbinder's work has seldom been noted until recently, probably because it often appears marginally in a literal sense: in Fassbinder's films, the freeze-frame as a specific form of visual standstill can be found as a figure of pause or sudden interruption usually at the beginning or end of his films.

As I would like to demonstrate in this chapter, in Fassbinder's work, this form of standstill in light of its complexity and variability does not solely represent a kind of banalized repetition of a modern stylistic figure in the wake of the Nouvelle Vague, but rather is tied to a specific idea about film and a kind of media theory. Furthermore, it implies a certain critique of the consensus of the contemporary society, which sometimes even assumes a utopian dimension. In so doing, it is located within a literary modernism, where the sense of the moment is bound to reflection, becoming an interface for relating past and present. Moreover, this form of interruption surfaces in Fassbinder's films as a closing figure, but also at the opening of some of his films, where it has the capacity to bind itself to other forms of suddenness.

Without supplying a comprehensive list of freeze-frames in Fassbinder's films, I have selected a few moments of visual standstill from his extensive work to show the variation and complexity of this figure to develop a theory of interruption in film. I would like to begin with one of the most famous films, DIE EHE DER MARIA BRAUN (THE MARRIAGE OF MARIA BRAUN) (1978). This film, as we know, is literarily framed by photographs: a portrait of Hitler at the start and a series of large portraits of West German chancellors at the end introduce the notion of a temporary expansion of the narrative, placed in the postwar years. This series of "negative" monuments – Willy Brandt is missing – is often analyzed in terms of semantic content. For me, however, it seems just as essential that this insertion of the photographic in the movement image on a formal level forms a symptomatic correspondence to another form of standstill at the start of the film. Even before the credits, the opening of the film brings us the scene of a newly married couple and a registry official leaving a German registry office during an air raid. We watch as the excited couple throw themselves to the ground, imploring the official to sign the marriage certificate right there. A sheet of paper floats upward, borne on the gust of wind caused by exploding bombs, and then, in the middle of the visual field, there is a sudden standstill in the form of a freeze-frame, while the soundtrack continues to herald the horror of the approaching artillery. This is followed by the film title in red letters that fill the entire visual field, word after word, as if it were a page in a book. At the end, Fassbinder's name appears alone on a white backdrop.

With this standstill, the floating sheet of paper is simultaneously captured and displaced by the film. Due to the non-sync between image and sound, of visual interruption and auditive flow, we are confronted from the very start with two various temporal modi: the time of the film narrative (the postwar years) and the time of the making of the film (the 1970s). At issue here is Fassbinder's time-place: when the author tells stories and histories, they are always primarily in the present tense.

In ICH WILL DOCH NUR, DASS IHR MICH LIEBT (I ONLY WANT YOU TO LOVE ME) (1976), there are numerous suspensions of movement toward the end of the film. As a whole, the narration is structured around flashbacks that are all motivated by conversations in a prison. The conversation in the beginning of the film is accorded therapeutic value for the (anti)hero Peter (Vitus Zeplichal), as well as symbolic capital for the psychologist, who intends to write a book about the story. Slowly, in the form of flashbacks, a story develops around a young man's psychic repressions, his "blockage", Oedipal confusions and a system of alienated exchange relations.[17] At the end of the film, a series of three visual standstills introduces the passing of the final titles in white letters. These visual stand-

stills astonishingly do not only serve as a curtain or backdrop for the final credits – this is Daney's critique of several films that have allowed the freeze-frame
to petrify into a clichéd figure.[18] Quite on the contrary, Fassbinder's final standstills are structurally tied to the psychologist's last question, which goes unan-
swered. In this series of *blockages* of the image (a kind of figurative displacement
of the protagonist's own symptoms), an *over the shoulder-shot* from behind the
psychologist is at first briefly arrested, framing a slight bottom view of Peter,
who, in that moment, stands up as the question is posed. The movement is then
resumed, and, in a counter shot, we see Peter's hands banging on the cassette
recorder on the table. This gesture becomes the object of the second interruption, accompanied by the continuous sound that repeats the sentence that was
just recorded. LEBEN SIE EIGENTLICH GERNE? (DO YOU LIKE LIVING?). After this,
the "frozen" image "melts", the movement resumes once again and Peter leaves
the frame. The third and last standstill occurs in this final shot and corresponds
to the beginning of the film: the camera pans towards the window, while behind
the bars a landscape opens in the twilight. This final shot marks the end of the
story, but also indicates that the story doesn't end for the protagonist, who still
has many years of imprisonment ahead of him.

It is telling that the same type of serial interruption can be found at the end of
another melodrama, where the story also ends in a disciplinary institution. In
WILDWECHSEL (JAIL BAIT) (1972) Hanni (Eva Mattes) is, by the end of the film,
all alone in the column-lined hall of a courthouse, while she waits to be called to
the witness stand to testify against Franz (Harry Baier), her former lover, whom
she had murder her father. The final credits pass over the frozen moments of the
final shot, showing Hanni, outdoors, hopping across the stones, oblivious to
everything as she plays with a cootie catcher. The riddle of her attitude toward
the accused is underscored by a gaze toward her warden (Irm Hermann), as
well as by the brief appearance of another witness. The issue in this interruption, as in ICH WILL DOCH NUR, DASS IHR MICH LIEBT, is the Truffautian idea of
an expansion or transgression of the narrative frame. On the other hand, in the
serial decomposition of a movement, the imaginary capture of a character is
established, just as in Godard's SAUVE QUI PEUT LA VIE (SLOW MOTION) (1980),
in that filmic time divides between an actual and a virtual mode (between present and past).

The series of visual standstills in ICH WILL DOCH NUR, DASS IHR MICH LIEBT
exhibits two significant aspects. First of all, we should emphasize the relationship of the suspension to the physical movement of the hero, who with a rough
gesture escapes the confessional setting (or *dispositif*, in a Foucauldian sense).
This outbreak counters the long series of motionless and blocked moments of
hesitation, with which the hero's Oedipal speeches are embodied throughout
the film. When movement is inscribed into the body as an outbreak of pathos,

more truth is seemingly implied by the formal relationship between standstill and movement than in the exchange of words that is usually central in Fassbinder's films. On the other hand, there is a complex relationship between the visual standstill and the apparatus. The image is frozen while the sound of the recording device repeats the words that were just stated as always already recorded, preformed, reiterated speech, an emblem of therapeutic control that (quite in the Foucauldian sense of *dispositif*) maintains the disciplinary system of the prison in another form. Here, confession is shown within an agency of power (or *dispositif*) that is explored in connection with a media apparatus. If, during the entire film, Peter's speech is transmitted as "blocked" speech, this blockage is ultimately related to the enigmatic image of the trauma of the deed that returns near the end, which is solved as a hermeneutic puzzle for the spectators. With a different apparatus, in this case a telephone, which is the object and symbol of his blockage, the hero is able for the first time to tear himself away from his compulsive petrification, in an *acting out*, to kill a restaurant owner whom he suddenly perceives as looking like his father. The body's stance, media apparatus and visual standstill coincide at the end of this film in a figuratively condensed constellation.

Certainly, the most striking freeze-frame in Fassbinder's work is found at the end of MUTTER KÜSTERS FAHRT ZUM HIMMEL (MOTHER KÜSTERS GOES TO HEAVEN) (1975). The violence and suddenness of this final interruption may be modernistic, whereas the motionlessness of the aerial views at the beginning awakens the desire of the spectator to watch a story begin that can be read as a homage to classical cinema. The final shot of the film shows Mutter Küsters in a medium-long shot, frozen in horror as she is confronted with the reversal of her political leanings. Her struggle for dignity ends, to her own surprise, with a hostage-taking organized by a group of radical activists who use her like the political party had earlier done.

The all-too spectacular event of the hostage taking, which ends the story, is ultimately told with intertitles on the "obtuse" side of the freeze-frame that further highlights the frozen stare of Mutter Küsters: cf. the intervention of the police, the death of Mutter Küsters, as well as the newspaper's chief editor, whom she feels has victimized her. The visual standstill here appears as a suspension of both filmic narration and motoric action. This arrest leads the spectator without a transition from visual projection to mental projection using text. The end is presented as a screenplay, which reasserts the projective function of the latter. By leaving out a spectacular ending, the visual standstill insinuates the virtuality inherent in any screenplay. Incidentally, the American version of the film has a happy ending.

A comparable example of narrative virtuality and contingency is found in DESPAIR (1978), where Dirk Bogarde, after murdering his doppelgänger, with the police giving chase, attempts to escape the fiction. In the final tense scene, he suddenly turns to face the audience, asks for their help, confirming his own identity as a mere actor. The last shot is a freeze-frame that fades to white and opens up a reflective layer of the film, underlining the arbitrariness of the ending.

If the opening credits of Maria Braun have become a site of the signature, then the final credits of Mutter Küsters serve as the scene of writing. The figure of standstill in Fassbinder's films always leads beyond this purely reflexive dimension, binding itself to other privileged instants. On the structural level of the narration, for example, the freeze-frame in Maria Braun is tied to the bombing that occurs during the wedding. This figure of suddenness and standstill corresponds structurally to the explosion at the end, through which the recently reunited couple is annihilated. In Mutter Küsters, the final standstill that serves as a disruption of the visual movement is linked to the sudden move toward terrorist activity, which repeats and replaces the husband's desperate act of violence that the radio had announced at the beginning of the film. The list of visual standstills at the end of his films is long, but there are also more discrete freeze-frames in other Fassbinder films.

As Karl-Heinz Bohrer[19] argues from his aesthetic theory of "suddenness" with regards to language and literature, the figure of suddenness places the spectator in a perceptive situation within which the uniqueness of what is seen counters standard modes of perception and dominant values. The radical temporalization that characterizes the pregnant moment (or privileged instant) lends it a simultaneously subjective and utopian dimension. It is on precisely this level that Fassbinder links the visual standstill to other figurations of suddenness. The clearest layer of correspondence to figurations of standstill is that of the *mise-en-scène* of bodies and machines.

Fassbinder in his early films was already emphasizing the link between the *mise-en-scène* and the setting in motion or the arresting of the body through suddenness. In Das kleine Chaos (The Little Chaos) (1966), where Fassbinder plays a sadistic petty criminal, the criminal "orders" his invisible victim, shouting *"Rauf, runter!"* ("Up! Down!") showing himself in a half close-up. The idea of the director controlling the body is further radicalized by the image of the blows of the fist and the shootings that literally throw bodies out of the visual field (in Das kleine Chaos, Liebe ist kälter als der Tod (Love Is Colder Than Death) (1969), and Whity (1971)). Like his violent slaps (Katzelmacher (1969), Warnung vor einer heiligen Nutte (Beware of a Holy Whore) (1971)), these blows and shots are often quite surprising and serve to dynamize a stationary configuration.

These sudden dynamizations always generate narrative consequences, as in the restaurant scene in Wildwechsel where Franz spits into his palm and then suddenly wipes the spit onto the overly-made-up face of his girlfriend Hanni. She leaves the visual field with her makeup smeared across her face. Such an inexplicably brutal instant occurs not only in connection with violent gestures but also in moments of pathos. There is, for example, a long shot in WARNUNG VOR EINER HEILIGEN NUTTE, where Fred (Kurt Raab), who has collapsed along with his buddies in a state of exhaustion and drunkenness, suddenly gets up to tame the uncontrolled fury that seems to be slowly building by leading the group in singing a religious song by Schubert, assuming the role of a conductor, rousing his drunken buddies to join in the chorus.

As far as machines are concerned, the ambivalence of the mechanism of standstill and movement appear even more clearly than in the scenic outbreak of a body from a statuary pose into kinetic gesture. In Fassbinder's work we find that the omnipresence of audio devices has often been noted – jukeboxes, record players, and tape recorders. Their running or pausing is sometimes characteristic of shots or entire scenes, or are even responsible for structuring entire films, as IN EINEM JAHR MIT DREIZEHN MONDEN. Here, Irene awakens the trans-vestite Elvira by removing a record needle stuck in a groove, thereby causing a dramatic silence. At the film's end, another song is heard skipping in a groove, highlighting a freeze-frame as the last shot, in which we see the sister Gudrun disappearing, as a witness to Elvira's childhood trauma. This is also echoed later when the playing of a tape with Elvira's voice on it announces her death.

In MUTTER KÜSTERS, the recording equipment and bugging operations repre-sent the control and power of the media. After her first public speech before Communist party members, Küsters departs, only to discover that her speech was recorded without her knowledge. A similar situation involving audio equipment and power is found in ICH WILL DOCH NUR, DASS IHR MICH LIEBT, but the association with the visual standstill is more obvious. The visual inter-ruption in MUTTER KÜSTERS paradoxically represents the definition of an al-ways-already-recorded image, a kind of "robotic image" (Serge Daney) that serves as a mobile idol. It is no accident that at the beginning of LOLA (1981), in a certain sense as a motto for the film, a photograph of Adenauer is shown, revealing the chancellor leaning on the armrest of a sofa beside one of his favor-ite objects, a music box including a radio, record player, television, and tape deck. Another example is the "sound terror"[20] that accompanies the mendacity of images that Eddie Constantine mentions at the beginning of DIE DRITTE GEN-ERATION (1979).

The ambiguity of the always-already-recorded image and sound in Fassbin-der's films is bound to the affixation of each speech act by power, whether it is the language of love or politics. At the same time, the idea of control in Fassbin-der's work also encounters a dimension that Jean-Luc Godard in his HISTOIRE(S) DU CINÉMA (1997), in paying homage to Fassbinder, calls the "control of the universe", that is the productive power of a filmmaker. From this standpoint, we can say that in Fassbinder's films at issue is the question of bringing things to a standstill and suddenness. The freeze-frame here serves either as a blockage loaded with symbolic character that announces eternal repetition – that would be the nihilistic version – or can be seen as a virtualization of the filmic narrative itself – that would be the utopian version of his poetics of expulsion.

If, for the film analyst, as Thierry Kuntzel writes, the filmic lies neither in movement, nor in standstill, but somewhere between the two, the utopian moments of standstill in Fassbinder's oeuvre can be understood as something in-between, as an interval between privileged instant and any-instant-whatever (or between pregnant and fleeting moments), as an opening towards a non-measurable time or towards a space in which the imaginary force develops and where the image is temporalized, not as eternal, but as becoming.

Translated by Brian Currid, revised by Christa Blümlinger. Reprinted with the kind permission of Bertz+Fischer Verlag, from the digital, English version of the book *Word and Flesh: Cinema Between Text and the Body*, eds. Sabine Nessel, Winfried Pauleit et al. (Berlin: Bertz+Fischer Verlag), 2008.

Notes

1. See for instance Laurent Guido/Olivier Lugon (eds.), *Fixe/animé, croisements de la photographie et du cinéma au XXe siècle*, Lausanne: L'Age d'Homme, 2010
2. Jean Epstein, "L'intelligence d'une machine" (1946), in vol. 1 of *Ecrits sur le cinéma, 1921-1953*, (Paris: Seghers, 1974), 255, 289 and 282. On the relation between the inanimate and life in Epstein, see also Laura Mulvey, *Death 24x a Second: Stillness and the Moving Image* (London: Reaktion Books 2006), 175.
3. André Bazin, "The Ontology of the Photographic Image" (1947), vol. 1 of *What is Cinema?*, (trans. Hugh Gray, Berkeley, CA: UC Press, 1967), 14.
4. Laura Mulvey argues similarly to Raymond Bellour, who upon commenting on Rossellini's LA MACCHINA AMMAZZACATTIVI (1948), establishes the dualities of the narrative (tradition and modernity, God and devil, life and death) in the relationship between standstill and movement by way of the figurations of the photographic. See Laura Mulvey, *Death 24x a Second*, 176; as well as Raymond Bellour, "Le spectateur pensif" (1984) and "L'interruption, l'instant" (1987), in *L'Entre-Images. Cinema, Photo, Cinéma, Vidéo* (Paris: Edition de la Différence 1990), 75-80 and 109-133, Eng. trans. "The Pensive Spectator", *Wide Angle* 9, no. 1, 1987, 6-10; and "The Film Stilled", *Camera Obscura* no. 24, 1990, 99-123.
5. Garett Stewart, "Photogravure: Death, Photography and Film Narrative", *Wide Angle* 9, no. 6, 1987, p. 11-31 (here: p. 19), see also Garett Stewart, *Between Film and Screen: Modernism's Photosynthesis*, (Chicago: University of Chicago Press, 1999), 27-73.

6. See Mary-Ann Doane, "The Close Up: Scale and Detail in the Cinema", *Differences: a Journal of Feminist Cultural Studies* 14, no. 3 (fall 2003).

7. See Serge Daney, "From Movies to Moving" (1989), in Tanya Leighton (ed.), *Art and the Moving Image: A Critical Reader,* (London: Tate Publishing & Afterall, 2008), 334-349.

8. Gilles Deleuze, *Cinema I: The Movement-Image,* trans. Hugh Tomlinson and Barbara Habberjam, Minneapolis: University of Minnesota Press, 1986, 2.

9. Roland Barthes, "The third meaning", *Image, Music, Text,* trans. Stephen Heath, (New York: Hill and Wang, 1977).

10. Gilles Deleuze, *Cinema 1: The Movement-Image,* 5.

11. According to Bellour, the ambiguity of the freeze-frame lies in that it only apparently interrupts the movement, without breaking up the movement of the *défilement* of the images in the projector. See Raymond Bellour, "The film stilled", *Camera Obscura* no. 24 1990, 99-123, here: 101.

12. Bellour, "The film stilled", 105.

13. Philippe Dubois, *L'Effet film, figures, matières et formes du cinéma en photographie* (Lyon: Galérie le Réverbère, 1999), 3-4; see also Philippe Dubois, "Photography Mise-en-Film. Autobiographical (Hi)stories and Psychic Apparatuses" in *Fugitive Images, From Photography to Video,* ed. Patrice Petro, (Bloomington: Indiana University Press, 1995), 153.

14. Kuntzel locates the filmic, the object of film analysis, neither on the side of motion, nor that of standstill, but *between* the *two,* in the creation of the "projection film" ("film-projection") by the filmstrip ("film-pellicule") and in the denial of the material film in the projection film. See Thierry Kuntzel: "Le Défilement", in *Cinéma: Théories, Lectures,* ed. Dominique Noguez, (Paris: Klincksieck, 1973), 97-110.

15. See Serge Daney, "Réponse à l'enquête 'Cinéma et Photographie," *Photogénies* 5, n. p.; "Du défilement au defile," *La recherche photographique* 7 (1989), 49–51 (tansl. "From Movies to Moving", op. cit.); "La dernière image," in *Passages de l'image,* eds. R. Bellour, C. David, C. Van Assche (Paris: Editions du Centre Pompidou, 1989), 57–59; on Daney and the question of *arrêt-sur-image* see Raymond Bellour, "L'effet Daney ou l'arrêt de vie et de mort," *Trafic* 37 (spring 2001), 75-86.

16. For Daney, this modern form of sublation coincides with the end of the narrative cinema. He sees the "hallucinated" form both as an affixation of the spectator (as a kind of mental state), as well as the perception of film (in a phenomenological sense). See Daney, "Réponse à une enquête."

17. If the narrative sounds quite Freudian, the logics of the narration are more Foucauldian, as the film images unfold microstructures of power relationships.

18. See Serge Daney, " La dernière image", op. cit.

19. See Karlheinz Bohrer, *Plötzlichkeit. Zum Augenblick des ästhetischen Scheins,* (Frankfurt am Main: Suhrkamp, 1981), 76. (Eng. trans. *Suddenness: On the Moment of Aesthetic Appearance,* New York: Columbia University Press, 1994).

20. See Thomas Elsaesser, *Rainer Werner Fassbinder,* (Berlin: Bertz, 2001), 66. (*Fassbinder's Germany. History, Identity, Subject,* Amsterdam: Amsterdam University Press, 1996).

The Temporalities of the Narrative Slide Motion Film

Liv Hausken

The Mexican director Jonás Cuarón's first feature film AÑO UÑA (YEAR OF THE NAIL, 2007) is a 78-minute film narrative composed of still photographs with an entire range of filmic sounds edited into a narrative that spans a year in the lives of Molly (Eireann Harper), a 24-year-old American traveling through Mexico, and Diego (Diego Cataño), a typically and perpetually horny 14-year-old – naïve, romantic and troubled by a persistent ingrown toenail. The son of Alfonso Cuarón, Jonás Cuarón's film has been said to draw on many notions from his father's work (Y TU MAMÁ TAMBIÉN in particular) and the broader context of recent Mexican cinema; a cross-generational relationship, the trials of puberty and the fleeting moments that shape young lives. It has been characterized as a "piece of work that resembles the exotic child from a union between LA JETÉE and Y TU MAMÁ TAMBIÉN".[1] The reference to Chris Marker's film LA JETÉE (1962) is due to the stills. It as been suggested that it is "inspired in style if not content by LA JETÉE",[2] and even claimed to be "LA JETEE-style".[3]

Chris Marker's LA JETÉE (THE JETTY) has become a cult classic, inspiring various tributes including Terry Gilliam's 12 MONKEYS (1995). Set in a bunker in a devastated Paris in the aftermath of World War III, it tells the tale of a man, a slave, exposed to experiments into time travel, sent back and forth, in and out of the present time of the diegetic world, into the past and eventually into the future, to replenish the decreasing stocks of food, medicine and energies of the present world. The story is told using black-and-white stills, voice-over, music, and minimal sound effects, including a distant, whispering sound of a muttering German dialogue between the scientists (the men conducting the experiments).[4]

LA JETÉE is often referred to whenever there are sequences of stills in a film, like, for instance, in Ingmar Bergman's SCENER UR ETT ÄKTENSKAP (SCENES FROM A MARRIAGE, 1973) or Pernille Fischer Christensen's EN SOAP (A SOAP, 2006), to mention just two. Briefly put, LA JETÉE is not only the title of Marker's 1962 sci-fi film, but LA JETÉE also appears to be emblematic of a film style where photographic stills are used to compose a fiction film, the "La Jetee-style". I will suggest that we use the term *slide-motion film*.

Slide-Motion Film

In his dictionary with the pretentious title *The Complete Film Dictionary* (1997), Ira Koningsberg uses the term "slide-motion film" for "A film, generally a documentary, that uses a series of still pictures like a filmograph, but in which the camera seems to move among the picture's elements by means of panning or a zoom lens".[5]

The typical example of films that fits Koningsberg's conception of slide-motion film would be a documentary about a particular historical event, or a biography about an exceptional individual (a famous adventurer, or a distinguished artist) composed of singular photographs from different times and places, illustrating the story told by a voice-over. Only in exceptional cases is the voice-over is left out, as is the case in Ingmar Bergman's 1984 short film KARINS ANSIKTE (KARIN'S FACE), a 14-minute portrait of the filmmaker's mother Karin Åkerblom Bergman. The film opens with a close up of a passport, its identity information pages indicating a person's identity in terms of name, nationality, date of birth, hair color, eye color, etc. We are shown the passport photo of an elderly woman and the passport holder's signature before an intertitle is cut in to note that Karin got this passport only a few months before she died. KARINS ANSIKTE then slips into Bergman's family album, for the camera to visit, in some cases scrutinize, one old photograph after another, with the earlier ones as sepia prints, and more recent ones in black-and-white. There is no dialogue, no voice-over, only the occasional inter-title and a spare, delicate piano score. It is a collection of singular photographs presented in a film that does not treat them as illustrations of a verbal narrative. The film creates a space of reflection and association, where the audience – based on their assumed knowledge of Bergman's biography and his other films or, more generally, based on experience with family relations and photo albums – is invited to indulge in identification and memory.

A similar status is accorded (or allowed) the photographs in Anja Breien's nine-minute short film SOLVORN (1997)[6] that, in contrast to KARINS ANSIKTE, does present a voice-over but also fits Koningsberg's definition and is thus of interest here. The film is based on a collection of one-hundred-years-old glass-plate photographs discovered in the attic of the filmmaker's grandmother's house. They all appear to have been taken in the same, somewhat narrow geographical area, in and around the house over a period of few years. The voice-over does not tell a story that is illustrated by photographs. Instead, the voice-over questions the photographs and, even more profoundly, the photographer's desires, and the wishes and intentions of the unknown photographic practice of the filmmaker's grandmother. The film investigates the photographs in an exquisitely elegant way without explaining what they can tell, instead creating relations between characters, composing small sequences of action and developing architectural space out of the singular photos in a way that seems to invite the audience into the scene to reflect on what it was like to be there during her grandmother's time.

Both Bergman's and Breien's films feature photographs that have been filmed by a film camera. These photographs are, however, not just the object of a film camera, but also part of a filmic universe where they are just one component among many (cinematography, editing, genre, etc.). Koningsberg's definition of slide-motion film seems to imply a fundamental relation between two instances or dimensions, the narrator and the photographs, the first being the active dimension, the voice speaking and the camera looking, the other dimension being the things looked at, the photographs as relics to be examined or documents to be shown as illustrations or evidence. There are no doubts that both KARINS ANSIKTE and SOLVORN are based on photographs. They, however, also create a temporally organized space, where the photographs are not only objects for the gaze but also components in the creation of a film universe. In SOLVORN's case this is done in a way quite similar to AÑO UÑA, a film that arguably does not fit Koningsberg's definition of the slide-motion film.

Being a fiction film, AÑO UÑA has an unusual production history. It is based on analogue photographs of everyday life, family and friends, taken by Jonás Cuarón over a period of one year. He then collated the 8,000 shots before reassembling 2,000 to 3,000 of them into a fictional narrative.[7] The negatives were scanned, digitally edited and printed to 35 mm film. Combined with dialogue, voice-over, music and other sound well-known film elements, AÑO UÑA's film style seems quite ordinary for a narrative fiction film, except that it visually presents a series of stills. Moreover, even if each individual frame appears as a still image, they are organized in sequences and present their static objects as integrated into sequences of cohesive actions.

Its production history resembles both KARINS ANSIKTE and SOLVORN. They all have a collection of photographs as their starting points. Moreover, they all focus on one or on a few individuals and their closest, social relations. All three may even tell a story about their main characters. Looking at the photographs from his mother's life, Bergman creates a story about the pictures of Karin from her youth, her marriage to his father, her having children, before she seems "to disappear into the family pictures", as he puts it (in one of the film's inter-titles). SOLVORN, on the other hand, poses a series of questions to the pictures (and to why they were taken in the first place), but it also composes a story by the way the pictures are arranged. However, compared to AÑO UÑA, both of these stories are fairly vague, due to the scarcity of images, the lack of – or never completed – narrative sequences, and the lack of information that is provided for the audience about what the pictures show (this is a theme in SOLVORN, and more enigmatic in KARINS ANSIKTE).

AÑO UÑA does not present singular shots from different locations, like many of the frames in Bergman's photo album. Rather, it composes scenes and sequences from images of the same location, images of a limited set of characters performing their activities as part of a narrative universe, which is kept constant during the whole film. We find Diego in his room early on in the story, troubled by his toenail, fantasizing about his cousin Emilia. The scene is composed of stills of the kid in one single narrative situation, with just slightly altered positions, visually framed in nearly identical manners from shot to shot. His voice-over also supports the unity of the scene both as continued sound bridging the change of images and as an inner monologue directing the audience's attention towards the experience of the boy rather than towards the pictures as such. But the sheer number of images of the same object, presented in the same place in one and the same situation distinguishes it from the scenes composed in SOLVORN. Whilst SOLVORN creates a virtual scene from a small collection of photos of the same environment, AÑO UÑA make us look at the scene as if there had never been a photographer. The scene does not look staged, like most of the pictures in Bergman's album and many of the photos in Breien's film. The story does not appear to be the result of an investigation of images, like KARINS ANSIKTE and SOLVORN, even if its production history may show this to be the case. AÑO UÑA focuses on characters interacting, their motives and feelings and how they change during the story, rather than on the existence of photographs (like SOLVORN) or what a particular collection of preexisting photographs may reveal about a particular person's identity (like KARINS ANSIKTE).

The three films are all based on photographs. KARINS ANSIKTE and SOLVORN present preexisting photographs. But they create a filmic space where the photographs are only one of several ingredients. In AÑO UÑA, this second characteristic supersedes the first. The images in AÑO UÑA appear as series of photographic stills, but not as photographs. There are no cameras filming photographs and moving among the picture's elements. This is not a film presenting photographs of events, but a film about the events, the visual dimension of the film appearing as stills. AÑO UÑA appears, in other words, less a double layer of photographic presentations (photographs and film), with all the implications this may have for narration and temporality rather than simply a filmic presentation of events employing a slightly unusual form of visual expression.

The same can be said for LA JETÉE, a film with a visual image comprised almost entirely of optically printed photographs, containing only one brief shot by a motion-picture camera, but nevertheless a film in which the static frames appear as photographic stills, but not as photographs.[8] Just like AÑO UÑA, Marker's film does not seem to fit Koningsberg's conception of the slide-motion film. LA JETÉE is presented as a *"photo-roman"*, a photo-novel (from the film's titles). One might, therefore, expect to see a film using a series of still pictures, "but in which the camera seems to move among the picture's elements by means of panning or a zoom lens".[9] However, not only LA JETÉE, but the entire field of "photo-romans", filmic or televisual "photo novels" or "photo plays" (including the French series of short films simply called *"Photo-Romans"* which I will turn to later) seems excluded from the term slide-motion films, not because they are narratives, not because their stories are fictional, but because they do not appear as films presenting photographs. One could argue that we should leave Koningsberg's definition of the slide-motion film behind and reserve it just for those films he had in mind. However, the terms used to describe films like LA JETÉE – photo novel, photo play, and sometimes even photo montage – has some of the same problems as Koningsberg's term when it comes to understanding the filmic space as well as narration and temporality. The films are understood in terms of photography. For the photo novel, the photoplay, and the photomontage, the notions explicitly signal this as such. In Koningsberg's definition of the slide motion film, photography is implicitly a premise, which arguably is insufficient for both SOLVORN and KARINS ANSIKTE and presumably also for the other documentaries that fit into Koningsberg's definition.

The photo novel, the photoplay, and the photomontage are all notions used for films including photographic stills. These films are, however, more often, referred to as "films similar to LA JETÉE", a practice that must be considered a sign of the lack of a proper term. I will argue that a photo-related designation has more drawbacks than advantages. To understand a film like in terms of photography often implies paying little or no attention to its sound and editing principles. Moreover, naming it after something photo-related also reproduces unrecognized assumptions about photography that have an influence on the conception of the film that may not be beneficial. The tendency to consider a documentary effect as intrinsical to photography is an example of this. Instances of this can be found in users reviews for AÑO UÑA, like one at the Internet Movie Database (imdb.com) saying "Nobody knows what he [Cuarón] was actually documenting at the time [he was making the photographs] but the story Cuarón created ... is poignant and funny".[10] It can also be read in film reviews, like James Dennis's at the website *twitch*, who characterizes AÑO UÑA as "A work of fiction with no actors, a documentary with a fictional narrative."[11] This description actually echoes the introduction of the film, written in Spanish and English with white letters on a black screen: "From 2004 to 2005 I photographed my surroundings. At the end of that year, I ordered the images in such a way that they suggested the following narrative." In the next image, again with white letters on a black screen, we read: "These are documentary images. The moments and characters are real," and finally: "Only the story is fictional." Thereafter, we get the first ordinary film image, a series of stills showing a young woman coming down the stairs towards us, or towards the camera, as we hear the sound of a distant female voice saying something vaguely comprehensible in Spanish. It seems reasonable to see the three verbal slides as the filmmaker's expression. But why should Cuarón photograph to document anything at all? And if he did, why should the photographs be considered a documentary after they have been reworked and inserted into a fictional story?

In contrast to the viewer comments and film reviews of AÑO UÑA describing it as a film "composed of only photographs and dialogues",[12] placing the word "movie" in quotation marks or even proclaiming (enthusiastically) "'AÑO UÑA' isn't even a 'movie'",[13] or "Strictly it is not a film. It is more than a film",[14] I believe AÑO UÑA, as well as LA JETÉE and also SOLVORN and KARINS ANSIKTE should be named explicitly as films or movies.

Another possible description could be "still film".[15] This term has been used for works characterized as "nearly static films, like TEATRO AMAZONAS" and Douglas Gordon's "slowed" films.[16] George Baker argues that this notion is implicitly dependent on a tension between film and photography, film reduced to its "foundation of the still frame" and, at the same time, "linked conceptually to a field mapped out by the expansion of *photography*, to which ... neither of them [the examples mentioned above] will of course correspond".[17] To include films like LA JETÉE and AÑO UÑA under this label would imply a redefinition of the term "still film", involving both a rethinking of this conceptual link to photography and the idea of the film still as a "reduction" of film to "its foundation".

As an alternative, we could simply redefine Koningsberg's term slide-motion film. Whilst "still film" has the possible advantage of ascribing importance to the stillness of the images in a film, "slide-motion film" emphasizes its *motion*. Admittedly, one problem with redefining Koningsberg's term might be that "slide" refers both to the verb "to slide, or glide" and the noun "slide" pertaining to the photographic still viewed with a slide projector. To include AÑO UÑA, LA JETÉE and similar films under this label, the primary meaning of "slide" must be the transparent, photographic image mounted in a frame, the image as projected, the still on the screen, rather than the gliding movement of the camera, tracking across the surfaces of pre-existing images, that may also be part of the filmic expression I am describing here, but which doesn't define it as such. The motion involved, then, refers not so much to the movement of the camera as to the impression of movement produced by sequences of projected images (often supported by the sound). As Christian Metz once noted, "... even if each image is a still, switching from one to the next creates a *second movement*, an ideal one, made out of successive and different immobilities".[18] I consider this "ideal movement" as a formative notion of the filmic expression of AÑO UÑA,

LA JETÉE and SOLVORN, and arguably, it is also important for the understanding of the aesthetics of KARINS ANSIKTE.

So, I will suggest broadening the term and adjusting (or adapting) the conception of the slide-motion film so that it can be used as a label for *any* film – fiction or factual, narrative, descriptive, poetic or argumentative – which visually appears as a composition of stills, the stills being of *any* kind including the freeze-frame. Furthermore, instead of discussing these films by juxtaposing stasis and kinesis as if these qualities or modes of expression were exclusively connected to two different media (photography and film), I will propose that the slide motion film should be conceptualized as a *filmic* form of expression, as a particular form of stasis within the field of moving images. As Noël Carroll once argued, "... if you know that you are watching a slide, then it is categorically impossible that the image should move. ... Movement in a slide would require a miracle; movement in a film is an artistic choice and an always available technical option".[19] To associate the slide-motion film with the family of moving images provides it with a range of perspectives and conceptions that I believe will benefit the understanding of these films and their expressive potential. In the rest of this essay, I will deal with one of these problematics, the conception of temporality of the slide-motion film in keeping with the way it is redefined above. I will confine the discussion to the *narrative* slide-motion films because the complex relation between time and narrative must be understood as different from but interacting with the complex relation between time and photographically appearing filmic expressions. The fiction film AÑO UÑA remains my main example, as compared to the titles mentioned above as well as the series of thirteen short, fiction films, PHOTO-ROMANS (1988-1991), and a short, documentary called ONE DAY (2007).

Story and Narration in AÑO UÑA

AÑO UÑA tells the story of Molly who meets Diego when she rents a room in his parents' house in Mexico. The two immediately strike up a relationship despite the age gap. Both are at turning points in their lives: Diego in the turmoil of puberty and Molly on the brink of post-education adulthood. Diego, who early in the story is consumed by desire for his cousin, Emilia, redirects his obsession after Molly arrives. Molly enjoys Diego's flirtation, finding the attention and respect missing from her relationships with boyfriends. The relationship continues to grow until Molly returns to New York. Diego decides to run away and win Molly's heart. Molly realizes that although it is an impossible relation-

ship in many ways, Diego is able to cater to her needs where a string of arguably even less suitable boyfriends could not.[20]

Before we see the film titles, we read the above-mentioned paratext that declares: "These are documentary images. The moments and characters are real //
Only the story is fictional". We are introduced to Molly at the metro, an amateur photographer and exchange student from New York. We hear her voice
first in Spanish, thereafter in English, as she reflects on the subway tunnel system's potential for photo opportunities, complaining about her boyfriend's ha-
bits and mulling over her situation as a student in a foreign land. The position
of this voice is ambiguous: It could be considered an interior monologue – the
thoughts of Molly running through her head during the moments of the sequence of stills – or is it off-stage commentary – Molly's voice-over reflecting on
the scene we see later that same day or days or weeks later? Given that this is
the very first voice we hear and the fact that the very first thing she mentions is
her photography, this ambiguous position seems to destabilize the position/sta-
tus of the written text presented just prior to the film titles: was that the filmmaker's words or Molly's? Or is Molly playing the character of the photographer on which this film is based?

After a few moments, the inter-title with her name – Molly – establishes a
more stable status for her: this is a story about Molly told by someone (that
might be Molly herself or someone else) treating her as a character *in* a universe
rather than the narrator *of* that universe. Then we are introduced to a less-am-
biguous male voice, as it is more obviously an interior monologue, a boy's voice
reflecting on how his sexual fantasies about his cousin (Emilia) have caused his
falling out of shape for the soccer matches, an image we can see from a distance.
The second inter-title presents his name, Diego. A few scenes later an inter-title
indicates the first season: *verano*, summer, which appears as the story of Molly
and Diego starts at with the beginning of summer.

Still, the introductory text has the potential to keep the characters ambiguous:
How can the characters be real while the story is fictional? In narrative theory, a
character is often considered subordinate to the narrative's action. This theory
goes back to Aristotle's poetics – a normative poetics meant to prescribe the
Greek tragedy, but still influential on modern theories of narrative – in which
the fable (the story) has primacy over character (before reasoning, diction, song,
etc.).[21] Being secondary to story is still quite different from being independent
of it, however. Most scholars of narrative theory would agree that character and
story should be treated as interdependent. This is often seen as the thrust of
Henry James's famous dictum: "What is character but the determination of incident? What is incident but the illustration of character?"[22] A character is, in
other words, normally seen as part of the narrative and not an entity that exists
independent of the narrative. In my view, this interdependency is crucial in dis-

cussions of narratives about actual events, transforming actual people into characters. In fiction, the distinction between people and characters cannot be so easily ignored. In Año Uña, this distinction is most clearly marked with Molly, a name given to a fictional character, played, staged or given form by the actual person Eireann Harper. To declare "the moments … [as] real" must be understood as referring to the photographs (of which this film, along with other components, are composed) considered *as photographs of family and friends* from the filmmaker's own world (including Eireann Harper), and not photographic fictions (involving fictional characters like Molly). Hence, if "the moments … are real" there are no photographs of Molly, at least not before the photographs are ordered in a fictional story.

The Production of Pastness

In Año Uña, Eireann Harper's photographic traces (in front of the camera) are transformed into a photographic representation of the fictional character Molly. Just like in mainstream entertainment film, the audience normally pays less attention to the actor and focuses on the character, unless the actor is well known (a star), which is not the case here. However, in Año Uña, the photographic stills seem to inspire a certain kind of attention not towards Eireann Harper but towards the moments of photographic exposure. Given that the sequences of photographic stills are not considered familiar form of filmic expression for most audiences, it seems to reinvest the culturally formative figure of pastness connected to photographic images.

I believe that we come to Año Uña and any other slide-motion film not only with an experience of the narrative fiction film. The moment we start watching and notice the unusual nature of this filmic mode of expression, the experience of the slide-motion film is also prefigured in our experience of photography in a very specific sense, namely the experience of photography as temporal displacement. This photographic experience is what Roland Barthes discusses in his last books La Chambre Claire (1980) when he considers the *noema* of the photograph as "that-has-been" (or, "the Intractable"). Even if the photographic still of the narrative slide-motion film is *not* a photograph, I suggest that this specific temporal experience of photography contributes to our experience of the narrative slide-motion film, particularly when it comes to the experience of its temporality.

In Año Uña, every single frame is static and so are the objects within the single frames. The sequence of images, on the other hand, is continuously unfolding during the course of the film: it has a certain tempo, rhythm, and duration. Thus, the tension between the static and the unfolding in the *visual* dimension of this narrative slide motion film may, in temporal terms, be experienced as a tension between the pastness of the static frame and the presence and becoming of the succession of images.

The auditory dimension of the narrative slide-motion film is often similar to most mainstream films: The diegetic sound is continuously there, so we actually hear the steps of a character coming down the stairs even if the visual presentation of the scene shows only two or three images, one from the top of the staircase, one from the middle, and maybe one at the bottom. Although the diegetic sound in Año Uña is rather flimsy compared to both mainstream film and other slide-motion films (like Photo-Romans, which I will come back to later), the relatively rich "whereness" of the dialogue and interior monologue in Año Uña contributes to the production of diegetic presence. The often unnoticed muttering in La Jetée similarly produces a certain impression of presence despite the scarcity of sound in this film. The *sounds* of the diegetic universe in other words create the impression of presence and the unfolding of events in the narrative slide-motion films.

Fig. 1. Año Uña *presents a large amount of inner monologues, normally signaled by the content of the utterance and the social norms indicated by the narrative situation. Screen shot, color film*

The *extradiegetic* components of the slide-motion films also work with what the audience expects: in most of them, music highlights the action and facilitates the transitions between images. Año Uña contains very little extradiegetic music, but sometimes the diegetic music distracts viewers from the visual cut. Moreover, in AÑO UÑA, as in most slide-motion films, the sound of the voice-over contributes to the production of a continuously unfolding of the action by its more or less continuously sounding voice.

However, the voice-over also works *against* this impression of an unfolding presence, not by presenting qualities parallel to the *static* quality of the single frame, but, nevertheless, by producing an impression of *pastness*. The nature and degree of this impression of *pastness* varies considerably for the different slide-motion films discussed here. Before we look into these variations, it may be helpful to introduce another temporal figure relevant here, namely finality.

The Sense of an Ending

Analytically, it may be useful to distinguish between the filmic and the narrative in this respect. Any narrative film is a final product, and this finality is twofold: First, the film is final. During the screening of the film, the future of the events that unfolding, in the words of Peter Brunette and David Wills, is, "always a future that is foreseen, that we know will come to an end within the space of the screening". And, as they add: "its finality imposes a kind of past upon it".[23]

Secondly, the narrative is also final. Just like the film, a narrative discourse makes the events unfold into a future that is already in the past. All narratives, even oral narratives and stories in the making, are told and listened to in accordance with an "anticipation of retrospection", to borrow a phrase from literary theorist Peter Brooks (1984).[24] This is the general, temporal logic of the plot. However, the narrative of a final product, such as a film, is told retrospectively in a stronger sense than stories in the making: we don't just expect a point to the story that we may grasp along the way or at least make sense of when the telling comes to an end. The narrative finality of the film narrative implies that even when the narrated events are fictional, we experience the story as a reconstruction of something that has already happened (in the narrative universe). Hence, the *narrative* finality of any narratively organized filmic discourse also imposes a kind of past upon it.

The smooth editing of images of moving objects in mainstream entertainment film reduces the attention paid toward the experience of both filmic and narrative finality and pastness. The stills of the narrative slide-motion film seem to rupture the impression of the presence of the unfolding of events. The voice-over appears to strengthen the impression of both filmic and narrative finality and pastness. However, the voice-over's production of pastness varies for the narrative slide-motion films discussed here.

The Temporality of the Narrating Voice

The voice-over's production of pastness is normally threefold: The conventional experience of a voice-over as *post production*, as something added onto the film afterwards, telling about or commenting upon the actions from its position on the balcony, to paraphrase Michel Chion's expression,[25] involves an experience of temporal distance between the actions unfolding and the action verbally described.

Moreover, besides the experience of a voice-over as post-produced sound, voice-overs are often also considered narrating instances employing a narrative mode in which the characters in the narrative universe are referred to, be it "he" or "she" (third-person narrator), "I" (first-person narrator), and the less common "you" (second-person narrator). The voice-overs in most of the slide-motion films mentioned here are first-person narrators. A first-person narrator talking about him- or herself as a character in the story is often also termed an autodiegetic narrator. Confronted with a story of dramatic realism, an autodiegetic voice-over narrator is often experienced as comforting for an empathetic audience, because the narrator's ability to actually tell the story seems to ensure the character's survival. The story is, in other words, experienced *retrospectively*.[26]

This impression of retrospective narration is often strengthened by the voice-over speaking in the *past tense*: They talk about the events *as* something that have already happened in the past. This is the third dimension of the voice-over's production of pastness and an aspect of some of the slide-motion films discussed here.

The production of pastness in the slide-motion film varies according to the three dimensions of the voice-over mentioned above and to the discursive mode in which the filmic story is told. Let me elaborate on this by comparing AÑO UÑA to PHOTO-ROMANS, ONE DAY, and SOLVORN.

The Narrative Past of PHOTO-ROMANS

PHOTO-ROMANS is a French series of thirteen short films produced circa 1990 in cooperation with television networks in twelve European countries. They are all classic, urban short stories, with one or two main characters and a beginning, middle, and end.

The filmic expression of the series PHOTO-ROMANS is quite similar to AÑO UÑA and LA JETÉE: Visually, these short films present a series of photographically appearing black-and-white still pictures. These are mainly sequences of freeze-frames, sometimes combined with photographs mediated by a moving film or video camera zooming in or tracking across the surface of the picture. Sound-wise, they are like most live action films: they include music, diegetic sound, sound effects, voice-over and even dialogue – less common in slide-motion films, but present in AÑO UÑA.

Confronted with this series of short films, the first thing that struck me was the impression of the character's vague presence, or non-presence, but the impression of *having been* there. Unlike mainstream fictional entertainment films where we get an impression of a character's being presence during the unfolding of an event, these short films never create the impression of characters actually being present. It is as if the images present the character's presence in the past tense. It has often been claimed that film "has no past or future tense, only the present",[27] and that "The linguistic equivalent for cinematic presentation of the past is: 'This *is* how it was'; and for the future: 'This *is* how it will be'."[28] PHOTO-ROMANS, however, seems to present past events in their pastness.

The impression of past events being presented in their pastness in PHOTO-ROMANS can be explained as a result of the combination of several factors, the most important being that they are all classic narratives of singular events and that most of them also have a voice-over with all of the three above-mentioned characteristics: The pastness invoked by the filmic expression as such (the slide motion film) is strengthened by the pastness produced by the voice-over. But it also seems important that the events referred to are singular. Let me explain this by comparing it to the short film ONE DAY.

The Narrative Present of ONE DAY: The Reportage

ONE DAY (2007) is a 17-minute documentary in color (which is quite unusual for slide-motion films) that presents a 14-year-old boy from Kenya who lived on the streets until he was adopted in the slums of Korogocho outside Nairobi. It opens *in medias res* at an urban garbage dump where several youngsters are talking in Keswahili.[29] There is no music in this pre-credit sequence, but, eventually, an English male voice-over appears as we see a boy with a clean shirt singled out of the small crowd. The voice-over is an autodiegetic narrator speaking in a past tense, describing how he used to live in the streets. Thereafter, the image shifts to a different place, a slum. There is more extradiegetic music, an establishing shot, super titles that indicate place, date and year: Korogocho, Kenya, 11th of May, 2006. We hear a cock crow, and the film's titles appear before we actually see a close-up of the same boy looking straight into the camera, and hear the voice-over state: "My name is Thomas Munene. I am 14 years old."

In festival programs and short film overviews, this film has been presented as "A stills documentary. A normal day in an unusual life. Thomas (14) has lived half his life as a street child in Nairobi. He has been adopted by a family living in the slum."[30] This "stills documentary", "still film", or as I will suggest, "slide-motion film" (in the broad sense I have already described) does not tell a story about one, single day in Thomas's life. Instead, it represents a typical day in the boy's life. After the credits, the film commences with a cock crowing at the break of day and ends with the boy going to bed and turning off his light. In between sunrise and sunset, Thomas has been our guide through his life, a reporter who presents his new family, takes us to his school on an average day, brings us along on one of his Sunday trips to visit his old friends at the dumpster in Nairobi. The voice-over varies between past and present tense. In both cases, the voice-over describes general situations rather than specific events, about how his life used to be living on the street, and how it changed after a family adopted him. There is no footage of his life on the street. Everything we see is from the present. One gets the impression that the film crew simply followed him for a day, except that the school visit and the trip to Nairobi probably happened on different days. Even when we see and hear Thomas interacting with his classmates at school and with his friends at the dumpster, this present day imagery and the voice-overs general presentation of what his days looks like, what he likes and what he wishes for the future, creates a strong experience of temporal presence. The title of the film, ONE DAY, therefore implies the future more than just a single day, a future of hope for his friends at the dump and for himself, because he wants to become a journalist and also hopes that he will eventually meet his biological family again (which is confirmed in the epilogue that he narrates four months later). Even if the voice-over sometimes speaks in the past tense and most likely has been post-produced, the voice-over does not appear retrospective in this film. Thomas is looking back on his life, contrasting his days now with how it used to be. But the voice-over, the many illustrative images, the hope with which he describes his situation, and the general comments and reporter's style of Thomas's voice-over seems to work against the culturally formative figure of pastness connected to photographic stills.

The color film may also be important in this respect. There is nothing about color film as such that signals present tense. However, most slide-motion films are black-and-white, and after the introduction of color film, choosing to shoot in black-and-white film has certain connotations of "old time footage", "documentary" or "art". Without going into any details, these categories of black-and-white photographic imagery often connote confirmation of what something or someone looked like and contemplation (reflection), and therefore also distance to what is seen. If the footage appears old, the distance is connected to a historic past. There is a historic past in ONE DAY, although it is a recent past. The film refers to a specific past in the life of an actual person. But this historic pastness is not indicated by the footage as such and nor by any old auditory record. In SOLVORN, the situation is quite opposite.

The Historical Past of SOLVORN

Like ONE DAY, SOLVORN is also a documentary that refers to a rather vague historic past. The film presents a collection of photographs made by a specific photographer between 1908 and 1913 in one particular geographical area, but, except for the fact that several of the characters are named in the voice-over, the details of these pictures remain vague and unspecified: Was there a specific occasion that these images show? Do they present a typical situation or something that happened only once? Like ONE DAY, the voice-over narration in SOLVORN also produces a strong sense of presence. Despite that, the voice-over in SOLVORN is obviously added to the imagery as part of the film's post-production, that it employs a retrospective mode, uses the past tense, and the second-person pronoun "you" and a curious attitude regarding why the pictures were made in the first place (what motivated the grandmother's photographic practice and what made her stop taking pictures in 1913), creates a strong emphasis on the voice-over as contemporary with the audienc. The form of address seems to establish the audience as a witness to the filmmaker's voice-over monologue or unidirectional dialogue with her dead grandmother, while she is looking at, and showing us, her grandmother's pictures.

However, in contrast to ONE DAY, the historic pastness in SOLVORN is clearly marked by the older footage. Its age is indicated by the style of the photographs and the way the people are portrayed (their clothing and poses) as well as by the voice-over, which informs us about the one-hundred-year gap between the film and the production of the glass-plate photographs. The historic distance between the filmmaker's era and that of the photographer is also underlined by the strong emphasis on the presence created by the voice-over's form of address and the lack of information about the photographs. The sense of narrational presence, in other words, accentuates the experience of historical pastness in SOLVORN.

The Narrative Present of AÑO UÑA: The Chronicle

As we have already indicated, the filmic expression of AÑO UÑA is quite similar to LA JETÉE and the series PHOTO-ROMANS: it is a narrative fiction about individual events. It does not illustrate a typical life situation (like ONE DAY) nor is it about the historic past (like SOLVORN). Its production of pastness is, nevertheless, less strong than in PHOTO-ROMANS. The fact that it strangely enough turns from black-and-white film into color film one-third of the way into the film may be significant here. More importantly, however, is the combination of several first-person narrators who often speak in the present tense, and the unclear distinction between voice-overs and interior monologues.

There are numerous interior monologues in AÑO UÑA. This narrative mode is most obvious in the case of Diego. Diego's voice is often heard when seen alone in a room, filled with sexual fantasies or troubled by his toenail. Given the privacy of his thoughts and the visual presentation of him being alone, Diego's voice most likely should be recognized as giving the auditory equivalent of his thoughts. However, due to the impossibility of lip-synching in a slide-motion film, the distinction between interior monologues and ordinary monologues may be difficult to distinguish. The grandmother's birthday party in AÑO UÑA may be indicative: On her 70th birthday, Diego's grandmother is at the center of everyone's attention while she is looking through some images and reflects on what she sees. Her slightly hushed voice may be perceived as a depiction of her thoughts being overheard by the audience, but it is unclear whether some of those sitting close to her can also hear what she is saying.

In Molly's case, it is not only the distinction between these two different diegetic modes – monologues and auditory representations of thoughts – that may be difficult to distinguish. It is also difficult to ascertain the difference between diegetic and extradiegetic modes, that is, whether or not what she says is part of the action we see unfolding or a reflection upon it made at a later stage. It seems reasonable to consider most of the first-person narrators in this film as part of its narrative universe (that is, diegetic narrators, perceivable by the other characters or not). Molly's voice, on the other hand, seems to float between narrative modes, in and out of the diegesis, never far away in time, but often reflecting upon her situation at a slight remove in time and/or emotion. We follow Molly from when we first meet her coming down the stairs in a subway station somewhere in Mexico until she returns to New York as if we are getting an overview of her whereabouts and overhearing her thoughts as dictated to her diary.

The private chronicle of AÑO UÑA, its many present-tense narrators and their somewhat uncertain status (thoughts, talks, comments) creates a certain temporal instability between the intimacy of the present and the temporal distance of the diary or the somewhat retrospective narrative. Compared to the production of presentness in ONE DAY, with its illustrative narration and reportage style and its focus on the hopes for the future, the presentness of AÑO UÑA appears more as a moderate version of the production of pastness in PHOTO-ROMANS. The pastness invoked by the filmic expression as such (the slide motion film) is moderately intensified by the pastness produced by the voice-over and the singularity of the events marked as past rather than typical and repeatable.

Fig. 2. In the slide-motion film, the visual composition of the image and the quality of the voices gives the strongest indications of who is speaking and whether or not the others can hear his or her voice. Screenshot from AÑO UÑA, *black and white*

The Social Temporality of the Narrative Slide-Motion Film

We have seen how the production of pastness in the narrative slide-motion film varies according to the status of the voice-over and the discursive mode in which the filmic story is told. However, compared with mainstream entertainment films, where both filmic and narrative finality are normally experienced as a balanced play between past, present and becoming, the narrative slide-motion film ruptures this balance by pointing more clearly towards the pastness of the photographic stills. In AÑO UÑA, as in the other slide-motion films discussed here, the photographic stills seem to instigate a certain attention towards the moments of photographic exposure. These moments are past moments. I will now argue that the pastness of these moments is experienced as inscribed into the historical and existential time of the audience. Allow me a short detour via photography.

"The date belongs to the photograph," Barthes declares in *La Chambre Claire*:

> not because it denotes a style (this does not concern me), but because it makes me lift my head, allows me to compute life, death, the inexorable extinction of the genera-tions.... I am the reference of every photograph, and this is what generates my aston-ishment in addressing myself to the fundamental question: why is it that I am alive *here and now?*[31]

In principal, the photographic still is *datable*: it is possible to *assign a date* to the moment of photographic exposure. The point here is not whether or not the image *is* given a date. Neither is it a practical matter (a question of whether or not we are *able* to ascertain the production date of a particular photograph, or any other object for that matter). The question is whether or not the datability of the image makes it part of a social and cultural history of human beings. Many photographs are considered culturally important and, as such, are included in our common cultural heritage. However, photographs are normally included in the public conception of culture and history in a more fundamental way, through the temporality of the photographic trace. No matter what is depicted in an actual photograph, the temporality of the photographic trace is inscribed in our socially constituted calendars, the calendars of our social and political histories, the calendars we relate to in our everyday life, the calendars of birth-days and anniversaries.

I will suggest that the photographic trace is experienced as a technical effect which via its historicity (that is, its character of datability in a socially and cultu-rally constituted world of real objects) is also given an existential dimension. Further, I will argue that the social and cultural reality of the photographic trace is important if we are to understand the temporalities of the narrative slide-mo-tion film, even if the still is a freeze-frame in a film, and even if the narrative is fictional like in AÑO UÑA, LA JETÉE, and PHOTO-ROMANS. No matter what the image depicts, and independent of the status of the depiction as fiction or fact, the single frame seems to incite the experience of the photographic stills as hold-ing back or withdrawing the photographic moment from the otherwise unfold-ing of an event and to inscribe this sequence of moments into the (historical and existential) time of the viewer.

In narrative fiction films like AÑO UÑA, LA JETÉE, and the PHOTO-ROMANS series, the voice-overs support the impression of pastness evoked by the static frames (even if this varies among the different examples). As sound, on the other hand, the voice-over also seems to have all the various sounds and the succession of images as its ally. There is, in other words, a tension between pastness and presence (or becoming) across the simple division between sound and image in the narrative slide-motion film that is made perceptible by the stills, but which is potentially there in all moving images. Sometimes this tension in filmic expression is intensified by the temporality of the narrative mode, as in PHOTO-ROMANS, which is a series of classic short stories that is somewhat ruptured by its filmic style. At the other end of the spectrum we find LA JETÉE, a film about memory and loss told as a time-travel story, arguably a perfect theme and genre for a smooth exploration of the expressive potential of the slide motion film. AÑO UÑA can be placed somewhere between these two extremes. Its mundane love story and chronological narrative makes it similar to the stories of PHOTO-ROMANS. However, the rather loose narrative structure of the film as well as its resemblance to a road movie (the traveling, the characters being at turning points in their lives, their evasive actions) and the way it adopts the narrative mode of the chronicle seems to fit more smoothly into this particular filmic expression.

As we have seen, there is a great amount of variety between narrative slide-motion films, which also involves their complex temporalities. Given the complexity of the temporality of the narrative slide-motion film I have sketched here, the temporality of this filmic mode of expression cannot be reduced to the cultural figure of pastness connected to the photographic still. However, I will argue that, along with the notion of the *ideal movement* "made out of successive and different immobilities" (Metz), the *pastness* of the moment of photographic exposure should be considered a formative notion of the filmic expression I have suggested that we call *slide-motion film*.

Parts of this argument were presented as a paper at the SCMS conference in Philadelphia, March 6-9, 2008. I am particularly grateful for all the useful comments from our panel respondent Mary Ann Doane. I also express my warm thanks to the participants at the workshop preparing this book at Lysebu Conference Hotel, Oslo, September 4-5, 2008.

Notes

1. See Dennis, James (17 November 2008), "*Año Uña* (Year of the Nail) Review", available at: http://twitchfilm.net/reviews/2008/11/ano-una-year-of-the-nail-review.php [last accessed January 11, 2010].
2. See, for instance, the photography blog Contact at: http://contactcollective.blogspot.com/2009/08/la-jetee-and-ano-una-stills-as-film.html [last accessed January 11, 2010].

3. See http://leonardo.spidernet.net/Artus/2386/ps.htm [last accessed January 11, 2010]

4. Contrary to what is normally reckoned, it is actually dialogue in this film, but admittedly, not used for the same purpose as in the classic entertainment film.

5. Ira Koningsberg, *The Complete Film Dictionary*, 1997 p. 367.

6. The title, SOLVORN, refers to the name of a village at the Western part of Norway where the photographs on which the film is based were originally taken.

7. See the interview by Georgie Hobbs "Año Uña: Photo Montage Film" at Dazed Digital.com, published 24 November 2008: http://dazeddigital.com/ArtsAndCulture/article/1475/1/A%C3%B1o_U%C3%B1a_Photo_Montage_Film, last accessed January 18, 2010.

8. The stills were taken with a Pentax Spotmatic and the motion-picture segment was shot with a 35mm Arriflex.

9. See Koningsberg 1997 p. 367.

10. See larry-411 (13 March 2008) "Keep an open mind and you'll be rewarded" available at http://www.imdb.com/title/tt0984969/usercomments [February 1, 2010].

11. Dennis, James (17 November 2008), "Año Uña (*Year of the Nail*) Review", available at http://twitchfilm.net/reviews/2008/11/ano-una-year-of-the-nail-review.php   [last checked January 11, 2010].

12. See pei_jin_lin (26 September 2008) "An experience of time in a highly intimate and original style", http://www.imdb.com/title/tt0984969/usercomments [accessed January 11, 2010].

13. See larry-411 (13 March 2008) "Keep an open mind and you'll be rewarded" available at: http://www.imdb.com/title/tt0984969/usercomments [February 1, 2010]

14. See pei_jin_lin (26 September 2008) "An experience of time in a highly intimate and original style", http://www.imdb.com/title/tt0984969/usercomments [last accessed January 11, 2010].

15. See Douglas Crimp 1979/1984, p. 183. Cf. also George Baker 2008 p. 185.

16. See Baker 2008, p. 185.

17. Ibid., p. 185.

18. Christian Metz, "Photography and fetish", [1985] 1990, p.157.

19. Noël Carroll, "Towards an Ontology of the Moving Image" in Cynthia A. Freeland and Thomas E. Wartenberg (eds.) *Philosophy and Film*, Routledge, London, N.Y., 1995, p.73.

20. As many have remarked, there are some similarities between this story and the story of Alfonso Cuarón's film Y TU MAMÁ TAMBIÉN (AND YOUR MOTHER TOO). In Y TU MAMÁ TAMBIÉN, two over-sexed and under-occupied seventeen year old boys meet a 28-year-old woman, flirt with her and invite her to accompany them on a trip to a beach they are unsure actually exists. Soon the three are headed out of Mexico City, making their way toward the fictional destination.

21. See Aristotle [384-322 BC] 1987 p.10-11.

22. See Henry James, "The art of fiction", in Shapira, Morris (ed.), *Henry James: Selected Literary Criticism*, Harmondsworth: Penguin, orig. publ. 1884, 1963 p. 80. See also Shlomith Rimmon-Kenan, *Narrative Fiction: Contemporary Poetics*. London: Methuen, [1983] 1992, p. 35.

23. Peter Brunette and David Wills, *SCREEN/PLAY. Derrida and Film Theory.* 1989, p. 115.

24. Peter Brooks, *Reading for the Plot*, 1984, p. 23. The context of the expression is, "Perhaps we would do best to speak of the *anticipation of retrospection* as our chief tool in making sense of narrative, the master trope of its strange logic". This is, in my view, probably the most interesting, but very much neglected insight of Brooks's book.

25. See Michel Chion, *Audio-Vision: Sound on screen*. New York: Columbia University Press. [1990] 1994, p. 68.

26. Sometimes this experience is ruptured, creating some sort of narrative shock, as in one of the shorts from Photo-Romans, called The Return, which has an autodiegetic voice-over and tells the story about a woman who ends up getting killed in the last scene. Given the otherwise dramatic realism of the film, the murder comes as a surprise, partly because it signals an impossible (or unrealistic) narrational position for the voice-over.

27. Thorold Dickinson (1971) *A Discovery of Cinema*, Oxford, p. 111.

28. R.P. Kolker and J. Douglas Ousley (1973) "A Phenomenology of cinematic time and space", *British Journal of Aesthetics*, vol. 13, p. 391.

29. Thanks to the filmmaker Inger-Lill Persett for this information (email correspondence, March 4, 2010).

30. See: http://docs.google.com/viewer?a=v&q=cache:iQVq8lxnJkcJ:www.novare.no/kff /dagsplan2007/pdf/NK5.pdf+inger-lill+persett&hl=no&gl=no&pid=bl&srcid=ADGE ESh1ZrnHsbYC-_GwvaYLe4r9vwCUFDbflff5XviiwlMEDCp9Pl6SdzAwe4prvxfFI VLLrFc6bsAq9Rav46HWriG4RmH6UXzT2_GMy8VX1AGO–uczQ3ovLNY1cF1z2 O9orSrpahM&sig=AHIEtbSm-84jrPOoEsTTTkHqp_b1EOsOow [last accessed March 29, 2010].

31. Roland Barthes, *Camera Lucida* [1980] 1993, p. 84.

The Cinematic Turn in the Arts

Stop/Motion

Thomas Elsaesser

The Museum and the Moving Image: A Marriage Made at the documenta?

One of the most significant phenomena in the world of contemporary sound-image media – seemingly far removed from the almost daily revolutions on the Internet, and yet intimately connected with them – is the extent to which the moving image has taken over/has been taken over by museums and gallery spaces. There are many – good and not so good – reasons for this dramatically increased visibility in the contemporary art scene of screen, projection, motion and sound. Some are internal to the development of modern art practice, if one accepts that, for many of today's artists, a digital camera and a computer are as much primary tools of the trade as a paintbrush and canvas or wire and plaster-of-Paris were a hundred years ago. On the other hand, there are also reasons internal to the cinema for such a seemingly counter-intuitive rapprochement: not least the much-debated (i.e., as much lamented as it is ridiculed) "death of cinema", whether attributed to television, the video-recorder, the end of European auteur cinema or to digitization and the Internet. Cynics (or are they merely realists?) may rightly conclude that the ongoing *musealization* of the cinema suits both parties: It adds cultural capital to cinematic heritage and redeems its lowly origins in popular entertainment, and it adds new audiences to the museum, where the projected image or video installation – the statistics prove it – retain the visitors' attention a fraction longer than the white cube, with its framed paintings, free-standing sculptures or "found objects".

On reflection, however, matters are not at all straightforward, when the moving image enters the museum. Different actor-agents, different power-relations and policy agendas, different competences, egos and sensibilities, different elements of the complex puzzle that is the contemporary art world and its commercial counterpart inevitably come into play. In short, from a historical point of view, the museum and the motion picture are antagonists, each with its own institutional pedigree, and during the past century, often fairly contemptuous of the other. Shifting from the institutional and the discursive to the aesthetic, the contrast is even sharper: however snugly the "black box" can be fit into the "white cube" with just a few mobile walls and lots of dark fabric, the museum is no cinema and the cinema no museum: first of all because of the different time economies and temporal vectors, which oblige the viewer in the museum to "sample" a film, and to assert his or her attention span, oscillating between concentration and distraction, against the relentless forward thrust and irreversibility of the moving image in the cinema, carrying the spectator along. But museum and movie theatre are also poles apart because they belong to distinct "public spheres", with different constituencies, popular and elite, collective and individualized, for the moment (of the film's duration) and for immortality (of the "eternal" work of art).

Given these incompatibilities and antagonisms, the forces that in the last three decades have brought the two together must have been quite powerful. The dilemma of contending public spheres having to come to terms with each other, for instance, can be observed quite vividly in the fate of (often politically committed) avant-garde filmmakers from the 1960s and 1970s. Since the 1980s, their films could no longer count on screenings either in *art-et-essai* cinemas, film clubs or even hope to find a niche on late-night television programs. As financing from television and state subsidies began to dry up, some found careers as teachers in art academies, and others welcomed a second life as installation artists, commissioned to create new work by curators of international art shows like Kassel's documenta. Especially after Catherine David in 1997 invited filmmakers from France, Germany, Belgium and Britain to documenta X (among them Harun Farocki, Sally Potter, Chantal Akerman, Ulrike Ottinger as well as H.J. Syberberg and J.L. Godard), the cross-over has continued at the Venice Biennale, the Whitney Biennial, at Carnegie Mellon, the Tate Modern, Berlin, Madrid and many, many other venues. These filmmakers-turned-installation artists are now usually named along with artists-turned-filmmakers such as Bill Viola, Fischli & Weiss, Johan Grimonprez, William Kentridge, Matthew Barney, Tacita Dean, Pippilotti Rist, Douglas Gordon, Steve McQueen or Sam Taylor-Wood.

Without opening up an extended balance sheet of gain and loss arising from this other "death of (this time, avant-garde) cinema" and its resurrection as installation art, a few observations are perhaps in order. First, the historical avant-gardes have always been antagonistic to the art world, while nevertheless crucially depending upon its institutional networks and support: "biting the hand that feeds you" is a time-honored motto. This is a constitutive contradiction that also informs the new alliance between the film avant-garde and the museum circuit, creating deadlocks around "original" and "copy", "commodity" and "the market", "critical opposition" and "the collector": films as the epitome of "mechanical reproduction" now find themselves taken in charge by the institution dedicated to the cult(ure) of the unique object, whose status as original is both its aura and its capital. Second, as already indicated, several problematic – but also productive – tensions arise between the temporal extension of a film-

work in a gallery space (often several hours: Jean-Luc Godard's 260-minute His-
TOIRE(S) DU CINÉMA, Douglas Gordon's 24 HOUR PSYCHO, Ulrike Ottinger's 363-
minute SOUTHEAST PASSAGE, Phil Collins's 2-hour RETURN OF THE REAL), and
the exhibition visitors' own time-economy (rarely more than a few minutes in
front of an installation). The mismatch creates its own aesthetics: for instance,
how do I, as viewer when confronted with such overlong works, manage my
anxiety of missing the key moment, and balance it against my sense of surfeit
and saturation, as the minutes tick away and no end is in sight? Some of these
extended works, in confronting viewers with their own temporality (and thus,
mortality) are no doubt also a filmmaker's way of actively "resisting" the quick
glance and the rapid appropriation by the casual museum visitor: regret or a
bad conscience on the part of the viewer being the artist's sole consolation or
revenge. Other time-based art, on the other hand, accommodates such random
attention or impatient selectivity by relying on montage, juxtaposition and the
rapid cut: artists have developed new forms of the collection and the compilation, of the sampler, the loop and other iterative or serial modes. In the film
work of Matthias Müller, Christian Marclay or Martin Arnold, it is repetition
and looping that takes over from linear, narrative or argumentative trajectories
as the structuring principles of the moving image.

Returning to the institutional aspect: one of the most powerful forces at work
in bringing museum and moving image into a new relation with each other is
the programmatic reflexivity of the museum and the self-reference of the modern artwork. Entering a museum still means crossing a special kind of threshold, of seeing objects not only in their material specificity and physical presence,
but also to understand this "thereness" as a special kind of statement, as both a
question and a provocation. This "produced presence" of modernist art is both
echoed and subverted by moving image installations, often in the form of new
modes of performativity and self-display that tend to involve the body of the
artist (extending the tradition of performance artists like Carolee Schneeman
and Yvonne Rainer, as well as of video art quite generally), even to the point of
self-injury (Marina Abramovic, Harun Farocki). Equally relevant is the fact that
installations have given rise to ways of engaging the spectator other than those
of either classical cinema or the traditional museum: for instance, the creation of
soundscapes that convey their own kind of presence (from Jean Marie Straub/
Danielle Huillet's synch-sound film-recitations to Janet Cardiff/George Bures
Miller's audio walks), or image juxtapositions/compositions that encourages
the viewer to "close the gap" by providing his/her own "missing link" (Isaac
Julien, Stan Douglas, Chantal Akerman) or make palpable an absence as presence (Christian Boltanski), each proposing modes of "relational aesthetics" (Nicolas Bourriaud) that are as much a challenge to contemplative, disinterested

museum viewing as they counter or critique cinematic modes of spectatorship (voyeurism, immersion, as well as its opposite, Brechtian distanciation).

However, what the marriage between museum and moving image most tellingly puts into crisis is the relation between stillness and movement, two of the vectors that have always differentiated painting and photography from the cinema and sound. The museum space here is able to take key elements of the cinema – such as the face and the gesture, or action and affect – and articulate them across new kinds of tensions and (self-) contradictions, also conducting a more general interrogation of what constitutes an "image" and what its "viewer" (Bill Viola, Dan Graham, Christian Marclay, Chris Marker and many others).

Suspending Movement, Animating the Still

Before developing some of the consequences of the dividing line between still and moving image having become "blurred" – the blur being one of the concepts I shall touch upon in passing – it may be useful to look at how this "suspended animation" has been theorized and contextualized in a recent study, Eivind Røssaak's *The Still/Moving Image: Cinema and the Arts*.[1] Røssaak's inquiry into the current state of the moving image situates itself strategically at the interface of several crossroads and turning points: the photographic/post-photographic/digital divide, but also the divide between "attraction" (or spectacle) and "narrative" (or linearity). It takes on board the dissensus between the commercial film industry and avant-garde filmmaking, just as it thematizes the institutional divide between screen practices in cinema theatres and screen practices in the museum space. To quote from the author's programmatic introduction: "In recent decades there has been a widespread tendency in moving image practices to resort to techniques altering or slowing down the speed of motion. Creative uses of slow motion, single frame advances and still frame techniques proliferate within digital cinema, avant-garde cinema and moving image exhibitions. This project investigates this tendency through a focus on aspects of three works that are representative for the tendency, show different aspects of it and are widely influential: Andy and Larry Wachowski's THE MATRIX (1999), Ken Jacobs's TOM, TOM, THE PIPER'S SON (orig. 1969, re-released 2000), and Bill Viola's THE PASSIONS (2000-2002)."[2]

As can be seen by the choice of works – all three situated both at the threshold of the new millennium and in different ways referring back to another moment in time, of which they conduct a form of archaeology – Røssaak raises a number of pertinent issues, while concentrating on "movement" and "immobility" as the key parameters. Aware of the self-conscious historicity of the works chosen, the author can focus on some aspects of the aesthetic regime put in crisis, without having to examine the full historical and critical ramifications, as briefly sketched above, when considering the moving image meeting the museum. "Immobility" thus becomes a shorthand or cipher, thanks to which different theoretical-aesthetic investigations into the nature and fate of "the cinematic" today can be deployed, while allowing the focus to firmly remain on these three specific, yet significantly distinct examples of filmic and artistic practice.

The strategic advantage of *The Still/Moving Image* for someone within film studies is that several of the key concepts are well established in the field and will be familiar to readers with an interest in cinema studies: "cinema of attraction", "media archaeology", "structuralist film", "found footage" are terms with firm connotations gained over the past two decades. Other concepts are more vague or metaphorical ("spirituality", "negotiation", "excavation", for instance). While this can lead to problems of coherence and consistency, with occasionally abrupt shifts in the levels of abstraction, the usefulness of the book lies above all in the judicious and felicitous choice of contrasting-complementary case studies, each of which is given a highly original historical placement and subjected to a complex and multi-layered historical hermeneutics. The theoretical framings, taken from art history (G.E. Lessing, Ernst Gombrich), new media theory (Lev Manovich, Mark Hansen) and film studies (Sergei Eisenstein, Raymond Bellour, Tom Gunning), are combined with empirical research (in archives, on site and in museums), which in turn lead to insightful observations on a wide range of works (from Mantegna to Franz Kline, from Tintoretto to Hogarth, from Hieronymus Bosch to Eadweard Muybridge), spanning five centuries and encompassing sculptures, altar pieces, paintings, etchings and chronophotography. Such a broad sweep does not only offer valuable context and historical background to the three works discussed in detail; it locates movement and motion in artworks across several moments of transition in the history of Western pictorial representation, thus contributing to the new discipline of "image-anthropology", as championed, for instance, by Hans Belting and inspired by Aby Warburg.

The first chapter on THE MATRIX is, in one sense, typical of the thesis as a whole, in the way it homes in on a selected part of the work, but then offers an in-depth reading of the detail thus isolated. This, in the case of THE MATRIX is the so-called bullet-time effect, which occurs three times in the film, taking up no more than one minute of the film's overall 136 minutes. On the other hand, this bullet-time effect in 1999, when the film came out, was the most talked about special effect since JURASSIC PARK's dinosaurs, and quickly became a *locus classicus* among fans, "nerds", and philosophers. Defined both by its extreme permutation of time (slow enough to show normally imperceptibly fast events) and space (thanks to the camera's – and thus the spectator's – point-of-view, able to move around a scene at normal speed while actions or people are shown in suspended animation or immobility), the bullet-time effect can be related back in its technique to Muybridge's chronophotography, but in its effect of motion frozen in time, also to Andrea del Verrocchio's statue of Colleoni on horseback. Linking CGI effects to both early cinema and Renaissance sculpture and thus to a long art-historical discourse about the representation of motion and time in the visual, photographic and plastic arts is a commendably illuminating contribution to several disciplines.

Equally full of surprises is the chapter on Tom Tom the Piper's Son. Here, the many layers of correspondences and interrelations between the 1906 Billy Bitzer film and Ken Jacobs' 1969-71 version are explored, all of them adding to the central discussion of movement and stillness. Røssaak shows that Jacobs's repetitions, decelerations and "remediations" of this "found object" from early cinema – itself, as it turns out, a "remediation" or "re-animation" of a famous print from 1733, William Hogarth's Southwark Fair – keep doubling back into the very same problems already encountered by Hogarth (how to represent the asynchronous and yet collective movement of crowds) and Bitzer (how to isolate and thus "arrest" in both senses of the word, one of the participants – Tom who stole the pig – in the milling masses of spectators and players). Each of the three artists deals in his own way, and appropriate to his time and medium, with multiple planes of action, their consecutive phases, and the tensions between guiding but also refocusing the spectator's gaze and attention. Even the modernist allusions in Jacobs's work now make sense as part of the movement/stasis/focus problem, which artists have posed themselves repeatedly over the centuries. But the references to abstract expressionism also afford an intriguing glimpse into the New York avant-garde scene of the 1960s and 1970s, with its intense cross-fertilization between artists, theorists and filmmakers. The brief section on copyright and the legal status of the moving image at the turn of the 20th century between "paper" and "photography" (the famous "paper print collection") makes Bitzer's original material and Jacobs' rediscovery of it a particularly interesting case of the persistence of issues of ownership and common property when it comes to our image heritage and its preservation: all issues central to the museum's role as potential guardian also of the cinema's history.

The book's key notion, "negotiating immobility" is, however, most aptly exemplified in the third chapter, which deals with Bill Viola's installation The Passions, and particularly the piece called The Quintet of the Astonished, a large rear-projected digital image of five people gradually and almost imperceptibly changing expression over a period of almost half an hour. Here, another formula from early cinema scholar Tom Gunning is put to good use: "the aesthetics of astonishment". While Røssaak sees it mainly as a refinement and clarification of the better-known "cinema of attractions", which due to its often indiscriminate application has now also come under attack, I think the term "astonishment" goes beyond the visual register of spectacle and "show", as well as avoiding the problematic binary divides between "norm" and "deviancy" (especially when "cinema of attractions" is played out against "classical cinema" of "narrative integration"). More helpful, also for Røssaak's case of how we perceive stillness and movement in relation to each other, seems to me the possibility that "astonishment" can identify what Gestalt-psychologist and others have referred to as "cognitive dissonance", that is, a level of discrepancy, say, between eye and mind (as in: "the eye sees as real what the mind knows to be impossible"), or between the body and the senses (as in cases where the classic divide between mobile spectator/immobile view [museum] and immobile spectator/mobile image [cinema] is subtly displaced and rearticulated, which happens when the moving image enters the museum). Bill Viola himself suggests as much when he talks about the high-speed photography of THE PASSIONS' continuous, if complexly choreographed movement, replayed and dilated by extreme slow motion as "giving the mind the space to catch up with the eye". Røssaak handles an extremely suggestive analytical tool in this chapter, which conveys very well one of the key techniques of Viola (besides his own version of the bullet-time effect) for producing both cognitive dissonance and motor-sensory imbalance: namely that of the *"desynchronized gazes"* among the five figures, which create the oxymoronic sensation of a cubist temporality. As spectators, we do not know whether to stand stock-still in front of the projected image or mimetically mirror the slow motion of the bodies, thus finding ourselves, precisely, caught in "negotiating immobility", i.e., trying to adjust to a "different" motion of "life" – or if you like, experiencing "ecological time" – in the midst of our hectic lives, dominated by timetables and the tick-tock of mechanical clocks.

Towards a Politics of Slow?

What is more natural than Røssaak ending his book with a gentle plea for "the politics of slow": a worthy sentiment, no doubt, but hopefully also not just intended as a "reaction" to the generalized speed and acceleration of modern life. We do not want to make the museum merely a refuge, and art a compensatory practice. Especially if it is a question of "politics", we need to see the "critical" dimension in movement itself – process, becoming, the possibility of transformation – lest immobility comes to signify not the absence or suspension of movement, but its arrest, with all the connotations of politics, policing and power this implies: "freeze" is, after all, what the cops say to a suspect in Hollywood movies. And one thing that the cinema is definitely not, in the world of the fine arts is a "suspect", and one role the museum should not play is that of the cop (from THE MATRIX), "freezing" the cinema, either in time or in history, the way he unsuccessfully challenges Trinity, the film's Protean heroine. "Negotiating immobility" must not become either a euphemism for the museum as mausoleum, or a code word for resistance to change.

And yet, resistance has been the mark of art for much of the 20th century, including that of cinema. In the contest of motion and stillness, however, what is "the dominant", to which the artist is compelled to offer dissent? Is it the stasis of the photograph, overcome by the cinematic image that brings life and animation, or is it quick editing and the montage of fragments, with its overpowering rhetoric of agitation and propaganda, demanding of the artist to counter it with images that absorb and focus, rather than mimic the frenzied onrush of a speeding train, as in Dziga Vertov's MAN WITH A MOVIE CAMERA? If speed was once perceived as the mark of modernity in the 1910s by Marinetti and the Futurists, or hailed by the Russian avant-garde of the 1920s as thrilling to the promise of technology and the impatient rhythm of machines, then the destructive energies unleashed by "lightning wars", supersonic aircraft or rocket-propelled missiles have also reversed the perspective: just as "progress" is no longer the only vector taking us into the future, so speed may not be the only form of motion to get us from A to B. The modernist paradox seems inescapable: we are obsessed with speed, not least because we are fearful of change, a fear of the relentlessly inevitable which we try to make our own – appropriate, anticipate and inflect with our agency – through speed. In the cinema, a *static high-velocity vehicle* par excellence, we seek out that which moves us, transports us, seduces and abducts us, propels and projects us, while keeping us pinned to our seats and perfectly "in place". Paul Virilio has expressed it most breathlessly, in his "aesthetic of disappearance": Velocity, understood as space or distance, mapped against time or duration, reaches its absolute limit in the speed of light, where space and time "collapse", i.e., become mere variables of each other. Is the cinema, as an art of light, asks Virilio, not always at the limits of both time and space, at the threshold of "disappearance", whose negative energy is stillness? Gilles Deleuze's opposition of the movement image and the time image intimates, among other things, not only a break in the relation of the body to its own perception of motion in time and space, but also a moment of resistance, a reorientation, where perception neither leads to action nor implies its opposite, while stillness does not contradict motion.

These "dromoscopic" considerations are to be distinguished from what has been called "the aesthetics of slow", indicative of a kind of cinema that has reformulated the old opposition between avant-garde cinema and mainstream narrative cinema around (the absence of) speed. Possibly taking its cue from

David Bordwell's characterization of contemporary Hollywood, the "cinema of slow" sees itself as a reaction to "accelerated continuity", where slowness – however expressed or represented – becomes an act of organized resistance: just as "slow food" is a reaction to both the convenience and uniformity of fast food, appealing to locally grown ingredients, traditional modes of manufacture and community values. No longer along the lines of "art versus commerce", or "realism versus illusionism", *slow cinema* (also sometimes referred to as "contemplative cinema") counters the blockbuster's over-investment in physical action, spectacle and violence with long takes, quiet observation, an attention to detail, to inner stirrings rather than to outward restlessness, highlighting the deliberate or hesitant gesture, rather than the protagonist's drive or determination – reminding one, however remotely, of the "go-slow" of industrial protest, but also the "organic" pace of the vegetal realm.

Yet "slow cinema" can also be seen as a way of already thinking the musealization of the cinema into the contemporary practice of cinema, making the classic space of cinema – the movie theatre – into a kind of museum (of the Seventh Art), understood (in the counter-current that not only preserves the anti-cinema of the avant-garde, but also the "cinema of disclosure" of Europe's post-war new waves) as the site of contemplation and concentration. The aural *silentio* of the museum's ambient galleries, conveyed in measured pace and the stillness of the image, would return us to an inner-space that is both womb and refuge, both protest against and a retreat from a world, increasingly experienced as spinning out of control.

Different Ways of Thinking of the Moving Image

We are thus faced with two conceptions of the moving image in light of its century-old history. If we consider the classical view, arguing from the basis of the technical apparatus, there is no such thing as the moving image, neither in photographic, celluloid-based moving images nor in post-photographic video or digital images. In photographic film each static image is replaced by another, the act of replacement being hidden from the eye by the shutter mechanism in the projector; in the analogue video image and the digital image, each part of the image is continually replaced either by means of a beam of light scanning the lines of the cathode ray tube, or refreshed by algorithms that continually rearrange the relevant pixels. Motion is in the eye of the beholder, which is why cinema has so often seen itself accused of being a mere "illusion", an ideological fiction, only made possible by the fallibility of the human eye: regardless of whether this "failure" was compensated by "persistence of vision" or the "phi-effect".

The other view could be called Heraclitean. Given that "everything moves" and that change and thus motion, whether perceptible to the human eye or not, is the very condition of life (animal, vegetal and even mineral) at the macro-scale as well as micro-level, the cinema (as moving image) is not an illusion, simulation or imitation of life but its approximation, by other (mechanical, mathematical) means. Henri Bergson is the much-quoted philosophical guarantor of such a view, at least as understood and interpreted by Gilles Deleuze. For Bergson, there is always priority of movement over the thing that moves, embedded as it is in duration, which, however, no image can represent. In *Creative Evolution*, Bergson even criticizes the cinema for passing static images off as movement, but Deleuze – with Bergson contra Bergson – argues that an image is always "in motion", not merely because the eye restlessly scans, probes and touches even the (still) image in the very "act of seeing": the still image is a "stilled" image, slowed down to the point of imperceptible motion, or stilled because it is taken out of the flow or extracted from it, but carrying with it as its virtuality the signs and traces of the movement to which it owes consistency, energy and substance.

While Deleuze's Bergsonism is part of his overall philosophy of "multiplicity" and "becoming", with roots in Spinoza and Nietzsche, his "revolution" in the way we can think about images in general and the cinematic image in particular is well suited for the recasting of the relation between stillness and movement also in the digital age. Before the advent of the digital image, photography and the cinema were traditionally seen as each other's "nemesis": each could speak to a particular truth, repressed or hidden in the other: the cinema – based as it initially was on the *chrono*-photograph – made us aware of the temporality en-closed or encased in the still image, which the cinema could liberate and re-animate, as it did in the very early performances of the Lumière Brothers, whose films habitually started with a projected photograph, suddenly springing to life. Conversely, photography has always been the cinema's *memento mori*: reminding us that at the heart of the cinema are acts of intervention in the living tissue of time, that the cinema is "death at work", in the famous phrase of Jean Cocteau. Film theory in the 1970s even went a step further: since cinema, in the very act of projecting moving images, represses the materiality of the individual frames that make up the celluloid strip, its "apparatus" cannot but be an instrument of power, at the service of an "idealist" ideology.

In art history, the 1970s also saw a revaluation, if not the incorporation, of photography into the canon of Western art. Photography's ability to hold a moment in time and freeze in it not just a past, but to sustain a "future perfect" has been the source of its peculiar fascination to art historians, taking their cue from

Walter Benjamin, Susan Sontag and especially Roland Barthes, whose insistence on the "tense" of the photograph is nonetheless unthinkable without the cultural experience of cinema against which it formulates a silent protest. Cinema is thus also the "repressed" of photography in the 20th century, at least in its intellectual-institutional discourse. As David Campany put it:

> Still photography – cinema's ghostly parent – was eclipsed by the medium of film, but also set free. The rise of cinema obliged photography to make a virtue of its own stillness. Film, on the other hand, envied the simplicity, the lightness, and the precision of photography.… In response to the rise of popular cinema, Henri Cartier-Bresson exalted the "decisive moment" of the still photograph. In the 1950s, reportage photography began to explore the possibility of snatching filmic fragments. Since the 1960s, conceptual and post-conceptual artists have explored the narrative enigmas of the found film still.[3]

As Campany goes on to point out, filmmakers in the 1970s like Andy Warhol, Michael Snow and Stan Brakhage "took cinema into direct dialogue with the stillness of the photographic image".[4]

Working on the Moment: Stillness in Motion and Motion within Stillness

These dialogical-dialectical relations between photography and cinema may well have come into another crisis with the effective disappearance, in the digital image, of either material or ontological difference between still and moving image. Instead, attention is gradually being refocused on the aesthetic possibilities that arise within digital imaging for the degrees, the modulations and modalities of stillness, arrest and movement, such as suggested earlier around the "bullet time" effect in THE MATRIX, but now in the realm of the fine arts. As Chris Dercon, commenting on the work of Jeff Wall, has remarked:

> The moving image has liberated exhibition spaces from the illusion of the static world. Things we generally associate with the visual arts suddenly start to move on a large scale. Or should we say that suddenly we have become aware that there are static images? As a result of the new applications of photography, cinema and video, we can now really reflect in our museums on what stillness is. From Jeff Wall's point of view, the stillness of still pictures has become very different, otherwise one couldn't explain the current fascination with still photography.[5]

In consequence, just as digital photography can now produce the "photographic mode" as one of its options or effects, so the aesthetics of both photography and cinema have to be re-thought in terms of particular historical "ima-ginaries", rather than being defined by specific properties inherent in each me-dium, least of all the criteria of stillness and movement. Such an idea of photo-graphy and cinema as merely different applications or culturally coded uses of a new (or rather, age-old) mode, namely that of the graphic image (including the photographic image), of which the digital image would merely be the latest installment, as it were, no doubt challenges our concepts of the photographic and the cinematic in all manner of ways. For example, it places the relationship between movement and its suspension into a temporal frame that belongs more to the spectator rather than to the object. Cartier-Bresson's "decisive moment" that needs to be "captured" before it disappears "out there" and "forever" is turned against its own metaphysics of time (i.e., the manifest palpability of time we call the moment), when compared to Jeff Wall's photographic light boxes or the video portraits of Gillian Wearing, where an elaborate staging of the "instant" or the "moment" (whether taken from a Hokusai woodblock print, a London mews, or a sunlit afternoon street in Los Angeles) produces and post-produces time (i.e., the temporal attention and extension the viewer gives to the work). It comes to constitute *the artist's work on the moment* rather than registering *the moment's work on the artist*.

A quite different example of such "work on the moment" occurs in CHUNGK-ING EXPRESS (1994), directed by Wong Kar Wai, who, together with his camera-man Christopher Doyle, might be said to realize a "photographic imaginary" but using cinematic means: not by inserting stills into his film, freezing the frame, or composing his films of photographs, as one finds them in the films of the Nouvelle Vague, from Jean-Luc Godard (A BOUT DE SOUFFLE) to François Truffaut (LES QUATRE CENT COUPS) and Chris Marker (LA JETÉE). I am also not thinking of the scenes in CHUNGKING EXPRESS that feature "stains" of motion blur in an otherwise sharp image – though these shots deserve more comment, not least because they play another variation on our theme, insofar as the blur records objects and people still in motion when the image has already been fixed. As the trace of a movement that exceeds another movement, the motion blur in the photographic-cinematic mode was often regarded as either a techni-cal flaw or an index of a special kind of authenticity. The sharp image, from which any trace of motion (and thus its temporal index) is banished, came to be the paradigm of normative representation. From the vantage point of the "digi-tal", on the other hand, the blur can realize a "layering" of degrees of stillness and motion repressed or deemed unacceptable in the photographic (or the cin-ematic), while nonetheless embedded as a possibility and an absent presence in the very opposition of stillness and motion.

However, I have in mind another scene: in order to convey the co-presence and overlap of two temporalities – one iterative and in the modality of "duration", the other focused on the moment; one external and impersonal, the other subjectively inflected with anticipation and boredom – Doyle shot a scene of passersby in a busy shopping street, while inside a bar, one of the protagonists, Cop 633, sits drinking coffee, with the amateur stalker Faye gazing at him in rapt absorption. What we see, however, is the non-encounter between the man and the woman taking place in a drifting, slow-motion dreamy haze of un-requited longing, while the people outside speed past these ghosts, lost to desire and ennui – a powerful metaphor for the life that escapes them, as they seek ways to live it more intensely, in a city that never rests. It is the sort of slowing down of movement we associate with Bill Viola, but instead of being "done digitally", Doyle shot the scene with an analogue camera, asking the actors to go into slow-mo mode, as if in a Kung Fu movie, while filming the crowds at normal speed – except that there is nothing "normal" about a scene so effec-tively combining two different "sheets of time" in the single image: time stands still for some, while it rushes past for others. Realizing an effect now considered typical of the "digital", and doing so with the resources of the cinema, Wong Kar Wai and Doyle anticipate one of the changes that the digital was to bring to the parameters of motion. Demonstrating a different kind of materiality and malleability of time in the image, they also implicitly confirm that we should not attach these changes to digital technology per se. Such scenes herald a new aesthetic of duration beyond movement and stillness, arising from both film and photography, but perhaps to be realized by neither.

Having become a "way of seeing" as well as a "way of being", the cinema has made itself heir to photography, one might say, not by absorbing the latter's capacity for realism, or by turning the still image's irrecoverable pastness into the eternal present of the filmic now. Rather, by handing its own photographic past over to the digital, it might fulfill another promise of cinema, without thereby betraying photography. The particular consistency of the digital image, having less to do with the optics of transparency and projection and more with the materiality of clay or putty, carries with it the photographic legacy of im-print and trace, which as André Bazin saw it, is as much akin to a mask or a mould as it is a representation and a likeness. Bazin's definition of the cinema as "change mummified" may have to be enlarged and opened up: extended to the digital image, it would encompass the double legacy of stillness and move-ment, now formulated neither as an opposition in relation to motion, nor as a competition between two related media, but in the form of a paradox with pro-foundly ethical as well as aesthetic implications: the digital image fixes the in-stant and embalms change: but it also gives to that which passes, to the ephem-eral, to the detail and the overlooked not just the instant of its visibility, but the dignity of its duration.

Here, then, lies the task for the museum, as it comes to terms with time-based art increasingly supplementing if not substituting for the lens-based art of the last century. With photographs now digital and intuitively understood as segments stilled from the flow of time, both film and photography, whether digitally produced or merely digitally understood, are an archive not only of moments, epiphanies and illuminations, or actions in the mode of the movement, cause and consequence, but also of sensations, affects and feelings that are experienced as transitory, inconsequential and ephemeral. Hence the ethical task of their *sustainability,* ensuring that they endure: in memory, as intensities, as the shape of a thought, even as their perception exceeds the eye and encompasses the whole body as perceptual surface. This "duration of the ephemeral" would not be in the service of slowing down the pace of life, nor an act of resistance against the tyranny of time, but would grant to the fleeting moment its transience as transience, beyond stillness and motion, beyond absence and presence.

Notes

1. Eivind Røssaak, *The Still/Moving Image: Cinema and the Arts* (Lambert Academic Publishing, 2010) is a revised edition of *Negotiating Immobility: The Moving Image and the Arts* (Ph.D. dissertation, University of Oslo 2008).
2. Quoted from the blurb of Røssaak's dissertation (*Negotiating Immobility: The Moving Image and the Arts,* 2008).
3. David Campany (ed.), *The Cinematic (Documents of Contemporary Art),* Cambridge, MA: MIT Press, 2007, 'Introduction' p. 1.
4. Ibid., p. 11.
5. Chris Dercon, 'Gleaning the Future from the Gallery Floor', *Vertigo* vol. 2, no. 2, spring 2002, online at: http://www.vertigomagazine.co.uk/showarticle.php?sel=bac&siz=1&id=574 (last accessed September 30, 2010).

After "Photography's Expanded Field"

George Baker

In what follows, I would like to do at least two things that my essay "Photography's Expanded Field" did not do. First, I would like to present an extremely close reading of a specific artist's practice as it is opened up and indeed was formed by the precise interpenetration of photography and cinema that I explored in my earlier essay. In fact, I will treat in detail a project by the Los Angeles-based artist Sharon Lockhart entitled PINE FLAT that came to fruition in 2005, the year of my essay's publication (and was thus not at all covered). Second, and more importantly, I offer this close reading as an amplification of the formal mapping of photography's expansion that my earlier essay hoped to broach. By amplification, I mean radicalization, in a way; what I hope to do here is deal not just with the forms and possibilities opened up by the expansion of the medium of photography, but with the *meaning*, and perhaps too the motivations, for the insistence with which many artists today emplace their practice *between* mediums, or engage in the cinematic opening of the still photograph that has been my concern. Another way of stating this radicalization would be to say that my concern today is less with the "objective" or structural mapping performed in my earlier essay; the interpenetration of forms, the expansion of mediums like the photograph has too a "subjective" logic, and it is to the desiring politics of the expansion of photography that I hope to turn.

In the first "episode" of Sharon Lockhart's recent film PINE FLAT, we see a pine forest blanketed by falling snow. We then hear – but do not see – a young girl, whose plaintive cry echoes through the winter landscape: "Ethan...! Where are you...?" And then: "Please Ethan! Come back...!" It seems like a game of hide-and-seek that has perhaps gone awry. But this cry of loss strikes me as significant, given the origin of PINE FLAT in what we might call photographic strategies of "objective chance" and the "found object". Looking in 2000 to get away from her home and work in Los Angeles, Lockhart drove some four hours north, into the foothills of the Sierra Nevada Mountains. There, she came across a rural community by chance and decided to stay, because it struck her as deeply "familiar".[1] While her previous work was known for an engagement with ethnographic representation that led to far-flung projects in Japan, Mexico, and Brazil, now Lockhart's attention was held by a locale that reminded her of a different sort of distance, a temporal one, as she claimed the community was similar to sites where she had been raised. Over the course of the next four years, the artist visited and re-visited the town, setting up a portrait studio where she created images of the local children, and collaborating with them on a film where they are portrayed in the pristine surrounding landscape.

The large format images in the portrait series, entitled *Pine Flat Portrait Studio*, are hardly outmoded in terms of their literal form or medium. Instead, it is the photographs' *conventions* – and perhaps their subject, rural youth, as well – that bespeak the past, as Lockhart engages the history and address of a specific kind of vanished, non-art photographic portraiture, produced in rural locales in the late-nineteenth and early-twentieth centuries by commercial photographers from August Sander in Germany to Mike Disfarmer in the United States. While Sander photographed his subjects in the context of their environment (something Lockhart engages more in her film than in her photographs), Disfarmer isolated his in an extremely Spartan studio setting, with all his subjects posed on a bare concrete floor against the same dark, blank backdrop. It was as if Disfarmer's subjects existed in a mournful void, the industrial setting and technique of the photograph emerging as the most extreme opposition to the rural Arkansas population.[2] Lockhart replicates this scenario exactly, and follows Disfarmer's reliance only on natural light and thus longer exposure times, allowing the subjects perhaps to "grow" into their image, almost to "bloom". Provoking an observing attentiveness with an extreme focus on detail, we would seem to be in the presence of an embrace of that leave-taking before the world – a kind of involuntary documentary impulse – that theorist Kaja Silverman has characterized as the "author-as-receiver". And yet the images present problems for us, in ways beyond the fact that their conventions are "appropriated".

In each photograph, the children adopt a pose; they do not present themselves "objectively" or analytically, all in the same position. Hands are placed on hips, or stuffed into pockets; arms are crossed defensively, or hold an attribute, like a drawing pad or a hunter's rifle or a lollipop. While the criticism of PINE FLAT has emphasized that Lockhart entered into a form of collaboration with her subjects that is characteristic of all her projects – which, for the most part, revise problematic conventions of human portraiture – we cannot be sure of the origins of the pose, whether it comes from the artist or subject; the attributes may also have been the children's idea or were potentially provided for them by the author. We face a similar quandary with regard to costume, which ranges here from everyday jeans and T-shirts to elaborate biker outfits and combinations even more outlandish than the general tendency of children to mix-and-match clashing pieces (witness a young girl seemingly buried beneath her accoutrements, which include a catcher's mask, cowboy boots, fringed turquoise riding chaps, a hunter's vest and an out-sized plaid flannel shirt marked with the word "Wrangler", a cowboy nostalgia brand popular with American children in the 1970s). It is entirely unclear, in other words, whether the photographs are to be understood as fictions or as documents, whether they engage in performative acting or testify to an unselfconscious "being", whether they approximate Disfarmer's models from the past or locate an untouched pocket of rural existence in the present.

And Lockhart's film presents us with a similar set of problems. Working in 16mm, Lockhart's medium in this instance *is* deeply obsolescent; however, here too there is a paradox. PINE FLAT connects its outmoded analog form to the pristine subject of youth and nature – however potentially threatened in our postindustrial present. The form is almost classical: Lockhart films episodes that are all ten minutes in length, with six of individual children and then six more of the children gathered into groups. The ten-minute expanse corresponds to the full length of a single reel of 16mm film. During the time in which the film is allowed to roll to its depletion without interruption or cuts, Lockhart's camera remains absolutely still. It is also insistently frontal or "objective". In this, the camera's fixed and passive gaze registers the non-heroic, non-narrative activities of the children, as they perform simple tasks – like reading a book in a field, sleeping near some mountain rocks, listening to the forest sounds while hunting, or waiting before a verdant valley for a slowly approaching school bus – throughout the full duration of the scene. All of the "open" passive attributes of the author-as-receiver seem in effect. And yet, while Lockhart supposedly "scouted" her pristine locations with the children, and perhaps discussed with them what activities they might enjoy based on their own proclivities, we again are not faced with a film of "found" documentary footage, even though this is its address. All of the episodes were staged for the camera. It is as if Lockhart does not recognize the opposition between fiction and documentary at all.

Such has been the ambivalence of Lockhart's images from the very beginnings of her career. The vast majority of her earlier portrait projects were focused on children or young adults. In her *Audition* series from 1994, Lockhart photographed children locked in an awkward but deeply touching embrace, as if she were trying to capture the non-replicable moment of one's "first kiss". However, Lockhart produced five of these images, each with different children but in the same locale. Impossible then to read as documentary or photojournalism – hardly examples of the "decisive moment" – Lockhart's images instead deployed the Hollywood or theatrical conventions of the audition, and each image was the result of the children's attempt to replicate a prior image, in this case the climactic "first kiss" scene from one of François Truffaut's films about children, L'ARGENT DE POCHE (1976). They thus presented a series of "memories" we might characterize as "falsifying" – we might even say "exteriorizing". Lockhart's photographs for the later project *Goshogaoka* (1997) followed a similar logic. We see a series of individual or group portraits of Japanese girls, members of the same high school basketball team, seemingly captured while the team was playing or practicing. However, Lockhart's images were arrived at only after the girls chose favorite sports photographs of (mostly American) basketball stars upon which to model their actions and their poses.

Lockhart's photographs thus dismantle many of the assumptions both of art portraiture and ethnographic documentation, the two discursive formations to which her work seemed oriented. Modeling pose and costume upon prior images was not her only strategy. As in PINE FLAT, the settings in which the act of portraiture occurs became an over-riding concern–the photograph's "world" in other words. This was enacted most poignantly in her Brazil projects that led up to the film TEATRO AMAZONAS (1999). Following anthropologists on research trips in the Amazon basin, Lockhart produced a series of images that moved laterally away from direct portraits of the ethnographic "subjects" of the field research. In her series *Interview Locations*, she photographed the homes in which the subjects had been interviewed, but absent of their inhabitants. Simultaneously, she requested treasured snapshots from the same families, which she then re-photographed for a series entitled *Family Photographs*. The result was a first series that gathered to itself so many images of seemingly abandoned homes, emptied-out domestic spaces, and another that spoke of time past in an anonymous voice, like rootless or discarded memories bereft of their individual owners.

Nostalgia whispered through both of these two projects inasmuch as the abandoned domestic interiors appeared like old black-and-white photographs of the kind Walker Evans had once made for his project *Let Us Now Praise Famous Men*; the re-photographed family snapshots also attached themselves to older imaging technologies and bygone times. But nostalgia attached itself even more deeply to those early works by Lockhart where her focus on youth portraits and on domestic interiors came together. All without titles, these now single images were filled with a general sense of languor and of suspension: a photograph of a young girl napping on or near a glass table, enveloped by its mirror embrace; a young woman in an old, fading home turned away from the camera. Rather than snapshots or documents, whose content they imitated, these images were elaborately staged, with locations scouted, costumes chosen, and lighting arranged again along the cinematic model. Similar images of children were made simultaneously in natural settings, looking forward in this way to PINE FLAT. But the peculiarity of almost all of these latter photographs, like the diptych *Julia, Thomas* (1994) or other *Untitled* images from 1996 – and perhaps attributing to their enigma and suspended sense of time – was how in each image the subject did not look forward but turned away, or turned back, to look along with the viewer into the black or fog-enshrouded distance of the photograph.

It has gradually become apparent that these early portraits take an opposite, but linked, approach to that evidenced in a series like *Audition*. For if the latter photographs approximated snapshots but had been modeled upon a cinematic "source", here Lockhart's cinematic portraits held a kind of mysterious dialog with prior documents, in this case family snapshots. Beginning in 1994, Lockhart had already adopted the strategy enacted later in Brazil for the *Family Photographs* series, engaging in a kind of "self-ethnography" as she began to re-photograph her own personal archive of her family's photo-albums. The series continues to the present day; Lockhart calls each of these images an *Untitled Study (re-photographed snapshot)*. In many of these "studies" we see Lockhart as a child in the arms of her father, or holding hands with her mother or sister, almost always turned away from the camera. Hardly any critical accounts have noticed or remarked upon these images. One exception is the early essay on Lockhart by Timothy Martin, who comments on their relation to the *Untitled* photographs of 1994-1996:

> Lockhart's pictorial language was now beginning to take the role of characterization upon itself, employing a cinematic sense of mise-en-scène as its chief device–though making no further overt reference to specific films. Nearly all of the untitled large-scale color photographs of 1995-1996 pursue this pictorial language to greater and greater degrees of scenic involution and mystery. And in nearly all of them the human subject is obliquely posed, many with back to camera: a figure of vacancy, stillness, and deferral within a picture of tense visual expectation. Curiously, a few of these poses echo those seen in the artist's rephotographed family snapshots, which she has produced from 1996 [sic] to the present day. In these nostalgic images, she, her sister, mother, and father appear as solitary or paired figures, typically with backs to camera, before natural vistas or more domestic placid scenery. The sense of longing and deferral in these images offers a powerful, though muted, personal counterpoint to the cinematic grandness of the large-scale photographs, which appear to derive from them in ways that remain essentially indeterminate and private.[3]

The *Untitled Study* series thus does not exactly amount to a set of image "sources". Instead, they are held in lesser-or-greater dialog with Lockhart's cinematic portraits – a strangely distanced relation to images of one's personal history coming into contact with a distanced, staged image of intimacy in the present. And this "dialog", I would say, continues into the present, as the natural scenery and the poses of the re-photographed family snapshots find a startling series of echoes in the current images from PINE FLAT. Indeed, now Lockhart has re-photographed a series of commercial portraits of herself and her sister produced in the 1960s and 1970s as *Untitled Study* images, documenting some kind of historical survival of the portrait practice engaged in by Disfarmer into her own personal history, which she then extends to the children in PINE FLAT.

And many of Pine Flat's filmed scenarios seem to follow closely from Lockhart's enigmatic family images, with pairs and trios of children playing in both, or with the snapshots of herself or her family members with back to camera now taken up in episodes of Pine Flat like "Bus" or "Snowy Hill". It is as if an initial analogy first occurred to the artist around the issue of pose–the fact that these enigmatic (failed?) snapshots of family members seen from behind created a correspondence with the situation of the viewer's orientation toward the image, with both viewer and photographed subject gazing toward a distant horizon, like the unfathomable vista of the enigma of the past itself. Both viewer and viewed were positioned similarly in relation to that unknown scene, and to a kind of thus infinitely deferred desire.[4] And then it is as if this initial analogy inspired Lockhart to seek out another series of affinities, "attuning" her earlier cinematic photographs or the current images from the Pine Flat project to these auratic images from her own past.[5]

Attunement, I want to claim, has become Lockhart's overriding artistic concern. More "aural" than visual, Lockhart's strategies of "attunement" expand the literal obsolescence of the analog into what we might call a conceptual strategy of analogy. To "attune" something requires two forms; it can never be a solitary endeavor. Attunement is the attempt to bring forms close, to have them "rhyme". It is a word we could use to understand Lockhart's insistent linkage of terms we normally perceive as oppositions, rhyming in her work document and fiction, past and present, viewer and viewed, subject and object, self and other– until the opposition will no longer hold. Attunement is a desiring and emotive mode; it is the form of Lockhart's disorienting version of "receiving", the way in which even while intensely manipulating her images, she makes space for the world outside. It is an action modeled on the workings of memory itself, the affinities through which desire can be displaced from past to present and vice versa. It is a device through which we might finally begin to understand that commonplace of the criticism of Lockhart's work that sees it as an uncanny combination of both distance and affect, of "objective" photography or "structural" film and the emotions – a combination that, moreover, Lockhart seems to signal precisely in the connotations of her project's title Pine Flat.[6]

This is because attunement, Lockhart has shown, can come from strangely readymade conventions, and unlikely, perhaps alienating places. It can emerge from practices of mass culture, Hollywood for example: Witness her photograph of actor Ben Gazzara (*Ben Gazzara, Los Angeles, California, March 21, 1998*), photographed in close-up, gazing almost longingly into the camera, head resting on his hands and on a pillow while he lies in bed. Evidently, the photograph of the aging actor was taken on a film set, for Lockhart has paired it with a second image of a young woman in exactly the same pose. This is Gazzara's "stand-in" during shooting, as Lockhart's title informs us: *Emilie Halpern,*

Stand-in for Ben Gazzara, Los Angeles, California, March 21, 1998. The result is immensely confusing, and yet intensely auratic: it is as if this commonplace cinematic practice during filming has produced a document of two individuals now deeply aligned, exchanging places with each other, "attuned" from one to the other. Possible scenarios proceed from this uncanny attunement, narratives having nothing to do with the story that we assume was being filmed: perhaps we face an amorous situation, a document of a couple in the intimate space of their bed. Or perhaps we face a memory, like those where we recognize an intensely personal attachment to a parent, but can't remember if we are thinking of an image of our "father" or our "mother", interchanging them within our minds. Or it is as if we see a scene of deep but loving identification, where a "daughter" takes the place and position of her "father". All of these scenarios seem legitimated by the images; none of them are definitive. And we hardly need to stop here. For the situation only becomes more expansive when we realize that these two photographs are themselves attuned to earlier images within Lockhart's oeuvre, by pose with the *Untitled* 1996 portrait of the sleeping girl near the glass table, for example, or by gaze with Lockhart's diptych of two teenagers standing before the sea, staring into the camera as if they were reaching toward each other as much as toward the viewer, across the gap of both space and time – *Lily (approximately 8am, Pacific Ocean)*, and *Jochen (approximately 8pm, North Sea)* (1994). And since all of these images may (or may not) be photographs aligned with Lockhart's own memory images, the attunement becomes more disorienting still.

In addition to alienating ready-made conventions, attunement can also emerge from dissonance itself; Lockhart's tactics seem dependent on such oppositions, and on the redemption implicit in overcoming them. Such was the task of Lockhart's film TEATRO AMAZONAS, where she filmed from the point of view of the stage an audience in Brazil gathered to listen to an "atonal" composition by Lockhart's frequent collaborator Becky Allen.[7] First, the project aligned the atonal composition with the community portrayed before us; a choral work for many voices attuned to a group of many faces gathered by Lockhart according to similarly "atonal" – or rather alienating and inorganic – procedures derived from sociology and statistics (a "scientific" sampling of the full range of the population in the Brazilian city of Manaus). As the burst of vocal music began to diminish over the course of the film – voice after voice eventually dropping out – the music's fading allowed the ambient "sound" of the community to emerge, to be "born". And so multiple dissonances came into alignment here, climaxing in what we might consider a foundational series for the artist: the attunement of the viewer and the viewed, of self and other, and of history and the present, as an audience in the past faces and models an audience gazing at the film at each moment of its present or future screening.

Music was included in Pine Flat as well, where an intermission linking the two halves of the film was filled with the sound of a young boy playing guitar and singing along to a prior "model", creating his own, tentative version of the angst-ridden pop-punk anthem "Stay Together for the Kids" by the California band Blink-182. We listen to the boy as he diverges from the original song, and even changes key from time to time. With this, Lockhart signals the processes of attunement that in fact run throughout the whole of the Pine Flat project. For here, it is the staged, "manipulated" image that registers the model of the author-as-receiver, producing an uncanny rhyming of past and present, a melancholic looking back (to a time of origins, or of the lost object) that paradoxically locates or models a new beauty in the world today, a new value in the present time.

Indeed, aside from considerations of artificial costume and pose, or potential models in image banks from other places, people, and times, the photographs in the series *Pine Flat Portrait Studio* manifest one manipulation more directly than any other: each of the images are "attuned" to all the rest. By precisely altering the distance of her camera to the children based on their relative sizes, Lockhart was able to photograph each child at the very same scale within the frame; the oldest and tallest of the children occupy the same space within the image as the youngest and smallest. The children thus all seem to literally "rhyme" as they are brought into physical correspondence with each other. The tactic seems egalitarian, but it is also deeply de-individuating, confusing the series' reliance on photographic objectivity and the portrait genre's role in the construction of identity. Arranged in a set diegetic horizontal line and mostly organized from younger to older children, the portrait series' attunement of all its images works against this ordering device as well. For we seem to perceive the slowing of the linear march of time, or witness it halted in its tracks altogether. Photographs of sisters perhaps taken at the same time seem like potential images of the same person taken at two different ages; photographs of the same child taken at two different moments during the project's life become impossible to reconcile, as if aging bifurcated the child into two different subjects, or conversely, was held in abeyance, its physical signs such as growth all but cancelled out. In this, the portrait series finds itself beset by wayward analogies, unruly photographic correspondences and affinities, and begins to produce forms of what we might imagine as the kind of "falsifying movements" within time more characteristic of the medium of avant-garde cinema. The photographs thus attune themselves to film.

Conversely, the Pine Flat film attunes itself to photography. Each image within it remains largely static; cinematic movement lies suspended; the film seems to slow, to become, like a photograph, almost "still". In this, the photographic attunement of film appears like a turning back of Lockhart's medium upon itself, a return of cinema to its photographic pre-history, and in this turn backward the film begins to attune itself to its subject: to the look back at the rural and at youth, to the activities and temporality of childhood. A slowed image, positioned by attunement squarely between photography and film, opens itself to the in-between, suspended activities of the child: reading a book with rapt attention; napping quietly; waiting distractedly; playing on swings, moving languorously back and forth; treading water slowly in a country stream. Critics have remarked that all of these activities seem reminiscent of the unself-conscious attentiveness often depicted in pre-modernist painting, where a depicted subject seems to block out the surrounding world, and that the art historian Michael Fried has called "absorption". Moving from these absorptive activities to the peculiarity of Lockhart's mise-en-scène, which seems to drain each episode of any sense of contrast between figure and ground, the point has been made that Lockhart wishes to engage not only with painting, but with *modernist* painting, and with its self-reflexive and ultimately solipsistic project.[8]

But this hardly seems the case at all. What appears to embody a belated modernism, again amounts to a project steeped in new analogies, connections, correspondences. For Fried, "absorption" signaled a mode in which painting was able to throw off its narrative functions, and begin an ultimately monomaniacal focus on the self-reflexive logic of vision, paradoxically by negating the convention that a painting was meant to be beheld. Absorptive subjects were thus solipsistic; they cancelled out the presence of the spectator, turning inward upon themselves. Later modernist conventions of suspending oppositions between figure and ground, foreground and background, achieved this eradication of painting's narrative basis in an even more radical way, severing the painting from the task of depicting the world, securing its lonely autonomy. If Lockhart's PINE FLAT "rhymes" with this history of another medium, recalling the prehistory of modernist painting, it is in the spirit of canceling oppositions in a much different manner, oppositions that modernism needed to uphold. It is in the spirit perhaps of canceling modernism's melancholic withdrawal from the world altogether. Lockhart's film is anything but "autonomous", solipsistic, self-absorbed. It is not "lonely" but a document of cohabitation, togetherness, and collaboration. PINE FLAT is not "absorptive" (selfish) but "attuned" (generous), perhaps linking its form both to photography and to painting.

Lockhart surely *does* cancel all sense of figure-ground distinctions in her filmic images: grass spreads directly up the screen and merges through color matching with the trunks and leaves of trees; horizon lines are rigorously suppressed; snow and fog join figures with their hazy fields; we are often *too close* to a scene to allow distinctions to emerge. And this *closeness* spreads to the children, who fuse with these figureless fields inasmuch as we could say they become "attuned" to their environment. Like an untimely sibling of what Walter Benjamin once said about ruins, this vision of youth portrays its subjects as "merging" into their surroundings. Lockhart achieves this in part through details of pose and costume: blue jeans and a plaid shirt worn by the child in the episode "Bus" rhyming with the blue-green and purple foliage of the surrounding valley; or the position of the child's body in the episode "Sleeper" curled up into the same shape as the crook between two rocks, curved into the same form as the land. In the episodes of pairs or groups, the children – even when bickering – seem to ally themselves with each other. And as the children throw out so many ropes to their environs or their playmates, attuning and attaching themselves to their surrounds, we as viewers of Lockhart's film hardly find ourselves "detached" from the children before us, negated or separated by a scene of self-absorption. Instead, we are "attuned" to the children's absorption by Lockhart's filmic form; we are attuned to their attunement. As two children, for example, tread water in unison and look down, away from the camera, into the water's fluid depths, we too look down at them, positioned by the camera in such a way as to attune our gazing with theirs. And as the children wait, or listen, or play with no regard for the passing of time, we too find ourselves as viewers waiting. We find ourselves "attuned" to their attentiveness, joined in their temporal suspension.

Our attunement to the children in Lockhart's film provokes a sense less of detachment, than of care. It has thus been suggested that Lockhart's close attention to children, her camera's open, capacious gaze in the PINE FLAT project, should be conceived in some analogy to that of the gaze of a mother toward a child.[9] In her work's transformation of a camera eye that initially seems totalizing, perhaps oriented toward surveillance or visual domination, into one of passive attentiveness and care, we do sense the opening up of a maternal and protective logic within the project. But attunement, ultimately, amounts to a quiet but unruly form of desire; the normative familial metaphors, even the redemptive forms of maternal care, do not regulate all of its paths. Attunement, for example, is not the same thing as what psychoanalysis calls "identification"; not based on "misrecognition" nor the rapacious drive to possess – *to be* or *to have*, as the psychoanalytic narrative would put it – attunement places two forms into the same "key". It precisely does not equate them.

Instead, this mutual rhyming preserves a crucial distance, evinced in the distanced tactics of Lockhart's oeuvre. Indeed, in PINE FLAT, it is as if we gaze into the distance – not just of so many gorgeous natural vistas, but also into the intense mystery of the past. Ultimately, this is why the obsolete analog format of Lockhart's film seems so appropriate. It signals an analogy not just with the threatened reality of rural youth in our present culture, like a pocket of historically surpassed experience subsisting against all odds; it points to the attunement that the film's images open up with Lockhart's own memories, and perhaps also with our own. The project embodies a literal nostalgia, a seeming resurrection or retrieval of youth, of childhood, of a time long past. It seems to fixate there, and the static camera that Lockhart utilizes amounts to just one sign of this. But we face a strange form of nostalgic pining. Pining denotes a melancholic wasting away from longing – for home and for the past. In PINE FLAT, however, this pining becomes a way to turn the wasting away into a gesture of generosity. Now it is the pining for the past in PINE FLAT that displaces the hegemony of the author; it is a "wasting away" that makes space for the other. A giving up and giving over, such longing also hollows out the image of the past, exteriorizing it and depersonalizing it. We hardly know to whom these memories belong (it is why we hardly recognize them *as* memories). Thus exteriorized, they can be claimed by others in the present. Simultaneously, this pining interiorizes; the wasting away from longing opens up a hole within the self, the emptiness and loss of melancholia, into which the other – the past of the other, the memories of another – can be inserted, and where they can also be preserved. And so here, to pine away for the past becomes an opening up to the world. It follows the ramifications of attunement, the impossible correspondence, the distanced rhyming (the rhyming of distance) – where now the other can be installed within the self, and the self shared vertiginously with the other.

PINE FLAT amounts to a displaced self-portrait. But it is also an "other-portrait", an imaging of the shared space between the self and the other. Thus, in our attunement to the children of PINE FLAT, we do not "identify" with them, but we perhaps recognize ourselves in them. We are called upon to desire this self-exile. Following the work's disorienting logic, we almost see them as ourselves, but in the irretrievable past, and this becomes a motor for attachment in the present: we see and experience ourselves as them, now. These two vertiginously similar experiences may appear equivalent; they are instead attunements, attempts to bring close two things that will never be the same. The episodes of PINE FLAT emerge as what we might call documents of memory, and also fictions of reality. At the same time they also rhyme with the opposite of such experience (as, in Lockhart's work, oppositions always come undone). For PINE FLAT also embodies a collection of fictional memories and "realized" or performed, documents. It testifies to an attempt literally to give shape to the past – to reshape the past – as well as to allow its now-redeemed light to shine quietly upon the present. It is an attunement of the one to the other. This attunement of past and present joins all the other oppositions that structure Lockhart's work, the collaboration within her oeuvre of photography and film, document and fiction, memory and imagination, artist and subject, self and other, viewer and viewed. These oppositions are pairs, Lockhart shows us; and rather than hold themselves apart, they call out to each other. Attunement becomes here the very modality of longing: it is the voyage home that never reaches its destination, the intimate approach that will never end.

Notes

1.   Lockhart, cited in Inés Katzenstein, "Sharon Lockhart, Ethnography Home," *Pine Flat* (Bilbao: Sala Rekalde, 2006), p. 119: "For this project, I wanted to look at something that felt very familiar to me. I immediately felt connected to the landscape and the people of Pine Flat. It is very similar to the places I grew up." It bears remarking that it is unclear whether Pine Flat is the actual name of the place to which Lockhart retreated, who, in other statements, has intimated that she will keep the site's true identity a secret.

2.   This opposition is particular to Disfarmer's name as well, which was not his given one (he was born Michael Meyers), and expressed an extreme dis-identification with his rural Arkansas origins (which were also paradoxical, inasmuch as he was born into a family of German immigrants). We may wonder if Lockhart was attracted to Disfarmer's not-widely-known work precisely because of this dis-identification staged around the opposition between his rural subjects and industrial photography – we may wonder, in other words, if Lockhart was attracted to this opposition precisely because of a need to overcome it (as now, today, both are outmoded).

3.   Timothy Martin, "Documentary Theater," *Sharon Lockhart: Teatro Amazonas* (Rotterdam: Museum Boijmans Van Beuningen, 1999), pp. 18-19.

4.   The "Orphic" dimension of this turn away from the camera, which I am reading as a turning "back" to the past, could be stressed. It is one of the founding metaphors of Silverman's forthcoming study of analogy, *Flesh of My Flesh*; see especially her chapter "Orpheus Rex" and her study of similar poses in the chapter on Gerhard Richter, "How to Paint History."

5.   There is little "proof" that Lockhart sees her *Untitled Study* series as intimately connected to the *Pine Flat* project; rarely seen or reproduced, as if they were in fact "private," the *Untitled Study* works are just as rarely discussed, and the artist has not commented on any such relation. However, it is suggestive that the largest grouping of the re-photographed snapshots that to my knowledge have ever been reproduced appear at the back of the recent catalogue *Sharon Lockhart: Pine Flat* (Milan: Charta, 2006), along with the re-photographed commercial portraits of Lockhart herself, and a sampling of other early images like the *Untitled* works of 1995 and 1996.

6.   Which I am obviously translating thus: to "pine" or to long for in the language of the "flat," the objective, the distanced.

7.   Allen also recorded all the sound for the film *Pine Flat*. Here is another form, we might imagine, of attunement: the intense collaboration between two female artists, one working in the realm of the visual, and the other in the realm of music. Attunement, in other words, is also a way in which we can begin to understand Lockhart's constant impulse toward collaboration in all of her projects.

8. Michael Fried, *Absorption and Theatricality: Painting and Beholder in the Age of Diderot* (Chicago: University of Chicago Press, 1980). It is Mark Godfrey who has pursued the analogy of Lockhart's work with modernist painting most interestingly (and with whom I am only partially disagreeing here), in his essay "The Flatness of Pine Flat," *Pine Flat*, pp. 112-117.

9. Francis Stark discusses this maternal metaphor, distinguishing Lockhart's treatment of childhood from an artist like Larry Clark, in "Not Church, Not School, Not Home," *Sharon Lockhart: Pine Flat*, pp. 134-136.

On ON OTTO: **Moving Images and the New Collectivity**

Ina Blom

Part One: Cinema and Automatism Recontextualized (Report on a Reversed Film Production Process)

I

Here is how the movie project named ON OTTO (2007) starts: With a poster for a film that is yet to be made, a film that no one, at this stage, knows if it is even possible to make (Fig. 1). No names (of actors, directors, producers) are mentioned. But like all movie posters, it takes film itself for granted, in fact, takes the whole cinematic context or apparatus as absolutely self-evident. There is, and will be, cinema: beyond individual productions, cinema is something akin to a paradigm – a generative set of rules organizing the production of phenomena at once scientific, perceptual, aesthetic, technological, economic and existential. There will be titles, music, editing, stage design, sound. Something will be directed by, produced by, photographed by, acted by.

The poster advertises this certainty and spells it out in letters that visually frame "the cinema" that they promise: A screening space, seen from the back of the row of seats so that attention is directed towards the movie screen. On this screen the enormous head of a film diva – apparently caught at the moment of death – clings to the foreground of the screen-image: Due to the play of shadow and light, a lock of her hair actually seems to have spilled over into spectator space, as if to make contact. And the quest for contact is reciprocated. A boy, a lone figure among otherwise empty seats, points a fish in the direction of the screen, directly in the angle of the blonde coils of diva hair. Between the screen and this spectator, a space of action is established: the poster, none too subtly, marks this space with a red markered circle. Demarcating an "expanded" notion of cinema, the poster for ON OTTO announces a cinematic production process that will reformulate the place and status of so-called "moving images".

Fig. 1. Tobias Rehberger, On Otto, *poster, 2007. Courtesy Fondazione Prada, Milan*

II

To reiterate: The poster was actually the point of departure for the movie project named On Otto, whose final articulation – a city-like architectural construction, a labyrinthine cine-city of sorts – was first presented in Milan in 2007. And, if this project departed from the marketing devices that are normally seen as final or supplementary elements of a movie production, it is because On Otto was, in fact, a reversed production, an "impossible" or "illogical" project that started with the design of the poster and ended with the writing of the screenplay. In what follows, I will trace in some detail the production process of On Otto – up to and including the highly particular screening situation it presents us with. But it has to be stated right away that in this project there is no principled distinction between the production process and some final product that might be called a finished film and that might subsequently be studied in terms of a concept such as "reception". The project is essentially a process of production that is perhaps better understood as a specific process of construction. And what is constructed here is not a cinematic "work" in the ordinary sense of the term, but more precisely a social world or an instance of sociality emerging in terms of specifically cinematic materials, agents and ways of doing. To trace On Otto's production process is then not just a way of grasping how the features of an idiosyncratic work of art come together, but – more perti-nently – to be able to understand this instance of cinematic sociality, i.e., the social proposition launched by this project. Hence, the question of the role and status of moving images in this project is also a question of their function in the construction of this particular social world.

Tracing this production process, one rapidly comes face to face with one signifi-cant fact concerning the role assigned to moving images – in their generalized difference from still images. Usually, the difference between moving vs. still images is approached in terms of the difference or intermingling of distinct mediatic frameworks or technical support systems, such as film versus photo-graphy or film versus painting. In contrast, On Otto departs from a displace-ment and generalization of one key feature of moving images that is subse-quently deployed in the construction of a complex urban environment and associated with the operations of a social collective. In this project, the term "movie" does not just connote images that move automatically – i.e., images that are defined by an immanent capacity for movement that does not depend on the mobilizing perception or imagination of the spectator.[1] It is also, and just as importantly, the name for a whole series of other automatic mobilizations or automatisms that take their cue, so to speak, from the automatic movement as-sociated with cinematic images. In film-related philosophy, an expanded con-cept of automatism is primarily associated with Stanley Cavell's open-ended definition of artistic media: as Cavell saw it, such media are not given or defin-able a priori, but forms that arise out of the material conditions of specific art practices and that are unknowable prior to the creative act of artists.[2] The con-cept of automatism is here, so to speak, transposed from the notion of imma-nent movement in and of a cinematographic image to a more generalized con-cept of automatic creation well known in the history and theory of 20th-century art – the materialist concept of a machinic instance that produces, moves for-ward, all by itself, beyond the conscious control of any one artist, producer or otherwise transcendent instance, and beyond the framework of a formal defini-tion of media and media technologies. Experiments with automatic writing, ca-davres exquises and various types of chance operations were then also figures for collectivity at work in the here and now. It is this transposition that takes place in On Otto, where the centrality of the question of automatism is indicated in the title itself: Spoken aloud, On Otto sounds off as on auto, abbreviation for on automatic. Starting with the poster that announces the series of cinematic com-ponents, On Otto is a machine, a material assembly or agencement that pro-duces automatically – in the sense that production moves ahead beyond the control, will or intention of any one director or producer. [3] It does so thanks to its dramatic unleashing of the creative forces of a heterogeneous assembly of cinematic agents: dedicated film professionals as well as the non-professionals known as spectators, human agents as well as non-human agents.

These agents all belong to the sphere of ordinary film production: the audience, the promotional apparatus, the sound designer, the composer, the editor, the cameraman, the actors, the costume designer, the set designer, the storyboard writer, the writer of the screenplay, the poster, the trailer, the sound, the music, the images, the cuts, the costumes, the light, the locations, the set constructions, the drawings, the pages of writing, and the projection space. What is less ordinary is how they are assembled, or put to work. For this production is moving ahead thanks to the automatisms unleashed by a simple and absolute rule. It is a rule as simple and absolute as the unshakeable logic of narration which decrees that a film production start with a screenplay and then move methodically through the different moments of production and post-production, each moment working off and adding to and correcting the results of the former, until the final projection of a luminous image of a certain duration takes place – what is generally referred to as "a film". ON OTTO's rule reverses this order. Everything starts from the "wrong" end, all the while sticking to the same rigorous film industry methods, executed in each instance by the type of Hollywood professionals one would have called on to do a normal movie. And the viewing situation arising from this automatic process is not centered around a single projection but on a complex architectural construction formed and informed by a variety of cinematographic materials – a spatial articulation that seems to inscribe itself in the discourses of expanded cinema or cinema without film that has evolved in the context of avant-garde and new media art.[4]

Here is how the inverted production took place, step by step. Based on their personal interpretation of Rehberger's poster, Kuntzel & Deygas, known among other things for the cartoon title sequence in Spielberg's CATCH ME IF YOU CAN, created a movie trailer – after which composer Ennio Morricone and sound artist Randy Thom (FORREST GUMP) created a 90-minute sound and music mix. This sound mix triggered the editing work of Sylvie Landra (CAT WOMAN, THE FIFTH ELEMENT), which, in turn, spurred the cinematography of Wolfgang Thaler (MEGACITIES). Only now – *after* the cinematographer had done his job – were the actors (Kim Basinger, Danny DeVito, Willem Dafoe, Justin Henry and Emmy Rossum) called in. Next, Mark Bridges (MAGNOLIA) designed costumes and Jeffrey Beecroft (12 MONKEYS) created the production design, passing on the torch to J. Todd Anderson (THE BIG LEBOWSKY, FARGO) who came up with the storyboard. The production process ended as Barbara Turner (POLLOCK, THE COMPANY) wrote the screenplay. At this point the German artist Tobias Rehberger – the person responsible for initiating the project – created an architectural construction for the screening of this project.

The screenplay was, in other words, the last stage in the production. But – given the lack of logical continuity in the sequence above (what is the point of editing when no film has as yet been shot? how can actors "play" in advance of costumes, stage sets and roles?) it could not be an end product in the sense that a projected film is the unified artistic end product of a collaborative process that starts with a script. But then one can, of course, question the concept of a unified aesthetic product – "a film" – the way Joan Didion ridiculed the pretensions of film critics who earnestly read auteurial will-to-art into every spot on the cellu-loid. A finished movie really defies all attempts at analysis: as she put it, the responsibility for its every frame is clouded not only in the accidents and com-promises of production but in the clauses of it's financing. And so, to the re-viewers trying to understand "whose" movie it is by looking at the script, Di-dion coolly suggests they take a look at the deal memo instead. Here, perhaps, one could get a glimpse of the almost aesthetic excitement of the deal itself:

> Many people have been talking these past few days about this aborted picture, al-ways with a note of regret. It had been a very creative deal and they had run with it as far as they could run and they had had some fun and now the fun was over, as it also would have been had they made the picture.[5]

What these observations reveal is not primarily the alleged cynicism of the film industry. What they emphasize is the peculiar phenomenology of a cultural ob-ject that is not so much based on collaborative effort as on the assembled effects of a number of highly different crafts and aesthetic practices that are held to-gether so to speak at financial gunpoint. A "movie" could then very well be understood as a series of heterogeneous materialities and temporalities, each producing to the beat of its own logic, its own set of ideal requirements. All it takes for these materialities to come forth in their singularity is, basically, a dif-ferent organization of the material: in this case, a reversal of the production sequence

III

To see how these different cinematic materialities become self-producing enti-ties, it is necessary to trace the different steps in the production process in some more detail. Imagine, for instance, design team Kuntzel & Deygas having to make a trailer from little more than whatever may be conjured up by the film title (On Otto). Sticking to what they know best, that is, to shape, outline, de-sign, they focus all attention on the graphic outlines of the letters in the title, making the basic circles and crosses of the o's and t's into a tic-tac-toe game, but a tic-tac-toe game made out of bones, with sinister white shapes standing out against a black background. A suspense theme is evoked – but above all, the trailer demonstrates the independent power of the visual "theme", the purely atmospheric power of design.

Imagine, next, Randy Thom creating the sound for the yet-to-be-made film – a 90-minute soundscape subsequently enriched by a small catalogue of orchestra and choir themes composed by Ennio Morricone for what would appear to be a modern non-comedy movie of some style and gravity. Thom happens to be an experienced sound designer who has frequently complained about the lack of interest in the narrative potential of sound on the part of scriptwriters and directors. Rather than being used to direct attention, activate memory and focus action, sound work is essentially done only in retrospect, as a way of filling out the picture, patching it up and smoothing it out into a seamless whole. Now, Thom could orchestrate a full vindication of the injustices suffered by sound: A feature length soundscape *without* film. A soundscape composed, more precisely, in terms of a purely aural evocation of cinematic locations and action – the hollows of great halls, the packed dust-sound of the private apartment, the subdued din of the outdoors – and the multiple smaller sounds that that modulate and shape them into action-spaces. There are the generic cars passing on wet asphalt, showers splashing on bodies, stiletto-heeled footsteps and keys turning in locks, but also the growling of unknown machinery, vague crowds, indefinite animal life. In all events, cinematic sound here appears as an independent entity, only hinting at the many possible but essentially interchangeable images that would so to speak feed off it.

A similar logic of independence informs the separate contributions from the editor and cinematographer as well. Having as yet no specific footage to work with, Sylvie allowed editing to emerge as an entirely autonomous activity, i.e., as a way of imposing a certain "personal" sense of rhythm on a material that is now above all a function of this rhythm. To foreground this sense of rhythm, Landra cut together short sequences from hundreds of films, some familiar, others not, some cleverly arranged to go with Thom's soundscape and others haphazard-seeming, with passages even shown upside down. Once the rhythm of the edit took center stage, the imagery became supplementary, mainly indicating the vast and seemingly anonymous stock of footage passing through the hands of an editor,

In contrast, Thaler's cinematography played up the weight and specificity of photographic imagery, foregrounding a camera that seemed to soak up the world as one grandiose photographic vista after another. With long footage edits from his own personal archive, his camera seemed to seamlessly pass over continents, seasons, cities, faces and genres, as if an issue of *National Geographic* was slowly brought to life. Here, Thom's soundscape seemed to mainly function as a non-specific backdrop to the image sequences; if it was fore-grounded it was mainly to draw attention to the very activity of photographic recording. At one point, an abstract whirling sound is interpreted by Thaler as the spinning reel of a small handheld film projector used in an Indian street context. When, a few minutes later, the same whirling sound reemerges as the backdrop to a desert landscape, we recall the Indian street scene and reread the lush desert images as the actual film material spinning in the tiny projector. Sound may serve narration – but, in this case, the narrative is that of cinemato-graphy itself, its technical and material reality and contexts of use and abuse.

At this stage in the production process it becomes abundantly clear to all in-volved that no *one* film will ever come out of this project. The poster will not generate film in the singular. There will be multiple costumes made for scenes that as yet do not exist and perhaps never will. There will be production design for potential spaces hidden within incompatible layers of footage and elusive sound signals. The possible strategic choices of storyboard and script are end-less. The cinematic assembly or *agencement* is at every twist and turn present, yet On Otto awakens you to the fact that such an assembly is not the composite or sum of the elements that compose it: it is above all a mobile *distribution* of materials.

But even with this distributive assembly of cinematographic materials, actors are still called in to do their job. The job of an actor is notably to embody, to give life and soul to a character as yet existing only on paper. They are points of identification and in most cases also focalizers in the visual narrative. In this case, however, there are as yet no specific characters to embody, nobody in par-ticular to "play". Instead the actors seem to give life to the media relation out-lined in the poster that started off the automatisms of On Otto. The screen im-age of the dying blonde shown on the poster is taken from one of the final scenes of Orson Welles's 1948 film noir classic, The Lady from Shanghai. The five actors; Basinger, Dafoe, De Vito, Henry and Rossum, are simply filmed by a still camera, one by one and close up, as they watch Welles' movie from begin-ning to end in a cinema space, the screen action reflected in the expressions of their faces. Five singular feature-length movies result from this, as singular as the facial expressions of each actor.

It is a curiously intimate form of presentation. To see the iconic face of Kim Basinger balancing for 90 solid minutes between acting and just being, between "giving" absorption and just falling in and out of it like any normal viewer, is to observe an entirely new form of cinematic "life" coming into existence (Fig. 2). This notion of cinematic life had already been apprehended by the movie pos-ter, which repeats a trope from early video art. The image of a zone of contact

between the screen and a fish (held out by the young spectator) recalls the asso-
ciations between signaletic and biological life that were continually staged in
the 1960's work of video pioneer Nam June Paik: Aquariums containing live
fish were built in front of TV screens or TV apparatuses were constructed as
aquariums that allowed you to see the fish through the screen. These constructions played off the fact that images of aquarium fish were used by many TV
channels to fill the pauses between programs, as if to indicate that the channel
was still, and in fact always had been, "alive". Paik seemed to suggest that the
"live" emissions of TV, its real-time feed of signals, were not primarily a presen-
tational form, but a token of the deep complicity between the new time-based
media technologies and life processes in general. [6]

Fig. 2. Tobias Rehberger, On Otto, *film still (Kim Basinger watching* The Lady
from Shanghai*), 2007. Courtesy Fondazione Prada, Milan*

In On Otto, the positing of this new form of cinematic life depends on the distribution or refraction of the singular moving-image object named film, taking
its cue from the way in which the filmic image itself is refracted in the famous
hall of mirrors climax scene in The Lady From Shanghai. In this innovative
scene, bodies and perspectives are serialized and multiplied in a way that is
reminiscent of the early image experiments of video art. The stage for a final
shootout, the hall of mirror and its effects makes it impossible to determine
whether the bullets hit images or persons. As a consequence, we never know if
any of the characters actually die: as the film concludes, the dead-looking

blonde (Rita Hayworth) lifts her head and cries: "I want to live!" Psychoanalytic theory uses the concept of the mirror to explain the process of identification – the individual discovery of (and adaptation to) a stable and ideal world-image that includes your own self. The apparatus theory of film has, for its part, has long referred to this psychoanalytic model in order to explain film's identificatory grip on us, and hence its unique force as an instrument of ideology.[7] On Otto is a cinematographic project where the mirror image of the unitary projection is not just "broken", reflecting wildly and senselessly in every direction, but where the very idea of mirroring (and the whole associated semiotics of messages, codes, ideological meaning) is brought up only to be dismantled. A different model is needed to explain the way in which this project evokes the existential reality of moving images and the politics that may be associated with their force and appeal. Henri Bergson's refutation of the (at once) realist and idealist distinction between matter and representation, perception and reality may have some relevance here. Watching Kim Basinger, media icon and living person, pure image and "real" material body, at once watching and acting her own watching of the image of Rita Hayworth (for 90 minutes), in many ways recalls Bergson's notion of our bodies as "images that act like other images, receiving and giving back movement": in relation to a material world defined as a flow of images, the human body and its perceptual apparatus is above all a center of action, an object destined to move other objects and not the sort of apparatus that, in the act of seeing, gives birth to a representation.[8] Having asserted the general existence of cinematic images, the poster explicitly hints at this problematic: in the lower right corner you find the legend *reality strikes back*, like an additional title. If the actors in On Otto are focalizers, they might then be seen as focalizers for this explicit shift towards an emphasis on image-bodes in action, enjoining us trace its wider ramifications for a conception of a world at once real and cinematic

Part Two: Automatism, Architecture and Collectivity

I

Every film is a society. It is a society in the sense that it is a complex collective production, the result of negotiations and collaborations between multiple persons, techniques, ideas, institutions and competences. However, by overturning the mechanistic principle of normal film production – the principle whereby each step in the production process (each application of knowledge and creativity) is potentially contained in the preceding one – On Otto raises the question

of the relation between cinema and collectivity to a principle. The real product of this work is then a specific collective formation – and not "film itself". And the most immediately available figure for this collectivity is an architectural expression – the city-like construction that both houses and is shaped by the multiplicity of cinematic materials let loose in this project (Figs. 3, 4, 5). In this city, passageways and avenues lead you in and out of labyrinthine constructions where sounds, moving images, design proposals, drawings, texts and audiences intermingle and overlay in numerous different ways and from a variety of angles and perspectives – depending on the movements of the spectators that visit the city or the cinematic personae or points of view that already inhabit it. This spatial organization radicalizes the familiar notion that film is always edited in three dimensions: its effects are played out in a dialectical operation where image, sound and the perceptual apparatus of the spectator confront one another. But even more pertinently, the architecture redefines spectatorial agency itself. In this city, cinematic materials are not just seen and heard by a specific class of human subjects named "spectators". Made up of percepts and affects, images and sounds are themselves quite literally posited as seeing and hearing, reacting and responding to other images and sounds. It is the architectural construction that allows this to happen, by, among other things, using projection screens as constructive elements (so that the image can be accessed from both sides) and by using sounds as territorial markers in a way that makes each

Figs. 3-5. Tobias Rehberger, On Otto. *Installation shots, Fondazione Prada, Milan 2007. Courtesy Fondazione Prada, Milan. Photo: Wolfgang Günzel*

aural territory confront and blend with others. The subtle articulation of insides and outsides, transparencies and reflections, open trajectories and closed circuits gives each image, text and sound element multiple extensions or modes of existence depending on their actual interaction with other elements. A decidedly modern city (reminiscent perhaps of the spatial complexity articulated in the city paintings of Picasso and Braque) everything is at once seen and seeing, heard and hearing.

II

Yet, the key question is of course how this specific cinematic articulation of collectivity is to be understood. An interesting perspective on cinema's collective dimensions arises from the ambiguities of the term *Aufnahme* as it is used in Walter Benjamin's essay on the work of art in the age of mechanical reproduction. Signifying at once *reception* and *recording*, it points not only to the collective mode of reception associated with the mass reproduction and distribution of media objects. As Samuel Weber has pointed out, Benjamin also saw the reproductive inscription that takes place in a film production as a specific form of recording proper to the mass itself. The mass should in fact be identified with recording and not just with reception: it should be understood as that which "takes up" or repeats the shock events in which the contemplative unity of time and place (the auratic moment) associated with great works of art is scattered or multiplied. In fact, this new notion of the mass character of recording opens up for a radical redefinition of aura: with cinema, focus shifts from the question of the unique identity of auratic *objects* to the question of the *temporality* of the unique presence implied by the concept of aura. It makes no sense, then, to speak of the mass in numerical terms, as a simple multiplication of contemplative subjects accessing reproduced media content: the concept of mass recording means that the mass must be defined in temporal terms, as a simultaneous repetition and dispersal of presence. And it is in these terms that the new recording technologies – the cinematographic apparatus of production – may be seen as staging an *encounter of the mass with itself*, giving the amorphous mass not an image or a representation of itself, but the *semblance* of a face, a purely virtual face vested less in the idea of collective identification than in the project of collective becoming.[9]

This analysis may seem pertinent in relation to On Otto – a production that not only highlights the collective aspect of the cinematic recording apparatus, but that also seems to associate this collective with the ineluctable automatisms of recording. On a purely technical level modern recording technologies are noted for the way in which supposedly intentional artistic processes (the thoughtful and controlled placing of paint on a canvas or words on a page) are overruled by a machine that "takes up" everything and anything, significant and insignificant, all by itself. Such automatism could also be seen to apply at the wider level of the cinematic apparatus: Individual decisions are "carried off" in a collective process that moves ahead with a force that gathers its own momentum and that can never be traced back to one singular artistic will or origin. In ordinary film production, this collective may have to face itself in the deal memo; in On Otto the cinematic collective is explicitly presented as *that which records*. Furthermore, this collective is defined through an equally explicit scattering of the very *moment* of contemplation: To walk around Rehberger's cinematic city, continually gathering and redistributing its huge array of cinematic "moments" in a process that is perhaps best described as a perpetually ongoing "spectator's cut", *is* quite literally to encounter a collective defined in temporal terms.

However, the *architectural* articulation of this collective adds another, and slightly different, dimension to the notion of a collective defined in temporal terms. Benjamin's concept of mass recording and its relation to the distribution of (shock) events are among the features that define cinema and its moving images as a time medium – i.e., a medium that produces and processes not images or representations but time itself. Cinematic time here is the critical or even revolutionary instance that systematically interrupts any mere *representation* of the historical past and its "given" collective identities: instead, historical time is re-activated as event-time. But the collective dimensions of cinema's time processing capacities may also be qualified along a different explanatory axis. To the extent that it is the human perceptual and cognitive apparatus that produces or "gives" any notion of time, film and other time media seem to operate in a special proximity to (or interaction with) human memory. According to Maurizio Lazzarato, these technologies mime the operations of thinking and memory, albeit in a very rudimentary way: their free contraction and distribution of temporal material resembles Henri Bergson's description of the memory as an ability to process past and future material within a continually unfolding now-time. And it is precisely through this capacity that these technologies has become the key social machines for a form of production that no longer draws value only from activity in the workplace but from all aspects of our lives – through our "free time" down to the level of the affects and sensibilities that characterize our cognitive activity. [10] Hence, the temporally defined collective may perhaps also be described in terms that evoke brain functions, the mental operations at work in sensation, perception, and memory. This proposition may, at the very least, be explored with reference to the highly specific association between architecture and film that On Otto sets up.

The association between architecture and film is not in itself new: in fact, film has been compared to architecture since its invention due to how it seems to mobilize both spatial and temporal modes of reception. First of all, stage sets and locations are vital parts of any film – at times they may even function as the protagonist or subject matter of the film itself. Second, it is generally recognized that film is not just a visual but also a spatial practice, in the sense that one has to take into consideration the cinema space itself and the phenomenological relation between the film and the spectator's body. Third, cinema has played a key role in the modern spectacularization of space – the formatting of complex geographical and geopolitical sites into the homogenized "locations" of the tourist industries, the kind of places that can be marketed for their untarnished "pastness" and quasi-ritualistic resistance to change. Fourth, there seems to be a structural relation between architecture and film based on the fact that both art forms are intimately related to the big state and capital institutions and in fact depend on the interest of these institutions for their existence. And, finally, it has been argued that film and architecture are structurally similar in the sense that both are received by a collectivity in a mode of distraction – received that is, in an incidental, absent-minded way, reminiscent of the attitude of a person drifting through a city and unlike the alert and contemplative vision associated with the viewing of paintings or sculpture. This was, at least, Walter Benjamin's perspective, which was no doubt informed by the non-organic compositions of the early cinema of attractions rather than the later narrative films of the Hollywood traditions.[11] According to Joan Ockham, this concept of distraction is the structuring principle of Jacques Tati's PLAYTIME, where the hypnotic glass spaces of international-style architecture emerge as the film's real protagonist as well as a visual metaphor for the luminous and "transparent" screens of film itself.[12]

This last emphasis on a *mode of reception* shared by architecture and film differs in significant ways from the specific association between architecture and film established in ON OTTO: the question here is a form of production involving the "work" of the human brain. A first cue to the logic on which this association is based can be found in the one-man cinema Tobias Rehberger built at Stockholm's Museum of Modern Art in 2000 – a construction that was initially conceived as the actual starting point of the ON OTTO production.[13] It was a superbly stylish piece of architecture, made in the type of slick 1970s style that evokes all of those expansive corporate environments endlessly caressed by movie cameras: In this way, it mimicked the design logic of the early cinema theatres, which were made to look like veritable palaces of cinematic fantasy, as if the movie had already started in the lobby. In fact, this cinema space seemed to have been conceived as the kind of construction that emerges when the image is no longer a representation existing at a certain distance from the viewing subject. The space was, quite literally, articulated as the second skin of a body placed so close to the screen as to be completely immersed in the moving image.

At this point, there is no longer a principled difference between perception and reality, images in space and images in consciousness: they belong to the same continuum. The one-man cinema seemed to illustrate Hugo Münsterberg's 1916 theory on the mechanisms of close-up that allow cinema to capture attention like no other time-based medium because the close-up objectifies, in our world of perception, our mental act of attention. When attention focuses on a special feature, the surrounding world adjusts itself, eliminating what is not in focus and making the object of attention more vivid. The spatial effect of cinema, given actual form in the Stockholm cinema, is that of an outer world, so to speak, woven into our minds, shaped not just by its own laws but also by our acts of attention.[14]

It seemed only logical that this extended cinematic body could itself be the object of spectatorship. Through tiny windows in the walls, outside viewers could inspect this specimen of mediatic life, a uniquely modern creature. But the Stockholm cinema was just a preliminary test case or point of departure: Rehberger's more fundamental idea was that an actual movie project should be developed based on the existential vectors of his one-man cinema – that is, on its peculiar infiltration of image, perceptual apparatus and spatial construction.[15] And this is exactly what takes place in ON OTTO, where Kim Basinger, Willem Dafoe, Emmy Rossum, Danny DeVito and Justin Henry are each being watched as specimens of mediatic life. At once actors, spectators and screens, THE LADY FROM SHANGHAI is here as if projected through their facial expressions – the automatic reactions – of bodies that are themselves already cinematic through and through. And the perceptual responses of these already-cinematic bodies are presented as the actual constructive elements of an architecture that should now be understood as being made up not just of building materials in the ordinary sense of the terms but – more pertinently – of "live" sensations, perceptions and cognitions. As Deleuze has pointed out, Sergei Eisenstein was interested in the capacity of cinematographic materials to directly engage the central nervous system, to deliver a sensorial shock that would provoke not just thinking in general but more precisely a self-reflexive "I think!": in this way a cinematographic "subject" of sorts would come into being.[16] Jean-Clet Martin seems to describe the spatial operations of this subject when he compares the non-distinction of reality and image in terms of a body's movement in a city: A city, which is obviously a definite and materially invariant site, enters into a variation and virtualization through the points of view of the bodies that act on it – bodies that in the moment of acting process the city through all sorts of memory materials, so that the extensive "trajectivity" of perception is redoubled by the intensive "trajectivity" of memories. Beyond the image/reality distinction, reality itself turns out to have several dimensions: it is constituted through the sharp point of a gaze that cuts through matter and also through a virtual, cumulative gaze that connects the elements "cut out" by perception along the lines of its own perspective.[17] Above all, "the city" in On Otto presents itself as a space continually formed by the work of perception, memory and thinking – an approach that differs radically from the traditional architectural focus on "built form".

Still it is difficult to neglect the heavily stylized dimension of Rehberger's cine-city, its unabashed evocation of all sorts of contemporary design trends and sensibilities. Built form may not be the end product here, but the effects of architectural "style" will still have to be accounted for. In fact, the specificity of its association between architecture and cinema seems to hinge on the fact that design styles are so to speak identified with the cinematographic capacity to trigger thinking. This dynamic can perhaps be explored more fully with reference to the many contemporary artworks (by Rehberger, among others) that initially come across as prototypes for elegant and trendy design solutions. But a closer look reveals that almost every single one of these designs are actually time machines, in the sense that they are fundamentally formed and informed by informational materials and production principles. There are, for instance, the many colorful and original "design" lamps that are also tele-visual in the most literal sense of the term, since they are connected to computer programs that make them at each moment transmit – in real-time – the quantity of daylight at some other time and place, for instance in a city on a different continent. Design is here not a value in itself, but a sensorial material or memory material that evokes the reality of design as a key site of self-relation or subjective becoming.[18] These "design" works then seem to trace a real if rarely discussed complicity between contemporary information technologies and the current overvaluation of design, a connection that makes it possible to think the precise way in which we "live" the media surround of the contemporary time machines. The activation of memory and affects in the processes of self-styling is just an aspect of the thinking operations that animate and are animated by the time crystallization machines – machines whose only real product is subjectivity itself. From this perspective, the sensory and cognitive apparatus of individuals are seen as intrinsic parts of the media apparatuses, part of the synapses or relays through which affective energy is accumulated and value created. Rehberger's cinematographic city may well look like the quintessential media playground or leisure palace – founded as it is on the manifold activation of perceptions, memories, affects and tastes. But by the same token it emerges as a place of production, a place where affective bodies are also working bodies. In brief, the specific association between architecture and cinema that is set up here seems to turn around the conditions of inhabitation and collective existence in a media society where the mind itself is put to work, or engaged in productive labor in the most concrete sense of the term and in an historically unprecedented way.

III

What is the collective spatial expression of minds put to work, engaged in a form of labor that exploits not work time in the traditional sense of the term but the all-encompassing time of memory and thinking? The term "labor", of course, evokes its own architectural landscape: the great 19th-century factory buildings, designed for efficiency, standardization and overview, quasi-palatial monuments that gave a new form of visibility and definition to the borderline areas between the countryside and the city. And, by extension, the development of huge landscapes of standardized worker housing projects, extending both horizontally and vertically and articulating (by their rational modular forms) the definition and management of the minimum needs of laboring bodies. By contrast, theme parks, tourist destinations, "sculptural" museum buildings, TV-studios, real estate development projects, computer game environments and the ubiquitous presence of everyday stylistics form a heterogeneous set of spatial articulations whose representative functions remain obscure. Yet, if the collective of cognitive workers may not consider their reality to be mired in a definite architectural form, it can, at the very least, have recourse to an architectural parable. This parable is a work of pure imagination – one produced at the peak of Western industrialization but with a strong intuition for the transformations about to take place within this mode of production. This parable has been recycled in recent years in precisely those artistic milieus most intensely preoccupied with constructing a new association between design, architecture and media technologies. In fact, it has not just been recycled but updated, tweaked and polished so that it could function better as a guide to the contemporary condition. In the years between 1879 and 1884, the eminent Italian sociologist Gabriel Tarde wrote a short novel, an exercise in utopian imagination that – like so many of the literary works produced by social scientists – was basically the fictionalized expression of his own social theories.[19] A new global society – a world where every corner of the earth is discovered and exploited, a society of unheard of riches where all sorts of aesthetic productions take pride of place over the mere satisfaction of needs – is confronted with catastrophe: The sun is suddenly extinguished. Once it no longer shines its light on the territorial expanses of the earth, life on the planet's surface becomes impossible and most people end up dying. However, a small population survives by escaping underground, carving out spaces in the deeper geological layers heated by the earth's burning core. Gradually a new society arises, but its mode of existence challenges the very premises of social explanation established by the economists and sociologists of the aboveground world.

This new mode of social existence is closely associated with the conditions of inhabitation determined by underground life. Once you go underground, territories can no longer be surveyed, monumental building forms can no longer exist, and axial construction and the hierarchical subdivision of space into center-periphery relations no longer make sense. Underground, you are always in the middle of things, in the same way that your mind is always in the middle of its own now-time. Wherever you find yourself in the expanding network of caves is always the centre: a society organized in terms of the extensive *forms* of aboveground architecture has been supplanted by an *intensive* mode of existence whose organizational principle is that of force rather than form. This concept of intensive existence was in fact key to a social theory that challenged the transcendental status given to the concepts of value, scarcity and need in usual economic accounts of human collaboration. For Tarde, any description of sociality should take as its point of departure the question of sharing sensations, perception, attention and memory rather than the question of how the means of subsistence are shared. The traditional deduction of the former from the latter would, in other words, have to be overturned. Society or collectivity should perhaps be described as a brain-like network of synaptic relays where human collectivity is first of all accounted for in terms of the "intensive" operations of mental forces such as desire, belief, sympathy and the capacity for imitation and differentiation.

> Certain Sophists, who were called economists and who were to our sociologists of today what the alchemists were to the modern chemists, had noted the error that society essentially consists of an exchange of services. From this point of view, which is quite out of date, the social bond could never be closer than that between the ass and ass-driver or the sheep and the shepherd. Society, as we now know, consists in the exchange of reflections. The tendency to copy one another accumulates and is combined to create a sense of originality. Reciprocal service is only an accessory.[20]

In the underground caves, the enormous surcharge of intellectual and aesthetic exchanges that was already a key feature of the pre-catastrophic aboveground world, found an architectural expression adequate to their central role in the definition of human society itself. In this parable, architecture is tantamount to social philosophy: if Tarde's text describes an architecture turned inside out, it is because it indicates a social ontology turned inside out. In a similar way, Tobias Rehberger's radical displacement of the moving image also contributes to an overturning of the principles of architecture that triggers the very question of how collectivity should be defined. In fact, the underground spaces that express the intensive exchange of reflections sound uncannily similar to the cavernous and labyrinthine cine-city created by Rehberger. Where Tarde describes "the most incredible and endless galleries of art", magical palaces lit by "countless lamps, some incredibly bright, others soft" glowing constantly "through the blue depths", Rehberger constructs spaces where insides and outsides are no longer sharply defined thanks to the omnipresence of all sorts of luminous moving image materials that reflect off one another and also function as sources of light.[21] Both present us with an architecture defined by the activation of perception and intellect, rather than the spatial "functions" derived from a life divided between labor and repose. Using cinema and its moving images as a cipher for what has often been referred to as a dubious "aestheticization" of politics, the public sphere, or life in general, On Otto momentarily overturns the logic of cinematic production as if to suggest how such aestheticization might point towards a new definition of the common (rather than being seen as a "problem" for politics per se.). In this project, moving images do not contribute to a finished aesthetic monument of the kind that will compete (at the Oscars, in Cannes) for visibility and representational value. And neither can they be associated with the much-deplored "spectacle" that bars access to material reality and history.[22] Rethought as a different kind of architecture, the big movie production here attests to the existence of a live brain network, ready to be connected with anything and anyone.

Notes

1. Here I rely on the definition of moving images given by Gilles Deleuze in, *Cinema I: The Movement-Image*, transl. Hugh Tomlinson and Barbara Habberjam (Minneapolis: University of Minnesota Press, 1986, 1-11)

2. Stanley Cavell, *The World Viewed, Reflections on the Ontology of Film* (Cambridge, MA: Harvard University Press, 1979, 105-108)

3. I prefer Deleuze and Guattari's concept of *"agencement"* to the English term "assemblage", or the Foucauldian *"dispositif"* which can more easily be misread as a composition of elements, or a totalizing system, than a dynamic and open-ended connection between heterogeneous entities. This, despite the fact that Foucault's "dispositif" may also be aligned with the underlying principles of the concept of "agencement", as Deleuze, in fact, did in his study of Foucault. See Gilles Deleuze, *Foucault*, transl. Sean Hand (Minneapolis: University of Minnesota Press, 1988) and Gilles Deleuze and Felix Guattari, *Rhizome. Introduction* (Paris: Editions de Minuit, 1976).

4. The classic reference here is Gene Youngblood, *Expanded Cinema* (New York: P. Dutton & Co. Inc, 1970).

5. Joan Didion, *The White Album* (New York: Penguin Books 1981, 167).

6. For a discussion of these issues, see Ina Blom, "The Touch Through Time: Raoul Hausmann, Nam June Paik and the Transmission Technologies of the Avant-

garde", in *Leonardo Journal of Art, Science and Technology*, # 3, 2001 (MIT Press: 209-216).

7.   Jean-Louis Baudry, *L'Effet cinéma* (Paris: Albatros, 1978).

8.   Henri Bergson, *Matter and Memory*. Transl. N.M. Paul and W.S. Palmer (New York: Zone Books: 1988, 19).

9.   Samuel Weber, *Mass Mediauras. Form, Technics, Media*. Alan Cholodenko (ed.) (Stanford: Stanford University Press, 1996, 78-107).

10. Maurizio Lazzarato, *Videophilosophie, Zeitwahrnähmung in Postfordismus* (Berlin: b- books, 2002).

11. Tom Gunning, "The Cinema of Attractions: Early Film, Its Spectator and the Avant-Garde" in Thomas Elsaesser and Adam Barker (eds.) *Early Film* (London: British Film Institute, 1989).

12. Joan Ockham, "Architecture in a Mode of Distraction: Eight Takes on Jacques Tati's *Playtime*" in Mark Lamster (ed.) *Architecture and Film* (New York: Princeton Architectural Press, 2000, 171-196).

13. For practical reasons, this idea could not be followed through: Rehberger was not able to contact everyone involved in the ON OTTO project to Stockholm during the period of exhibition, and so the poster was devised as an alternative starting point.

14. Hugo Münsterberg, *The Photoplay: A Psychological Study* (New York and London: D. Appleton & Company, 1916).

15. Interview with Tobias Rehberger, Frankfurt, October 2005.

16. Deleuze's discussion of Eisenstein and the cinematic circuit is found in *Cinema 2, The Time Image*, transl. Hugh Tomlinson and Robert Galeta (Minneapolis: University of Minnesota Press, 1989, 158-164).

17. Jean-Clet Martin, "Of Images and Worlds: Toward a Geology of the Cinema" in Gregory Flaxman (ed.) *The Brain is the Screen, Deleuze and the Philosophy of Cinema*, (Minneapolis: University of Minnesota Press, 2000, 61-86).

18. I discuss this topic in detail in my book *On The Style Site: Art Sociality and Media Culture* (New York: Sternberg Press, 2007).

19. Gabriel Tarde, *Underground. Fragments of a Future History*. Updated by Liam Gillick. (Dijon: Les Presses du Réel, 2004.) Tarde's novel has figured as a central element in a number of works by Liam Gillick. Its influence can also be traced in the manuscript for a science fiction radio play produced on the occasion of Rirtkrit Tiravanija's retrospective exhibition in London, 2005.

20. Tarde, 2004, 65.

21. Tarde, 2004, 55-56.

22. Guy Debord, *La Société du Spectacle* (Paris: Editions Gallimard, 1992).

The Algorithmic Turn

Mutable Temporality In and Beyond the Music Video: An Aesthetic of Post-Production

Arild Fetveit

> For the last twenty years, neither matter nor space nor time has been what it was…. We must expect great innovations to transform the entire technique of the arts, thereby affecting artistic invention itself and perhaps even bringing about an amazing change in our very notion of art. (Paul Valery)[1]

> …first we had the industry of the moving image, today we have the industry of the accelerated image. (Gene Youngblood)[2]

> …the body of the speaker dances in time with his speech….the body of the listener dances in rhythm with that of the speaker! (W.S. Condon and W.D. Ogston)[3]

> We listen to music with our muscles. (Friedrich Nietzsche)[4]

Paul Valery's words about innovations transforming the entire technique of the arts, quoted by Walter Benjamin in the opening of his essay, "The Work of Art in the Age of Mechanical Reproduction," still resonate today.[5] We are also in a time when we must take stock of sizable changes in artistic production, in part inspired by technological innovation. Today, the technological innovations which may be "affecting artistic invention" and perhaps even bringing about a "change in our very notion of art," are not the apparatuses of mechanical reproduction that reformed artistic production in the days of Valery and Benjamin – predominantly photography and film – but the computer and its operational logic, which keeps penetrating and reforming the spheres of cultural production.

The aspect of such changes that I specifically want to address here is a *mutable temporality*, especially prominent in music videos, which appears to be a new *aesthetic of post-production*. It is associated with a greater change in which creative performances in audiovisual works seem to be increasingly relocated, from the site of the profilmic scene where actors, set designers and dancers display their craft, to the site of post-production, where new kinds of computer-enhanced creative performances take place, and where an emergent algorithmic culture becomes increasingly prevalent.[6] The tendency is not only to "fix it in the mix" or in the editing suite, but to develop "the mix" or editing suite into the key arena for creative performance. It is when such changes seem to manifest themselves aesthetically in deliberate and particular ways that it becomes reasonable to talk of an *aesthetic of post-production*.

By addressing it as "an aesthetic," I aim to do two things. First, I aim to localize it at the level of aesthetic practice, akin to a poetics, which reaches beyond the actual means and techniques of production that are utilized, and is therefore not simply congruent with the works where certain technologies and means of post-production are used. Second, the emergence of this aesthetic is fundamentally imbricated with the technological developments afforded by the surge of new code written for cultural production in the aural and visual realms. These technological developments support *various* aesthetics of postproduction that are interconnected, yet different. An aesthetic of sampling, as well as a related aesthetic of remixing – reinvigorating older practices like collage, montage and appropriation – have been addressed.[7] Others might also be identified, or are yet to emerge. Thus the various aesthetics of post-production take a number of shapes across multiple fields.

In the field of art, the French critic and curator Nicolas Bourriaud intervened in 2001 with an inclusive notion of post-production.[8] He argued that the practices associated with post-production processes in audiovisual media – that is, the taking and combining of elements that are already there rather than the creation of something from the scratch – had become the new *modus operandi* in the art world. He asserts that, "Notions of originality (being at the origin of) and even of creation (making something from nothing) are slowly blurred in this new cultural landscape marked by the twin figures of the DJ and the programmer, both of whom have the task of selecting cultural objects and inserting them into new contexts."[9] This logic of creation – mirroring both the DJ and the *modus operandi* of the computer itself – is vital both for the specific aesthetic addressed here and for understanding the wider reach of the aesthetics of post-production, and its fallout in the art world in particular. Bourriaud also points to a wider cultural sensibility within which the aesthetics of post-production are lodged. However, this article, as indicated in its title, aims first and foremost to interrogate a limited aspect of this field, what I am calling mutable temporality, which enriches the field between the realms of still and moving images, as well as the dynamism of moving images as they render music "visible."

Thus, what has triggered my interest is a fascination with the mutable temporality – not to mention the spatiality – which appears as a new aesthetic of post-production. In the last decade, a new temporal dynamism has expanded and vitalized the playing field between the realms of still and moving images, with a key feature being the dynamic speed control of various sorts. A privileged playground for such forms has been the music video, like Jonathan Glazer's video for the Radiohead song, STREET SPIRIT (1996), Chris Cunningham's video for the Portishead song, ONLY YOU (1997), as well as his independent video project, RUBBER JOHNNY (2005), Max Giwa and Dania Pasquini's video for Craig David's song, THE RISE AND FALL (2003), some of Michel Gondry's videos, and videos by contemporary music video directors like Francis Lawrence and Dave Meyers. In these, and in many other contemporary music videos, we may find more or less prominent examples where the initial temporality of body movements as performed for the camera are partly overruled and controlled in the post-production process. The cinematic mechanism of automated reproduction, guaranteeing a temporal correspondence between the profilmic movements and the movements we eventually see on screen, grounds what we may call *ordinary audiovisual discourse*. In music videos like the ones mentioned above, this correspondence is suspended by a performative temporality staged in post-production, producing the mutable temporality explored in the following. What forms does this aesthetic take, what does it offer, and how can it be historicized? These are the main questions informing this article.

Hans Richter and Film as Rhythm

When considering the peculiar connection between music and image manifested in recent videos like Cunningham's ONLY YOU, which excels in visual rhythmicity, it seems appropriate to revisit the German Dadaist Hans Richter. As an artist taking up the new medium of film, which a number of avant-garde artists of his period did, Richter formed part of the sweeping changes in artistic production addressed by Valery and Benjamin, most prominently in the 1910s and 1920s. In a 1926 article, Richter claimed film to *be* rhythm, and explained how he sought the development of a common language for expressing human emotion through the temporal movement of abstract forms:

> The emotional world, as well as the intellectual, has laws governing its expression....
> Just as the path of the intellectual formulating power leads to thought, as a justifying
> moment of intellectual activity, so the emotional formulating power leads to rhythm
> as the essence of emotional expression.[10]

As we shall see, Richter's envisioning of rhythm as the essence of emotional expression seems perfectly attuned to the temporal sensibility by which Cunningham conducts his images to the music. This should not entirely surprise us. If we see our present audio-visual culture as one in which mutable temporalities have some prominence, and note the growing preoccupation with thinking about time and cinema as well as the realm between still and moving images, these characteristics also define the era of the early film experiments of Richter and other avant-garde filmmakers of the 1920s. Tom Gunning has commented on how a *cinema of attraction* is present both in early film and in contemporary production – how "the two ends of the Twentieth Century hail each other like long lost twins."[11] The historical ramifications of the avant-garde artists' work with a cinema of mutable temporality is beyond the scope of this article. But the following comment from Richter, which harks back to Valery's concern in the opening quote, and speaks to how we should conceive of the relation between technological and aesthetic invention, may help us to understand not only the interest in mutable temporality in early cinema, but also its demise. When describing his making of the short fine art film RHYTHM 21, in the early 1920s, Richter explains, "I did my shooting partly on an animation table, partly in the printing machine by stop motion and forward and backward printing. The printing machines at that time were not fully automatic...."[12] This absence of a fully automated reproduction process – which also applied to the hand-cranked cameras used in early film production – provided a technological grounding for an audiovisual culture of mutable temporalities. There are indications that the culture of mutable temporality in early film ran dry with the automatization of speed required by the lip-synch based sound cinema emerging in the 1930s. Temporal irregularities were deeply problematic for the sound, which, contrary to the image, becomes variable not only in terms of speed but also in terms of pitch. Of course, shifting temporalities still had an important afterlife in mainstream cinema though slow motion – in sequences that do not involve synchronized sound and lip-synch – and in experimental cinema through a series of more disruptive practices.

"Time Warp" Software

In current practices involving an aesthetic of mutable temporality, the pitch of the sound no longer needs to be affected. Digital technologies may compensate by keeping the pitch at the same level in spite of variations in the speed. In fact, a brief look at the contemporary technical support for an aesthetic of mutable temporality quickly displays a host of technologies for producing what is often referred to as a "time warp" effect. A few years ago, tailor made software made its spectacular time warp effects a selling point. Avid sold "Liquid Pro 7," by claiming to offer the creation of "fast motion and slow motion effects in real-time," which makes it "much easier to try various speed changes to find the perfect matching speed."[13] Algolith's "Time Warp plug-ins" claimed to provide similar features, and Real Viz's "ReTimer Professional" claimed to let one "control time for astonishing slow motion or fast motion effects...giving...ultimate flexibility during post-production."[14] Interestingly, these powerful "time warp" capabilities seem now to have taken a back seat as selling points in the marketing of post-production software, which indicates that such affordances are increasingly taken for granted as part of new and upgraded post-production suits.[15]

The developments in software production invite a new look into how, more precisely, innovation in cultural production takes place. Innovation now, it appears, takes place as much in specially-designed software as in particular art works. A new algorithm may be created for achieving an effect in a film, for example, and outputs from such an algorithm are readily exportable to other projects, either through the original software produced, or through other software producers' attempts to emulate the effects. The stunning mutable temporality of the "bullet time" effect in the Matrix trilogy provided a groundbreaking achievement that echoed through audiovisual culture in a number of more or less convincing imitations. The imminent and almost viral spread of this aesthetic was soon supported by specialized software offered as add-ons to widely circulated editing tools, though the original effect was not merely a matter of code, but a creative set-up and use of photographic still cameras drawing on pioneering experiments by the U.S. photographer Eadweard Muybridge and the French cartographer Aimé Laussedat.[16]

So far, we have seen how visions and technologies supporting a mutable temporality can be located in the early 20th Century avant-garde, as well as in the tools for digital post-production of the early 21st Century. The latter tools have been developed in concert with an emergent aesthetics of mutable temporality, which took off in the 1990s and now seems to be taken for granted as part of current audiovisual discourse. A number of precursors could be identified in a more conclusive history, which could consider music video alone, or also address art video and various uses of animation in the wider realms of film and television production.

Animation techniques like stop-motion and pixelation, technically positioned between photography and film, have a rich history of interrogating the landscape between still and moving images. These techniques have also been used in music videos. A notable example is the video for Duran Duran's ALL SHE WANTS IS (1988), directed by the photographer Dean Chamberlain. The video uses stop-motion animation and long exposure times to effect a curious discursive positioning between the realms of still and moving images. It uses mannequin stand-ins for the band members in a number of shots, which further iterates a tension between the still and the moving, as well as between the inanimate and the animate. The video was awarded the 1988 MTV Music Video Award for innovation. The following fifteen years saw a creative surge in music videos, often using animation in various forms to depict un-photographable fantasies, also involving play with mutable temporality.

Street Spirit

Jonathan Glazer's video for Radiohead's Street Spirit (1996) was groundbreaking in its use of acceleration and de-acceleration effects, as well as in the combining of two irreconcilable temporalities within the same frame, allowing subjects in the same space to move at different speeds. One or both of these effects is featured in almost every shot.[17] The video, shot in black-and-white, shows a 1950s trailer park at night with a thunderstorm looming in the distance. Members of the band are sitting on chairs outside one of the trailers. The opening shot shows the lead singer Thom Yorke standing on top of a trailer, letting himself fall backwards towards the ground. The video decelerates to slow motion and we never see him hit the ground. It cuts to him lying on top of the roof of a damaged car. In the next shot, Yorke is standing in the foreground, singing. His right arm has been digitally removed. It looks as if the footage of him has also been altered in terms of its speed. In the background, the guitar player, Jonny Greenwood jumps out of the trailer and seems almost suspended in the air as the footage of him slows down. Yorke is not affected by the slow motion effect. This is typical of the way in which irreconcilable temporalities are combined in the same frame throughout the video. A bit later, we see Yorke smashing window-panes with a hammer. He moves at a normal speed, but the windows break in slow motion. Shortly afterwards Yorke also encounters himself. While one Yorke jumps in slow motion, another Yorke strikes a stick horizontally under his feet at a normal speed. Between these various tableaus of irreconcilable temporalities, we see shots of Yorke singing, often in double exposures fading over each other, as well as tableaus with three female dancers slowed down and speeded up again, a man's face covered with tar, and guitar player Ed O'Brian falling backwards in his chair as the slow motion effect halts the fall. The video ends with Yorke jumping, while slow motion erases gravity and leaves him suspended in thin air.

The persistence through which the effect is used evokes a world in which speed is a strangely variable thing, to the extent that its inhabitants may share spaces with others, even themselves, but often accelerate into different temporalities. The use of slow motion is often congruent with a desire to study body movements in intimate detail, just like in Muybridge's motion studies and in Dziga Vertov's notion of the genius camera eye (rearticulated by Benjamin as an "optical unconscious"). In STREET SPIRIT, such an epistemological interest in the human body in motion comes in the background of a poetic interest in existential aspects of the human predicament. Key to the poetically surreal world articulated here is the mutability and dynamism of time, and how a hybrid temporality may render us worlds apart from the people around us who would seem to share time and space with us, but do not.

Various forms of hybrid temporality can be found in other videos, for example, in the video for the Goo Goo Dolls' HERE IS GONE (Francis Lawrence, 2002). In this video, several shots combine people from two groups, one moving in high speed, often in a staccato, produced by time-lapse photography, and another group of ghostly-looking characters moving in slow motion. One scene draws more explicitly on the idea of being in different worlds, as a woman in slow motion comes up to and carefully kisses another woman from behind who is seated at a table, eating. The woman being kissed does not notice. She occupies a high-speed temporality, portrayed by means of time-lapse photography. The divergent temporalities render them worlds apart, in spite of the intimacy of the situation. It evokes a sense of loss, much like the temporal divide in melodramatic stories where feelings of love and care are sadly expressed "too late."[18] Carol Vernallis, after having discussed the video with the director, suggests that it is of a ghost who "kisses a flesh and blood relative…transgressing the boundary between worlds," but this is hardly the only possible reading.[19] Whatever specificity is assigned to the group (ghosts, outcasts or other), the sentimentality produced through the hybrid temporality in HERE IS GONE is quite different from the poetic surreal world of STREET SPIRIT.

As is often the case in music videos, the rhythm of editing and of accelerations and decelerations in STREET SPIRIT do not coincide precisely with, and therefore do not interfere with, the beat of the song. Rather, the editing coheres with the song's mood the way it evolves, and with the deeper emotional logic of the song. A radically different approach to the way the visuals of a video intervenes rhythmically is demonstrated in Cunningham's music video, ONLY YOU (1997), for the Portishead song of the same name.

Mutable Temporality in "ONLY YOU"

In ONLY YOU the mellow and cinematic trip-hop soundtrack – based on a strong baseline, laid-back drums, sparse use of electric piano and guitar, audio samples and record-scratching – is topped by the intimate melancholy of Beth Gibbons' characteristic voice, relating thoughts on what seems like a relationship beyond repair. The video locates us in a desolate back-alley where we see a boy who comes floating in the air towards the camera and lands his feet on the street. His shoelaces are untied. They draw interesting patterns though the space. His hair does as well. Beth also comes floating into the space, singing. A third motif is an insistent zooming in on a window above them, where a man is standing looking out, as if monitoring the action below. The curious floating movements of the boy and Beth are generated by a series of effects. First, their bodies are shot under water. Visible traces of the water itself are then removed. What remains is the water's effects on the bodies' gravity, their logic of movement, as well as on their eyes and skin. This material is then further subjected to Cunningham's acceleration and de-acceleration effects and extensive use of slow motion. The movements generated through having them take place under water are quite uniquely fitted to the dreamy, cinematic slow motion-like atmosphere of the music. The under water footage offers a peculiar vantage point for controlling the movements later in post-production.

If the mutable temporality of STREET SPIRIT was based in slowing footage down and speeding it up, as well as in the hybrid temporalities inhabiting the same frame, in ONLY YOU, the mutable temporality takes a more explicitly musical approach. Cunningham, in effect, *dances* the bodies to the music by means of adjusting the speed of the footage in post-production. The implication of this dancing is not only to overrule the automated reproduction process audiovisual discourse is based upon. It is also to re-situate the human body as a malleable "puppet" body open to control by another performer, who, in effect, takes on the role of a master puppeteer. If the puppet answers to the master puppeteer, he again answers to the rhythmic pulse of the music itself. With its temporal performance so intimately answering to the logic of the music, this video realizes new potentials for an exploration of fundamental rhythmic pulses – pulses that may inform both body movements and musical beats, and facilitate correspondences between them – like we see in dance closely synchronized to music. The level of synchronization at stake in ONLY YOU is reminiscent of the extreme forms observable in the way Michael Jackson danced his funky pop, drawing on the tap dance tradition, or from a different continent, the aggressive, yet sweet care for the beat displayed by the British dancer Akram Khan when performing in the Indian *kathak* tradition. In Cunningham's video, such a synchronicity is brought to bear on the very different musical style offered by British trip-hop.

An even more important reference for the aesthetic in play here is the "scratching" practice developed by the modern DJ – by which the original temporality of the music is overruled in a rhythmic performance whereby the record is moved manually (a technique which is now often simulated electronically). From this DJ culture has also emerged a VJ (Video Jockey) culture, shaping an aesthetic congruent with what Cunningham offers in ONLY YOU.[20] The close relation between the scratching tradition of the DJ and the mutable temporalities effected in post-production is explicitly commented on in Dave Meyers' video for Missy Elliott's WORK IT (2002), through cross-cutting between a DJ scratching and bodies moving to his rhythm, as if indicating that the DJ operates as a master puppeteer. WORK IT follows up on several Missy Elliott videos that utilize mutable temporality in synch with the music.

THE RISE AND FALL and the Aesthetics of Post-Production

In the music video for THE RISE AND FALL, we can also observe a mutable temporality, and the presence of a master puppeteer, as it were, who conducts the movements in a way that is anchored in the music, as well as in a logic of body gesture. But there is also another logic at play that involves a different aspect of the aesthetics of post-production.

When making his song, Craig David sampled a main theme from Sting's 1993 hit, SHAPE OF MY HEART. Thus, Craig David's song positions itself already within a logic of cultural production defined through borrowing and re-circulation. Moreover, his use of an Auto Tuner to overrule the original phrasings in his vocal performance – which affords a human and intimate feel, touched by the algorithmic logic of the machine – ensures that both aural and visual elements are inscribed within the aesthetics of post-production. How, then, is the mutable temporality inscribed in THE RISE AND FALL, and in which ways are body movements overruled by the master puppeteer?

In the song, Craig David sings about the dangers of fame, how he can "lose it." We see him in a pub, where he gets two beers at the bar, and sits down with Sting at a table. Sting is singing the chorus part at the beginning of the song, as inserts of other pub guest looking at and discussing them illustrate the effects of fame. Among the other characters in the pub, there is a bartender with dreadlocks about to pour some coins into the cash register, a female waitress on her way to a table with a tray full of drinks, a group of people playing darts and another group having fun playing pool. A lot of slow motion is used, which adds to the calm atmosphere of the song and helps create the general mood of the video. As Craig David sings, "my life was never gonna be the same – cause with the money came another status – that's when things changed," things also start to change in the video. As if on a cue from the word "money," the image showing the coins pouring into the cash register from the hand of the bartender slows down to a freeze frame. Similarly, following the words "when things changed," and Craig David pointing to his watch as if to invoke the issue of time, we see an image of the waitress about to lose her tray with all the drinks, also slow down and freeze. The loss of the drinks is marked on the sound track as well, as if someone touched the turntable of a record player for an instant to make the speed dip. For this instant, both speed and pitch dip, to underscore "the fall" and the possibility of "losing it," perhaps also to ironically comment on the previously-mentioned problem with pitch related to slowing down footage. At this point in the video, the slowing down to freeze spreads throughout the pub. In the dart game, a thrown dart is frozen in mid-air. At the pool table, a prospective winner takes a shot at the 8-ball to pocket it in a corner, but miscalculates, so the ball is about to jump off the table when the image is slowed down to a freeze.

The camera then tours the pub where all life is now frozen. Craig David and Sting, however, can walk about the room, which is inhabited not merely by frozen people like in a wax museum, but also frozen acts with objects defying gravity – coins, a tray of drinks, pool ball and dart still frozen in mid-air. This is reminiscent of the way Morpheus and Neo, in THE MATRIX (Wachowski and Wachowski 1999), after the surrounding action is frozen, walk about the simulacrum of a world that just a moment ago seemed real, discussing the matrix as a system. When walking about his similarly frozen world, Craig David adjusts the black pool ball to a position just above the corner pocket. One by one, the petrified people and things start moving again as Craig David and Sting leave the pub: the coins fall where they should, the dart hits its target, the adjusted black ball hits the corner pocket to enthusiastic cheers, the fall of the drinks continues onto the floor.

Thus, like in STREET SPIRIT and in HERE IS GONE, hybrid temporality, as well as slow motion and variable speed are at stake. However, the hybrid temporality in STREET SPIRIT and HERE IS GONE, where bodies move at different speeds in the same frame, is rather different from the execution in THE RISE AND FALL, where action around the key characters is frozen. An aesthetic reminiscent of the one in THE RISE AND FALL is found in Michel Gondry's video for The Rolling Stones' version of LIKE A ROLLING STONE (1997). In Gondry's video, a combination of two simultaneously shot photographs is used as a basis for a 3D model in which a virtual camera can move. Gondry did not go on to construct a model for people to walk about in, but merely used a technique of sliding between the perspectives of the two cameras to produce its curious effect. The effect is actually prefiguring the bullet-time effect used two years later for THE MATRIX, which used many more cameras to get 360 degrees around its subjects. The two-camera effect employed by Gondry hardly operates with a range beyond 60 degrees. The compelling visuals of the video are based on a combination of this pre-bullet-time effect and an effect created by using "one picture out of five from a film and … an image warping" between these, as Pierre Buffin, from the visual-effects company that worked with Gondry, describes it.[21] This warping produces a "wobbly" effect reminiscent of a concave/convex distorted funhouse mirror.

The unreal atmosphere effected – curiously situating the video between the realms of still and moving images – is consistent with the point of view of the video's main character, the lost female "rolling stone" played convincingly by Patricia Arquette. Yet another effect relating to the 3D model based on two photographs used by Gondry is the one used in the video to David Bowie's song, NEW KILLER STAR (Brumby Boylston 2003), where a flickering back and forth between two perspectives on the same object also involves a rudimentary animation. The technique is much like in lenticular cards, but the flickering repetitions and animation effects also recall some of the works of the experimental filmmaker and artist Ken Jacobs, who has done much to explore the realm between still and moving images.[22]

Slow motion pervades music videos in general beyond those discussed here. It has a compelling power to examine movement, a power that is also celebrated in Benjamin's essay on the artwork in the age of mechanical reproduction. Citing Rudolf Arnheim, Benjamin talks about how "slow motion not only presents familiar qualities of movement but reveals in them entirely unknown ones 'which, far from looking like retarded rapid movements give the effect of singularly gliding, floating, supernatural motions'."[23] Expanding on this observation, Benjamin adds that a "different nature opens itself to the camera than opens to the naked eye…[The] camera intervenes with the resources of its lowerings and liftings, its interruptions and isolations, its extensions and accelerations, its enlargements and reductions."[24] Some of the fascination with slow motion in Benjamin's description points to instances of "gliding, floating," and recalls notions of weightlessness. Likewise, in THE RISE AND FALL, gravity is put on hold, and various objects are in effect rendered weightless, hanging, as movement is slowed down toward a standstill.

The intimate relationship between weightlessness and slow motion is probed, as we have seen, in another way in Cunningham's video to ONLY YOU, where the weightless unreality of the body is not only produced through the mutable temporality of post-production, but also induced by means of positioning the actual profilmic bodies under water, a liquid carrying much the same weight as the human body, whereby it is rendered weightless. This produces a temporality of movement modulated by the under-water weightlessness, which again is overwritten on a secondary level by the temporality created in post-production. Still, the initial logic of movement of the weightless body in water continues to be present in this palimpsest, though it is overwritten by the performative dancing of the body to the music.

In ordinary slow motion, time is set aside and overruled, in favor of laying out the spatiality of a movement, which in its normal tempo is hard to appreciate in all its detail. This can be observed in the spatial dynamic of facial emotion, as explored by Bill Viola in a number of art videos, or in exploding buildings in blockbuster movies or in the music video to Fatboy Slim's GANGSTA TRIPPIN (Roman Coppola 1998), or in fight scenes in a film like THE MATRIX. Thus, if the spatial tends to be privileged (over the temporal) as the original temporalities are sacrificed in ordinary slow motion, in ONLY YOU, a new temporality performed in post-production gets to trump and dominate the original temporalities which are still perceived deeper in the palimpsest. Thus, the originary temporal dynamics of the profilmic bodies in ONLY YOU are partly subdued, not so much in order to bring forth spatial details, but predominantly in order to bring forth an alternate temporal dynamics performed by a master puppeteer who eloquently demonstrates how rhythm is the essence of emotional expression. This situation can, for example, make it difficult to assess how fast the movement represented in the slowed-down format really would be were it not slowed down. The location of the characters, floating in mid-air in a back alley, furthermore operates to alienate the movements from its origins.

In THE RISE AND THE FALL, mutable temporality is employed to produce parallel temporalities, as well – those of the frozen and of the moving characters. In principle, this can also be regarded as a form of what I, with reference to *Street Spirit*, have called *hybrid temporality*, allowing irreconcilable temporal worlds to co-inhabit the same photographical picture frame as if it were showing a single world. Of course, such a world could not exist to be filmed and its filmic image may therefore be assigned to the category of *the impossible image*, not because of the spatial breaches as to how the world appears (which initially inspired this term), but because of its temporal breaches. If *the spatially impossible image* violates what is spatially possible, then *the temporally impossible image* violates what is temporally possible. The sense of the impossible also looms more or less strongly under vocal performances overwritten by the Auto Tune effect. In the case of Craig David, the effect seems moderately used, but it still makes the vocal output a palimpsest, and also a hybrid, where man and machine are both featured, in a singing cyborg that merges Craig David and his machines.

On a more general level, these examples illustrate how post-production processes now often endow photographical images, or recorded voices, with a ra-

relations between music and motion, where the gestural level, in part, orga-nized around attitudes, forms a bridge between these two spheres.

The British musicologist, Nicholas Cook, when discussing the relation be-tween image and music, argues that "the coupling of image and sound contex-tualizes, clarifies, and in a sense analyses the music."[31] Vernallis brings the clar-ifying and analytical powers of images more directly to bear on music videos when she notes that

> Meyers … uses particular techniques to draw attention to the heterogeneity of a pop song's rhythm arrangement. The first half of a musical phrase might be ornate, and the second half given over to a smoother flow of images: a bevy of kids on big-wheeled bikes, or a slow-mo shot of water pouring from a pail. These two contrasting types of visual articulation – busy or drawn out – offer different vantage points. We might first listen more intently to a particular detail, and next we might hear the mu-sic as a wash.… Meyers's broadly drawn and well-projected visual material can change the way we hear songs. The songs seem louder somehow. They gain a sense of clarity and immediacy.[32]

Thus, a crucial way the video might "analyze" the music is by its approach to editing and the sense of temporal flow in the imagery. As an overall approach, the music video can show attentiveness toward particular details, or it can pre-sent a more general "wash." Cunningham does not hold back on being particu-lar. He intervenes on a musical level, as if providing new instruments to the musical mix. But key to his visual analysis of the music, as it is in many music videos, is the bodily gestures displayed. Maróthy talked about how music has the power to switch "the individual into the circuit of universality." We may well conceive of the gestural as a key link whereby that can take place.

Such a switching of the individual into the circuit of universality, however, may take place in radically different ways, relating also to fundamentally differ-ent forms of life. This is evident when moving to the last example to be dis-cussed here, Cunningham's independent video project RUBBER JOHNNY. This moves us away from the post-industrial aesthetics of Portishead so well con-veyed in the music video ONLY YOU, to the freakish retrograde, yet futuristic post-human frenzy of a mutilated and morphing character, shape-shifting to the frenzied beat of Aphex Twin, moving faster than any human can. Still, on a fundamental level, Cunningham's video may be regarded as a *music video*, in the sense of a video attuned to music, where we in fact can *see* (as in the original sense of the word *video*) *music*.

The Posthuman Frenzy of Rubber Johnny

A grainy close-up of Johnny's face, taken with an infrared camera, opens the video. It seems he is being interviewed by an off-screen therapist asking, "Now, how are you feeling? Are you feeling OK, you feel well?" Johnny merely mumbles as a response. He seems both physically and mentally beyond the norms of the human. He is sitting in a wheel chair and sports an abnormal egg-shaped head on top of a small face, and seems otherwise feeble and weak. Yet, the therapist seems to sense that Johnny is capable of perceiving something he himself cannot, so he asks: "Are you seeing something…is there something you see over there? What do you see there, Johnny?" The meeting ends by Johnny hyperventilating and the therapist offering him an injection to calm him down. A transitory sequence starts as a neon light is lit, a rat walks over the logo 'Warp Film', a condom is pulled over a dildo and punctured. On the condom is written, 'Rubber Johnny,' which in Britain simply is slang for condom.

The punctured condom, with its world of rubber, does not sexualize the video as much as its puncture produces a certain attitude. The sexual theme and an atmosphere of rubber still provides a bizarre undertone in a new close-up of Johnny's face as he shows his tongue in a fast equilibrist motion parodying a standard trope of the porn movie. The movement is spastic and grotesque. It is produced at an inhuman speed and with a mechanical gestural logic that seems as robot-like as human, and which thereby evokes an impression of Johnny as a bizarre cyborg as much as simply deformed.

Johnny's play with his tongue leads to a peculiar music and dance sequence which – in contrast to the opening scene – positions him in full control of his surroundings. The sequence creates a completely new world for him. This is a world of ferocious speeds and a virtuoso bodily control in complete synch with the music. In this world, Johnny has mutated to become strong and athletic, catching and reflecting rays of light coming at him, as if from an attacking enemy's laser weapons in a computer game. He comes across here almost like a mechanized game character – as someone played as much as playing. The sequence is disrupted by someone in a doorway, outside the frame. A character that could potentially be Johnny's father addresses him in an aggressive and demeaning manner. This instantly reverses the mutation to an athlete and reconstitutes Johnny as a passive, deformed freak under control.

A new sequence radicalizes the video and its exploration of the limits of perception. The sequence is initiated by Johnny sniffing a long stripe of white powder. His body again moves with the music in a frenetic tempo. The at-times-mechanical body now reveals its organic aspects as the body virtually explodes into fragments, and is broken down to its constitutive parts: plasma, brain-mass and bones are thrown at the camera and hit a glass frame right before our eyes. Johnny decomposes and is reduced to pure plasma and an occasional organ in the form of an eye, an ear, a mouth. As if a still-life picture or a snapshot, such tableaus are held on the glass plate before the frenetic beat starts again, with visuals tightly in synch with the music. When the biological remains that is Johnny tear themselves loose again to revamp the ferocious movement, the plasma is stuck on the glass plate for a while until it pops back, like chewing gum. This connects to another rubber element here, namely that rubber quality inherent in the frenzy of the electronic music and in the dance the video articulates. Cunningham comments on the rubber quality in the music in an interview:

> The bass line in the track sounded like an elastic band to me and so I got the idea of someone shapeshifting like a piece of chewing gum, whilst raving. The title Rubber Johnny just seemed to fit the character and shapeshifting idea really well. It has nothing whatsoever to do with condoms, although it is a bonus that Rubber Johnny is a term that we used in the playground.[33]

On a more general level, "an elastic band," situated around the waist, is also key to the dynamism and elegance of dancers, vital for energetic rebounds. Thus, Cunningham dramatizes a key element in dancing in his Rubber Johnny character, who from a rubber-like music, in the words of Cunningham,"[is] shapeshifting like a piece of chewing gum."[34] However, this rubber quality, is in RUBBER JOHNNY orchestrated with a spastic energy reflecting both the mechanization of his body as well as its abnormal deformities, in a register far away from any form of harmonious human dance.

Perception and the Limits of the Human

What Cunningham comes to explore in the mutable temporality of *Rubber Johnny* is not merely a shapeshifting body capable of moving beyond human speed, or a music pushing the boundaries of our perception. The limits of human perception are thematized more fundamentally. The issue is first raised though the questions about what Johnny sees. Implicitly, an ordinary human like the therapist cannot see what Johnny can. An inserted picture of a Chihuahua, with its eyes much like Johnny's, white in the infrared camera's green imagery, ironically comments on our lacking perceptive capabilities. We are reminded that we are incapable of seeing what the dog, and probably also Johnny, sees. Issues of perception are also articulated by the infrared photography itself and its expansion beyond the visual field where we can only operate with technological aids that

can adapt signals to our visual register. Yet another element focusing on perception and its manipulation are the drugs involved, the therapist's injection as
much as the white stripe. One of the parameters through which drugs can be
assessed, is whether they are energizing or relaxing, whether they support high-
or low-speed activities. Another is whether they support presence or open alternate worlds of fantasy through changing our perceptions, even offering halluci-
nations. In RUBBER JOHNNY, drugs, at least the white stripe, may evoke a sense
of both the energizing and the hallucination-inducing, but first and foremost it
can be related to the speed of a certain kind of music, which through the aesthetic of post-production, has ventured beyond the realms within which a human musician can handle without special aids. The tempo is simply far beyond
what a human body can play.

The music for RUBBER JOHNNY is therefore largely produced by means of a
computer operating the instruments (or sound samples). This allows programming to take place at a human speed, where both the sense of rhythm and the
body of the player/programmer can keep up. The speed of the tracks can later
be played at a completely different speed, in this case much faster.[35] Thus, the
limits of human performance and perception also become an arena for the music here. The music pushes up against and partly beyond the limits, not only of
what the human body can play and dance, but also of what it can perceive.
Sound and image in the ordinary music video, according to Michel Chion, are
only occasionally synchronized.[36] Vernallis also notes this in her discussion of
the music video director, Francis Lawrence's work: "Editing is subtly articulated
off the beat and irregular. It makes the music the dominant voice – the image
serves as a coloration or counterpoint."[37] She also describes how Lawrence's
"softly articulated editing falls off the beat, bringing the song's rhythm to the
fore."[38] In RUBBER JOHNNY and ONLY YOU, Cunningham articulates a diametrically opposed vision. In RUBBER JOHNNY, synchronization is taken to the extreme, much further than in the already strongly synchronized ONLY YOU.
Thus, RUBBER JOHNNY, by means of music and imagery, pushes us to the edge
of or beyond human perception. Cunningham comments on his exploration of
the limits of perception by saying:

> I wanted to see how fast you can go before it becomes nonsensical, a mess. The edit-
> ing style in RUBBER JOHNNY is actually very old fashioned and simple. If you were to
> watch it at half speed you would see that.
>
>   It was incredibly difficult to edit this video and find that line, where it seems break-
> neck, but still flows and makes sense as a sequence. I would have to redo each shot
> about twenty times in order to find something that worked. It involved a lot of ex-
> perimentation. It was closer to animation than editing and I had to create the video
> two frames at a time.[39]

At times, works in video, music or other arts may also push beyond the edge Cunningham is balancing. They may radically transcend the limits of human perception. Rather than challenging the capabilities of our perception and balancing on the edge of the possible, they may, in a sense, leave their anchoring in human-embodied perception and instead make themselves available on a conceptual level.[40] But, in this case, James and Cunningham do not wish to leave the human scale, but rather push it to its limits. Therefore, they operate at, and slightly beyond, the threshold of human perception, but without leaving it altogether.

The Forms Afforded by Temporal Mutability

STREET SPIRIT and THE RISE AND FALL inaugurate, in their wildly different ways, worlds of hybrid temporality where bodies are miraculously accelerated and de-accelerated independently of each other while mysteriously sharing the same space. ONLY YOU articulates an intimately controlled universe, where the speed of the bodies is *danced*, as if from an immensely sensible and musical master puppeteer, while RUBBER JOHNNY displays a more action/reaction-oriented synchronicity where the controlling agency is more dispersed. The ecology of the musical groove, together with the visuals, allows questions of originary agency to fade into the background in favor of a circulation of energies and impulses that seem as much human as machinic, as emanating from the "shape-shifting" plasma in play. This cyborg dimension, where the machinic and the organic are fused in a new dynamism – albeit here ironically charged with the abject deformities defining Johnny – can also be traced back to some of the inspirations behind Benjamin's questioning of the relation between art and technology, in particular to Dziga Vertov. In one of his early manifestos, Vertov describes how the human is transformed and engulfed by technology, in this case, the cinematographic apparatus:

> I am kino-eye. I am mechanical eye. I, a machine.... Now and forever I free myself from human immobility, I am in constant motion.... My path leads to the creation of a fresh perception of the world. I decipher in a new way a world unknown to you.[41]

In Vertov's vision, as well as in Cunningham's, an interrogation of and change in perceptual forms are pivotal. The human becomes machine-like, liberated from human mobility or lack thereof, finding new dynamism in a merging with the machine, with technology. This merger yields a new and fresh perception of the world.

Within the nexus of the human body, technology and perception – where the human and the machine are brought together in cyborg-inspired visions – we can also find the Australia-based artist Sterlac's explorations of body and technology. He also seems interested in puppeteering the human body, as if installing a sort of post-production procedure whereby his limbs can be controlled. His most interesting project in this regard may be his MOVATAR (2000), which he describes as an "inverse motion capture system".[42] Motion capture is based on capturing the movements of one object, often a human body, and mapping that motion onto a virtual object, for example a 3D graphical model of a human being. Now, what Stelarc's MOVATAR does is to reverse the traffic of data. Rather than having movement data mapped from the real to the virtual body, he proposes to get data from a virtual body equipped with the artificial intelligence necessary to generate movement, and map that data onto one or more human bodies. In a presentation of the project Stelarc writes:

> Consider, though, a virtual body or an avatar that can access a physical body, actuating its performance in the real world. If the avatar is imbued with an artificial intelligence, becoming increasingly autonomous and unpredictable, then it would become more an AL (Artificial Life) entity performing with a human body in physical space.
>
> With an appropriate visual software interface and muscle stimulation system, this would be possible. The avatar would become a Movatar. Its repertoire of behaviors could be modulated continuously…and might evolve using genetic algorithms. With appropriate feedback loops from the real world it would be able to respond and perform in more complex and compelling ways. The Movatar would be able not only to act, but also to express its emotions by appropriating the facial muscles of its physical body.[43]

Starlac's project appears at a time when the mapping of movement data from one object to another has become an important device in the field of cultural production.[44] Motion capture technologies have long been used in the production of films and games, and the art world is rife with more playful mappings of data. Recent developments in image production seem to render motion capture techniques even more central, and thereby bolster the realm of post-production. With reference to THE MATRIX RELOADED (2003), Silberman, explains this shift in the following way:

> The standard way of simulating the world in CG [Computer Graphics] is to build it from the inside out, by assembling forms out of polygons and applying computer-simulated textures and lighting. The ESC team [ESC Entertainment is a special effects company] took a radically different path, loading as much of the real world as possible into the computer first, building from the outside in. This approach, known as image-based rendering, is transforming the effects industry.

A similar evolution has already occurred in music. The first electronic keyboards sought to re-create a piano's acoustic properties by amassing sets of rules about the physics of keys, hammers, and strings. The end result sounded like a synthesizer. Now DJs and musicians sample and morph the recorded sounds of actual instruments.

Instead of synthesizing the world, Gaeta cloned it.[45]

Manovich makes a similar point about the shift from simulation to sampling-based technologies, drawing heavily on the visual effects designer of THE MATRIX trilogy, John Gaeta, who is also discussed in Silberman's article (above). Later cases like THE CURIOUS CASE OF BENJAMIN BUTTON (David Fincher, 2008) and AVATAR (James Cameron 2009), as well as ongoing aspirations towards photographic realism in computer games by means of capture and synthesizing technologies, only reinforce this development.[46] Silberman's parallel to music production, where "DJs and musicians sample and morph the recorded sounds of actual instruments," also captures well the generalized post-production mode that permeates cultural production at present, where the interest in mutable temporalities is merely one element.

Valery was right in expecting innovations to transform the techniques of the arts, and thereby affect artistic invention even to the brink of changing our very notion of art. These changes are still being discussed, perhaps now most intensely in relation to the new status of photography in the art world and the term *post-medium condition*.[47] Likewise, it seems increasingly necessary to reflect on the ways in which current technological changes affect cultural production and perhaps also come to alter our notion of art. Today's technological changes are related to the computer with its procedural receipts offered by ever more finely tuned algorithms, along with increasingly developed storage, mixing and modification technologies. Thus, efforts to conceptualize current changes to cultural production often revolve around notions like archive, algorithm and post-production.

This chapter has explored a particular aspect of the aesthetics of post-production, the mutable temporality, which seems to become increasingly prevalent in contemporary music video, but is in no way limited to this format. When the music video in particular has been an arena where various forms of mutable temporality has been probed, it has at least two explanations. Music itself being our most important temporal art form, is therefore also an arena for the explorations of various forms of emotional temporalities. Such temporal experiences are not merely articulated in the music itself, but also in the image streams and pulses accompanying them in music videos. Another explanation may be found closer to the relationship between technology itself and the audiovisual language it supports. Music video has long been a playground for new technologies, for new algorithms and ideas. For the film director David Fincher, it was "the most terrific sandbox, where I could try anything."[48] Special effects companies are aware of this perception and have offered some of their new toys for music video directors to try out, as was the case when Gondry made the video for Like a Rolling Stone.[49] Although the attraction of new technologies, effects and algorithms will stay with us, there are also reasons to expect that the technologies supporting mutable temporalities may become less foregrounded as they increasingly become standard equipment in editing suits. With these medial resources firmly embedded in the algorithms of applicable software, as well as in visions about what the medium is capable of and what visual languages can convey, we can expect new works in this field to become less technologically driven and more free to explore artistic visions without becoming a vehicle of display for the new technological device. Thus, the artistic vision may stand out stronger, and not risk being reduced to a mere consequence of a new special effects tool. This means that the urgent charge of exploring new algorithms and technological solutions, offering works that carry their technological fingerprints – like Street Spirit, Like a Rolling Stone and The Rise and Fall – may give way to works that take the human predicament of subjective temporal experience even more seriously, as a field that warrants interrogation.

With contemporary life being increasingly networked and mediated, where we can conduct exchanges across various time zones with several friends simultaneously – one caught in a hurried morning, another enjoying the relaxation of a night approaching bed-time, where virtual and real presence increasingly comes to feel really real no matter whether we can physically touch each other or not – there are contemporary temporal and existential experiences to be interrogated and articulated. The prevalent practice of walking about with our own soundscapes in our headsets, cut off from the sounds of our immediate surroundings, can also bring alternate temporalities into our lives, and disconnect us from the temporalities of the world physically surrounding us.

Music videos have been important as sites for interrogating hybrid temporal experiences and forms of mutable temporalities – supported by the music itself as a temporal art. But may such issues also become increasingly interrogated in other formats and genre? Could we not expect various forms of mutable temporality to make a greater impact in cinema too? The realism of storytelling, as well as the pervasiveness of dialogue between characters we see speaking, can be counted among the factors holding back such a development. However, interestingly, a film like Christopher Nolan's Inception (2010) has a plot that lends itself to the relativization of time, and may be considered a major effort, after The Matrix, to warp time and to articulate not only a *spatially impossible image*, but also a *temporally impossible image*, where hybrid temporalities seem to inhabit the same space. The modernism of Alain Resnais certainly provided compelling hybrid spatio-temporal experiences in the doubling of Nevers and Hiroshima in HIROSHIMA MON AMOUR (1959). A film like Wong Kar Wai's FALLEN ANGELS (1995) also provides strong subjective temporalities in which voice-over, in combination with slow motion, effects a divide from the physical here and now. These few examples of wildly different films from different times and styles offer merely an indication of what cinema has achieved in terms of temporal hybridity. But in spite of the achievements, cinema, it seems, have come a longer way in exploring space. With the growing interest in subjective storytelling and the inner working of the mind, combined with the growing options for mutable temporalities, cinema may now be on its way to conquering the vicissitudes of time more forcefully. Still, there are crucial differences between music videos and movies, even if both exemplify audiovisual discourses. In traditional cinema, sound is fitted to the image; whereas in music videos, it is the other way around, the images are fitted to the music. Naturally, with the temporal art form of music at its center, as its raison d'être, music video absorbs the mutable temporality with faint resistance. Cinema, on the contrary, may partly have to leave the common representational strategy of lip-synch in order to gain the freedom to involve mutable temporalities. It is telling that Wong Kar Wai's style has been compared to a music video, and the effectiveness of the music video as a "sand box" for film directors coming of age now may also be telling for coming developments.

The growing importance of the aesthetics of post-production may more generally be anchored in a series of developments. Bourriaud's diagnosis of the form that cultural production now takes – especially in the world of art – as based on *post-production*, provides both a general diagnosis of cultural production and an analysis of the logic of production in the art world. Music production since the Beatles has largely been an art of the mixing table as much as an art of the instruments played. This situation is further radicalized by the singing cyborg afforded by technologies like Auto Tune. Manovich argues for the necessity of inserting a hyphen into the word *photography* to truly represent the photographic practices of current filmmaking, not merely in Hollywood science fiction, but increasingly across genres. John Belton adds to this picture by noting how "filmmakers used to say they would 'fix it in post[-production].' Now… they tend to say they'll 'make it in post'."[50] In accordance with this, Belton further observes how "PLEASANTVILLE combines color and black and white in the same frame, violating the integrity of the image. The image is revealed as not whole, but made up of parts."[51] All of this speaks to the growing mutability of our forms of cultural production, in which *the index* – which helped boost the credibility of images and sounds inscribed through mechanical reproduction to a higher status, above the merely *iconic* forms of representation – is becoming a less restrictive force in the formation of contemporary sound and image production. Post-production is the stage where this mutability is executed and realized.

The aesthetics of post-production, and more specifically, the aspect involving mutable temporality, is likely to stay with us and may also move more powerfully into the language of cinema, where the temporal may offer unexplored fields in an art form that has often been more spatial in its concerns. But the urgent charge toward investigating something new, as mutable temporality has been explored in music videos, will not endure, as the fronts of urgency keep moving. Counter-reactions like Dogme 95 – which shunned the "fix-it-in-post" mentality – and interest in more or less abandoned media, as well as an interest in traditional production methods, are also likely to remain. However, the new mutability in audiovisual culture, whereby it has, in a sense, become more algorithmic, is likely to see further blossoming, supported by the step-by-step migration of audiovisual production to digital platforms.

Notes

*   I want to thank Liv Hausken and Kiersten Leigh Johnson for helpful comments and suggestions, Kiersten also for improving my language.

1.   Paul Valery, "The Conquest of Ubiquity," *Aesthetics: The Collected Works of Paul Valery*, Volume XIII, ed. Jackson Mathews (London: Routledge, 1964) 225.

2.   Gene Youngblood, "Cinema and the Code," *Leonardo*, Computer Art in Context Supplemental Issue (1989): 29.

3.   W.S. Condon and W.D. Ogston, "Sound Film Analysis of Normal and Pathological Behaviour Patterns." *The Journal of Nervous and Mental Disease*. Volume 143(1) (1966): 338.

4.   Friedrich Nietzsche, quoted in Oliver Sacks, "The Power of Music." *Brain*, 129 (2006): 2528.

5.   Walter Benjamin, "The Work of Art in the Age of Mechanical Reproduction," *Illuminations* (London: Fontana, 1973) 211-44.

6.   Alexander R. Galloway uses the term "algorithmic culture" in the subtitle for his book on computer games. Though he is first and foremost concerned with the role of algorithms in games, he is also connecting his analysis to the wider gamut of an informational network society that realizes key elements in what Gilles Deleuze called "the society of control." Alexander R. Galloway, *Gaming: Essays on Algorithmic Culture* (Minneapolis: University of Minnesota Press, 2006). Lev Manovich discusses various forms of algorithmic manipulation, as he tends to call it, in *The Language of New Media*, a trait he sees as characteristic of new media. Lev Manovich, *The Language of New Media* (Cambridge, MA: MIT Press, 2001).

7.   Beyond exploring an aesthetic of sampling, Susanne Østby Sæther presents a valuable account of terms like "collage," "appropriation," "sampling," and related concepts in Susanne Østby Sæther, *The Aesthetics of Sampling: Engaging the Media in Re-*

cent Video Art. Dissertation (Oslo: Department of Media and Communication, University of Oslo, 2009).

8. Nicolas Bourriaud, *Postproduction* (New York: Lukas and Sternberg, 2002). I have used the term post-production throughout the chapter, also when discussing Bourriaud's notion of postproduction (which he has chosen to write without a hyphen).

9. Bourriaud 13.

10. Hans Richter, *Film ist Rhythmus.* Eds. Ulrich Gregor, Jeanpaul Goergen, and Angelika Hoch. (Berlin: Freunde d. Dt. Kinemathek, 2003) 87. (My translation.)

11. Tom Gunning, "Re-Newing Old Technologies: Astonishment, Second Nature, and the Uncanny in Technology from the Previous Turn-of-the-Century," *Rethinking Media Change: The Aesthetics of Transition,* ed. David Thorburn and Henry Jenkins (Cambridge, MA: MIT Press, 2003) 51.

12. Richter 87.

13. http://techetrends.blogspot.com/2007_08_01_archive.html (last accessed May 1, 2010)

14. http://avaxhome.ws/software/realviz_retimer.html (last accessed May 1, 2010)

15. The effect of Auto Tune, whereby a singer's pitch can be overruled for more or less compelling effects, should also be mentioned here. It does not change the temporality in terms of rhythm, but merely in terms of pitch. A separation of the two is, of course, reliant upon digital processing. However, Auto Tune is first of all a corrective means that can allow everyone to sing in tune. Its prevalence and effect over the last decade, as well as the strong reactions against it recently are worth exploring in their own right. (Christina Aguilera appeared in public in Los Angeles on August 10, 2009 wearing a T-shirt that read, "Auto Tune is for Pussies".) http://en.wikipedia.org/wiki/Auto-Tune (last accessed May 1, 2010)

16. Eadweard Muybridge created an elaborate setup of synchronized cameras for his movement studies from the 1870s. However, they were not usually set up to capture one moment from various angles, but rather consecutive moments from one angle. The French cartographer Aimé Laussedat at this point had already explored photographic mapping techniques for twenty years. The U.S. journalist Steve Silberman writes: "By taking multiple exposures of the landscape from different angles and triangulating them with clever algorithms, it was possible to generate a topographical map from flat images, similar to the way your brain generates depth perception from two separate 2-D inputs: your eyes. Laussedat's breakthrough was christened photogrammetry." Silberman also notes how, in the late 1990s "Arnauld Lamorlette, the R nonmilitary aircraft may fly over the city only on Bastille Day. Lamorlette found that by morphing between two photographs, he could generate a 3-D model: digital photogrammetry. BUF employed the technique to help director Michel Gondry create a music video for the Rolling Stones." Steve Silberman: "MATRIX2." *Wired Magazine,* May 2003, http://www.wired.com/wired/archive/11.05/matrix2_pr.html (last accessed May 1, 2010).

17. I call these shots because they appear as shots, as continuous recordings from a camera. However, in cases of hybrid temporality inside a frame, it becomes clear that what we see must be a montage of at least two shots or two different parts of a shot. The fact that they appear as single shots helps ground their paradoxical appearance.

18. Linda Williams, "Film Bodies: Gender, Genre, and Excess," *Film Quarterly,* volume 44, no. 4 (summer, 1991) 2-13.

19. Carol Vernallis "'The Most Terrific Sandbox': Music Video Directors, Style, and the Question of the Auteur." *Quarterly Review of Film and Video,* volume 25, issue 5 (October 2008) 408.

20. The VJ grew to be an important part of the club scene of the 1990s. VJ-ing has predominantly remained a performative art in the sense that it has mostly remained bound to live performances. Recorded performances have tended to circulate as "show-reels" for the various performers, rather than as works in their own right.

21. http://www.director-file.com/gondry/stones1.html (August 10, 2010).

22. See Michele Pierson, David E. James and Paul Arthur (eds.) *Optic Antics: The Cinema of Ken Jacobs.* London and New York: Oxford University Press, 2011).

23. Benjamin 235.

24. Ibid., 235-6.

25. Lev Manovich, "Image Future," *Animation* 1.1 (London: Sage, 2006) 25-6.

26. Charles S. Peirce, "Logic as Semiotic: The Theory of Signs," *The Philosophy of Peirce: Selected Writings,* ed. Justus Buchler (New York: Routledge, 1940) 106.

27. Ibid., 26.

28. János Maróthy quoted in Richard Middleton, "Popular Music Analysis and Musicology: Bridging the Gap," *Reading Pop: Approaches to Textual Analysis in Popular Music* (London: Oxford University Press, 2000) 106.

29. Janós Maróthy, "Rite and Rhythm: From Behavior Patterns to Musical Structures." *Studia Musicologica Academiae Scientiarum Hungaricae,* T. 35, Fasc 4 (1993-1994): 430. http://www.jstor.org/stable/902316 (last accessed June 1, 2010).

30. Ibid.

31. Nicholas Cook, *Analysing Musical Multimedia.* (Oxford: Oxford University Press, 1998) 74.

32. Vernallis, " 'The Most Terrific Sandbox': Music Video Directors, Style, and the Question of the Auteur," *Quarterly Review of Film and Video,* 25 (2008) 416-7.

33. Warp Interview With Chris Cunningham. http://www.director-file.com/cunningham/rubber.html (last accessed April 10, 2010)

34. Ibid.

35. In recent music production, a visual interface is increasingly used to expand creation beyond what our intuition can yield when working merely inside the aural realm. Thus, the artist plays around with sounds by means of visual representations. Afterwards the results can be subjected to an aural check. This method of production can expand the purview of aural creation, because, when playing music, a basic principle is that we can *recognize* more interesting things than we are able to *create* by means of playing.

36. Michel Chion, *Audio-Vision: Sound on Screen* (New York: Columbia University Press, 1994) 37, 167.

37. Vernallis 410.

38. Ibid., 406.

39. Se http://www.director-file.com/cunningham/rubber.html (last accessed November 30, 2010)

40. A case in point is John Cage's work *Organ²/ASLSP* now being performed in the St. Burchardi church in Halberstadt, Germany. The performance started at midnight on

the 5th of September 2001 – with a silence lasting until the 5th of February, 2003 – and is scheduled to finish in the year 2640. Thus, Cage has made a piece that requires a 639 year performance. At that speed, it is not perceivable as a combination of sounds that constitute a rhythm and a melody of any sort. No single person can hear the whole piece, nor even its beginning and its end. Thus, it is to be experienced first of all on a conceptual level.

41. Dziga Vertov, *The Writings of Dziga Vertov*, Annette Michelson (ed.), transl. Kevin O'Brien (Berkeley: University of California Press, 1984) 17.

42. http://www.stelarc.va.com.au/projects.html# (last accessed May 1, 2010).

43. Ibid.

44. Such efforts also take place within medicine directed towards appeasing disability and revealing functions of the human brain and body. Among the challenges is to have the brain control artificial limbs like it controls its natural ones.

45. Silberman.

46. Both The Curious Case of Benjamin Button and Avatar perfected capturing technologies, enabling actors to be able to control their digital characters more precisely, and avoid a "botox effect" stemming from a loss of data that might render the virtual actor somewhat muted. According to Silberman, this may be easier than we may initially think: "While the topography of the human face is the hardest to simulate digitally, it turns out to be one of the easiest to map photogrammetrically. It has fewer shadows and occlusions than, say, the city of Paris. The language of the face communicates maximum information through the subtlest inflections. The interfaces of our souls are designed to be read in a heartbeat." Ibid.

47. Rosalind Krauss, "Reinventing the medium", *Critical Inquiry*, 25: 2 (Chicago: University of Chicago Press, 1999) 289–305; Arild Fetveit, "Convergence by means of globalized remediation", *Northern Lights* Volume 5 (2007) 57-74; Michael Fried, *Why Photography Matters as Art as Never Before*. (New Haven: Yale University Press, 2008).

48. Carol Vernallis "'The Most Terrific Sandbox': Music Video Directors, Style, and the Question of the Auteur." *Quarterly Review of Film and Video*, volume 25, issue 5 (October 2008) 404.

49. Pierre Buffin, co-founder of BUF Compagnie introduces the co-operation on Like a Rolling Stone in this way: "We had already worked on different projects with Michel Gondry, such as video-clips like Björk, Lenny Kravitz or Terence Trent D'Arby. During his visits to BUF, we showed him the new tools we were developing and the new effects they could provide. One day we showed him our tool for modeling objects from two pictures, based on stereophotogrammetry." The situation invoked here – in which the expert maker and the expert user of groundbreaking tools meet up before the execution of an important task – seems strangely reminiscent of the congenial meetings between James Bond and Q early in every Bond film. http://www.director-file.com/gondry/stones1.html (last accessed August 10, 2010).

50. John Belton, "Painting by the Numbers: The Digital Intermediate", *Film Quarterly*, Vol. 61, No. 3 (Spring 2008) 59.

51. Ibid., 62.

Algorithmic Culture: Beyond the Photo/Film Divide

Eivind Røssaak

In recent film and media studies, there has been a growing uneasiness among scholars with regard to the destiny of the moving image in the digital age. This article will argue that an investigation into the altered relationship between still and moving images can tell us a lot about the new condition of the moving image culture. Traditionally, the relationship between still and moving images has been governed by a discourse on the dialectical or antitethical relationship between film and photography. Historically speaking, the art of photography predates the invention of cinematography, but projectionists and filmmakers have always utilized this relationship dramatically and aesthetically as a transitional relationship between forms of mobility and immobility. Tom Gunning has shown how the Lumière brothers would astonish their audiences with a special technique of exhibition where they transform a projected still image into a moving image by cranking the projector. Since then, the ambiguity between stillness and motion has always been a resource for resonance and wonder in cinema and, in particular, in experimental film from the constructivists and surrealists all the way up to contemporary filmmakers like Jean-Luc Godard and Chris Marker in Europe and Ken Jacobs and Ernie Gehr in the United States. In more recent digital cinema (especially science fiction films), and in moving image installations in art galleries and on the Internet, a new kind of exploration of this resource is emerging. It may be connected to the transition from analog to digital.

Within the analog world of film stock and celluloid, the relationship between the still and the moving image was often looked upon as a way of foregrounding the material basis of the filmstrip, the relationship between the tacit frames and the act of projection. Accordingly, within the digital world of bits and bytes, the relationship between the still and the moving image has changed. But is this focus on stillness and motion outdated? On the contrary, it seems as if the relationship between stillness and motion has returned within a new and perhaps more complex matrix of problems. Several studies among acclaimed film scholars such as Laura Mulvey, Mary Ann Doane, Bernard Stiegler, Timothy Murray, Geoffrey Batchen, Thomas Elsaesser and W.J.T. Mitchell, have in recent years tried to diagnose the situation by reflecting on and doing close readings of certain works. Significantly, their studies are not simply close readings in the formalist sense of the term; rather, they are investigations of a new situation. What has happened to the image? Scholars talk about a "naming crisis" in the realm of the digital image.[1] Is it still an image? Both scholars and artists seem to be urgently engaged in trying to assess this crisis – or new potential – of the image. A growing number of scholars such as Friedrich Kittler, Lev Manovich, D.N. Rodowick and Mark B.N. Hansen have also started to address these issues via the technical term "algorithm", which was a term only used by computer specialists and mathematicians just a few years ago. This chapter will specifically address the relationship between new media, algorithms and the construction of the image. While many scholars trained in the world of analog and photochemical photography lament the introduction of digital image production because they think it impoverishes the experience of time and history, this paper will explore some of the new affordances of the digital in relation to aesthetic experience and sensation.

Even film scholars not interested in this aspect of the digital image see many advantages of digital technologies. Today, it is hard to imagine that before the advent of the laser disk and the videotape, most film scholars were writing their analyses from the memory of the film they had seen in a movie theatre. For instance, Stanley Cavell writes in the foreword to his seminal work, *The World Viewed* (1971), that, "I wrote primarily out of the memory of film".[2] Laura Mulvey talks about a similar situation in the "Preface" to her *Death 24x a Second: Stillness and the Moving Image* (2006). These researchers and critics from the 1970s were confined to watching films in darkened rooms, projected at 24 (or thereabouts) frames per second. But new media changed this situation. "By the end of the twentieth century, ways of consuming cinema had multiplied and the regulation of its speed had been widely extended," Mulvey writes.[3] With the VCR, films could be stopped at any point, and with the DVD-player perfect freeze-frames were easily created. The pause button and the menu button have introduced new modes of analyzing film, thus opening up old films in new ways. In the essay, "Delaying cinema", Mulvey contends:

> The process of repetition and return involves stretching out the cinematic image to allow space and time for associative thought, reflection of resonance and connotation, the identification of visual clues, the interpretation of cinematic form and style, and, ultimately, personal reverie. Furthermore, by slowing down, freezing or repeating images, key moments and meanings become visible that could not have been perceived when hidden under the narrative flow and the movement of film. Although the alert spectator of melodrama may well have had the ability to read the cinematic language of displacement, consciously or subliminally, at 24 frames a second, today's electronic or digital spectator can find these deferred meanings that have been waiting through the decades to be seen.[4]

Mulvey's narrative almost exhibits a teleology at play. She discusses the transition from the constrictions of the movie theatre spectator to the new revelatory potential of the "digital spectator" as critic. Through a series of brilliant readings, she shows how new technology can alter cinematic hermeneutics. Nevertheless, Mulvey's newly liberated observer addresses the "same" object, namely classical cinema. Her interests lie in the way new media can enhance and deepen the encounter with the unique singularity of the classic feature film. She is not interested in the potential of the new; she is interested in the potential of the old – finally revealed. She uses new media to study the potential of old media, without paying attention to how new media have changed the conditions of visual culture. Indeed, these two aspects of new media are interconnected. New media do not simply deal with or offer "the new". They address and, some would even say, strengthen the distribution and hegemony of the old. Many have already done encyclopedic assessments of what is new and what has remained the same since the digital revolution with regards to narrative cinema.[5] What interests me here, is the changing vocation of the image after it became a technological object of a different kind, that is, a programmable object.

Programmable Objects

According to media philosopher Lev Manovich, a new media object is defined by its programmability.[6] All programmable objects are composed of digital codes and are subject to algorithmic manipulation. The algorithm is the necessary conversion point in the transformation of the analog image into a digital image. Algorithms are abstract, symbolized, step-by-step instructions normally written in pseudo-code or drawn in flow-chart diagrams. Alan Turing, one of the inventors of the computer, described algorithms as any set of instructions fed into a machine to solve a problem.[7] Put simply, algorithms describe how a computer can carry out the task you want it to do. They are expressed in a form called a program or software. They accept an input and produce an output. A text or an image that undergoes this kind of treatment, becomes a programmable object, or "softwareized".[8] Within the visual field, the question of representation and indexicality is threatened. Now, is the new image "real" or not? Some hardcore celluloid fetishists, like D.N. Rodowick, would even venture to say that "digital depictions are not 'images', at least in the ordinary sense of the term".[9] Even if digital imagining strives in most cases to be perceptually indistinguishable from the previous medium, namely, the photographic or photographic realism, the difference in the medium is crucial, and Rodowick's explanation is worth listening to even if I disagree with some of his more pessimistic and nostalgic conclusions.

In *The Virtual Life of Film*, Rodowick discusses the differences between the analog and the digital as two distinct ontologies. While the analog photochemical process is based on a principle of continuity between input and output, the information processing of the digital image is, ontologically speaking, based on a separation or discontinuity between input and output. Without this fundamental discontinuity, computer algorithms wouldn't work. "The ontology of information processing…is agnostic with respect to its output," as Rodowick phrases it.[10] It is the discontinuity between the input and the output that produces a new space for creativity and imagination – and chance and control. This space is addressed, not by light and shadow as in the photochemical process, but by computer algorithms, which carry out manipulations and alterations.

Algorithms is a key term here. Indeed, William Uricchio talks about today's "algorithmic turn" due to the new affordances of software such as photosynth. The "modern" *static* perspective, perfected by artists like Canaletto, isn't really challenged before the arrival of the "postmodern" *dynamic* and processual perspectives made possible by photosynth software, according to Uricchio.[11] But the algorithmic turn should also imply several elements of the less spectacular and the less visible. Alexander Galloway describes more generally *and* more specifically contemporary culture as an "algorithmic culture".[12] He uses the term to describe the culture of computer gaming as paradigmatic for understanding our new digital age. Video games are "informatic software" and belong to what he calls "algorithmic cultural objects".[13] Gaming is "oriented around understanding and executing specific algorithms".[14] In computer gaming, it is all about action and change. Each gesture, each action the player performs is connected to an algorithm. To Galloway, computer gaming becomes a metacritical reflection that reaches into the heart of computerized society.

Both Uricchio and Galloway make "processuality" and processing, that is, editing and otherwise manipulating existing digital images, central. Computer gaming, as an active intervention in the processual aspect of the technological image, becomes exemplary for the way more and more people interact, via algorithms, with available objects from our visual culture. Most of us do not write algorithms, we access them through application software. As I see it, playing around with digital editing software also is a "game" which is all about finding the best algorithm. Among the many well-known software packages are Adobe Photoshop and Final Cut Pro, which, in reality, consist of thousands of ready-made algorithms, and the user can activate these algorithms simply by importing an image and adding different layers or techniques using a variety of easily available tools to transform the image. The software industry even describes how their programs offer unique and robust graphics editing *experiences*. Some of the most advanced effects deal with manipulating the quality of the "medium" itself. Indeed, what we see on the screen – whether it is a digital image that looks like a painting (after the "fresco" effect is applied), a sculpture, a mosaic, a still photograph or an image which is somehow moving or is a combination of still and moving elements (easy with the programming language called Processing) – is now just an option inscribed by the algorithms. In other words, the photo/film divide, which was closely associated within the analog culture with certain stable substances or medium-specific qualities such as celluloid, paper or chemistry, has become radically problematized. Indeed, the *same* digital information can be instantiated visually, acoustically, or kinesthetically with the help of adequate programming algorithms; the information can be warped, streamed, or sampled, accelerated or slowed down, supersaturated or attenuated. Programmable objects can simulate any previous media object. We can, in other words, call the algorithmic culture a *transversal* culture, because it so easily creates lines of flight between or across different "old" media. Certain medium-specific qualities have become preliminary appearances easily available for alterations.

Algorithmic cultures address a new materialism that is not based in medium-specific divisions between photo and film or still and moving images, for example, but rather in mutable information codes. Within a coded environment, forms of appearance are optional and governed by the new machinic agency of the viewer/user. This is the new situation established by the computer and reinforced further by the Web's 2.0 culture, smarter software and more bandwidth. Film and photography are no longer medium-specific qualities, but are rather two of the ways that algorithms hide themselves. Significantly, we interact with the algorithms, but usually through an interface where the actual algorithmic instructions are hidden. As Galloway reminds us, now more than ever, the question is: *is what you see what you get?*[15] The answer to this fundamental question is both yes and no. The coexistence of both of these phenomenologically incommensurable positions addresses both the problem and the potential of the new algorithmic culture.

The New Ground of the Image

The German artist Andreas Müller-Pohle has explored the relationship between image and information in its many variants. A crucial narrative behind his largely conceptual image production is the transition from the analog to the digital. In one of his most famous series of works, *Digital Scores (after Nicephore Niepce)* from 1995, he has literally turned visual culture upside down by folding the computer language out of the black box (the machine) and into the white cube, the art gallery. In this piece, he reprocesses the information from the oldest existing photograph, Nicephore Niepce's so-called heliograph *View from the Window at Le Gras* from 1827. Niepce's heliography was made using a pewter plate coated with a solution of Bitumen of Judea, which was exposed in a camera for more than eight hours, then washed with oil of lavender and white petroleum to remove those parts of the bitumen not hardened by the light. To the left in the image, we see Niepce's pigeon house and to the right, a wing of the main building of his home. The light in this picture is magical. It is as if all of the normal shadows caused by the sun have been somehow erased. This is due to the fact that during the eight hours of exposure, the sun had crossed the sky and lit every object evenly. There is indeed *time* in this photograph, a time which encompasses a duration longer than most feature films.

In Andreas Müller-Pohle's *Digital Scores (after Nicephore Niepce)*, we no longer see Niepce's home or the pigeon house. The dots, the silver, the emulsion and the light are also gone. The visual information in the image has been turned into data, numerical representations. Müller-Pohle has taken the old image, the old medium of the heliograph, on a journey literally into the darkest corners of the digital machine. Niepce's heliograph (or at least the watercolor reproduction of it found in Helmut Gernsheim's 1983 *Geschichte der Photographie*) becomes a long winding digital code. Müller-Pohle displays the code on eight panels as a messy swarm of numbers and computational notations. Each panel represents one-eighth of one byte of memory. Niepce's eight hours of exposure has been transformed into eight panels of information. The time of the image has been spatialized into numeric code. In a gallery, the time of the image is "recaptured" as the time it takes to walk from one panel to the next.

Crucially, Müller-Pohle has reversed the image-making process and chosen to display the new matrix of the image. What kind of transformation are we witnessing? "We see not a photograph, but the new numerical rhetoric of photography", Geoffrey Batchen writes in a comment to this work.[16] However, this numerical rhetoric should not be confused with the old relational geometry used in the rhetoric of composition, which goes back to the time of Alberti. We are instead dealing with an attempt to display the language of the computer as the new language of the image. The visual aesthetic of the original photograph has been decisively displaced in favor of the machine's capacity to "remember" the image as numbers to be manipulated. The result fiercely demonstrates the fundamental anti-aesthetic hidden in the logic of the algorithmic culture. Contemporary image processing usually involves digital conversion and attunement at some stage in its process. If this process is arrested to reveal the codes conditioning these operations, as in Müller-Pohle's case, the impression will denigrate the image as we know it. Some would even say that an algorithmic culture involves a fundamental critique of the visual layer of our culture. If visual culture is reborn as programmable codes, it is, at the same time, non-visual. In a questionnaire on the future of visual culture studies, Laura U. Marks asserted, "I personally think that the period of visual culture is over. Thus it's ironic that all these programs in visual studies are starting up, just at a point when information culture, which is invisible, is becoming the dominant form of our culture."[17] Batchen thinks that information processing pushes us primarily into a kind of immaterialization:

> At least since 1989 and the introduction of Adobe Photoshop into the marketplace, photography has been in the words of the French philosopher Jean-François Lyotard, an *immatériel* ("the principle on which the operational structure is based is not that of a stable 'substance', but that of an unstable ensemble of interactions … the model of language"). Certainly, the identity of the photographic image no longer has to do with its support or its chemical composition, or with its authorship, place of origin, or pictorial appearance. It instead comprises, as Müller-Pohle suggests, a pliable sequence of digital data and electronic impulses. It is their configuration that now decides an image's look and significance, even the possibility of its continued existence. In other words, "photography" today is all about the reproduction and consumption, flow and exchange, maintenance and disruption, of data.[18]

I both agree and disagree with Batchen's radical conclusion. Since the initial stages of the digital revolution, we have learned that the immaterialization thesis of Lyotard and Batchen has its limitations. To a certain extent, it is due to a notion of programmability understood as conditioned by immateriality. It would be better to see the contemporary image as a technological object, which is processual. Even if digital photography comprises "a pliable sequence of digital data and electronic impulses", it still relies on a variable system of supports (capturing apparatuses with specific algorithms built in, software and hardware), which comprise the work process, or what Karl Marx would call "the hidden abode of production" where access is restricted or governed by what Friedrich Kittler has called "computeranalphabetismus".[19] Rather than Batchen and Lyotard's focus on the process of immaterialization with regard to digital media, we need this focus on a new materialism. In the hidden abode of contemporary production, the medium/matter distinction hasn't disappeared, but has simply been reorganized. We could use the distinction between the medium of storage and the medium of display as an illustration. Within analog culture, there is usually a causal relationship between storage and display, say between negative and print, but in algorithmic culture, the relationship has become not simply arbitrary, but dependent on the new interstice of software, or what I would call an algorithmically enabled work process. By using the term "algorithmic culture", I want to direct attention to this new and fundamental difference. An algorithmic culture is not an immaterial culture, but a factory where the work process abides in different layers of code and algorithms.

If we juxtapose the two images, the old Niepce heliograph and Müller-Pohle's *Digital Scores*, the question is, what controls the move or the transition between these two images? By using information theory, we can say that we see two types of information and two different types of media. They both direct attention toward a material substratum of production: dots in the case of Niepce and numbers in the case of Müller-Pohle. We move from dots to digits. If we formalize the impression we can put it this way: it is the same image, but represented differently. The first we would call a photograph, the second is a numerical representation of the photograph. The identity of media itself has changed fundamentally. Put more simply, we could say that in the case of Niepce, there is a causal relationship between storage and display, but in Müller-Pohle's case, the new storage medium of digital codes has itself become what is displayed. Müller-Pohle's experiment addresses the new "non-visual" layer of visual culture by arresting the technological nature of image processing at the stage "before" it becomes an image in the ordinary sense. He implicitly criticizes Bolter and Grusin's idea that the digital image essentially remediates earlier media, for example, realistic photography or analog film, but the heart of the matter is more complex: the diffusion of informatics within the production and recirculation of images actually – and essentially – negates and postpones the phenomenological output "level" of the image. In a paradoxical maneuver, Müller-Pohle displays the non-visual machinery of the before-the-image as a multiple, as eight potential images, as codes to be reprogrammed. The machinic ground of the image (codes and algorithms) has become a reservoir for a plurality of expressions.[20] The digital image becomes a new (non)ground for unprecedented spatio-temporal explorations.

The Image as Projectile

Ken Jacobs has used both analog and digital technologies in his found-footage film experiments. His TOM, TOM, THE PIPER'S SON (1969/1970) rephotographed Billy Bitzer's ten-minute silent short from 1905 into a 110-minute delayed exploration of the material. He uses what could be called an analog technique (rephotographing off the screen) to create a vertical effect. A recurring stylistic effect is namely the ways in which he digs deeply into each frame of the film to excavate the hidden life of the grain of the image.[21] Jacobs' film is widely recognized as a classic structural film and was added to the US National Film Registry by the Library of Congress in 2007. In 2008, Jacobs reworked Bitzer's old short with the aid of digital tools. He calls this version, RETURN TO THE SCENE OF THE CRIME. This time he limits it to reworking the film's short opening scene where the pig is stolen. However, this version is 93 minutes long, but instead of digging deeply into the frames in a vertical manner, he uses a technique that is comparative and horizontal. It is not primarily the grain of the image that he studies here; his comparative analysis of images and sequences often juxtaposes images or a series of images in different technical (digital) attires. In a fabulous sequence, the juggler's balls are transformed into still images "captured" from different fractions of the opening scene (fig. 1). It is as if the whole opening scene is folded into a spectacular explosion of past and present moments, creating an intensive time-space. The juggler scene suddenly comes to a halt, is then run backwards and then forward again. The sequence intensifies time and space in ways that eclipse the analog version of the same material.

Fig. 1. Still from Ken Jacobs's RETURN TO THE SCENE OF THE CRIME *(2008)*

These intensities have been further explored by Jacobs' student Gregg Biermann, who also refashions found footage, often using Hitchcock classics. I call his works "software cinema" because they so insistently explore a found sequence of film images according to a preprogrammed software feature or "spe-

Fig. 2. Still from Gregg Biermann's LABYRINTHINE *(2010)*

cial effect". In LABYRINTHINE (2010) Biermann works with 41 memorable and iconographic shots in Hitchcock's classic VERTIGO (1958). The shots are superimposed on top of each other, creating a hypnotic labyrinth of repetitions and transformations (fig. 2). The different moments overlap in a kind of contrapunctual proliferation lasting 15 minutes. This superimposition of images is unlike how we remember it from the classical (analog) techniques, where the images are partly transparent. The images are composite sequences of concentric rectangles. The rectangular screen no longer frames one shot at a time, rather, the screen becomes a theatre for a multiplicity of images where each new shot is born within the previous shot as a new rectangle, which gradually increase in size and finally covers the last shot. As it grows, new shots are born within the shot and this goes on according to a rhythmical scheme where each shot is repeated four or five times. As the film develops, several series of shots overlap. Cinematic motion as the movement of objects in space *within* the image is here competing with the movement *between* blocks of floating images. The blocks float like moving pictures *through* the screen like an approaching bullet or projectile. Ultimately, a labyrinth of movements appears both within the image (the image within the image) and between the images (the changing relationship between the images within the image). Continuity editing is replaced by a discontinuous and labyrinthine editing process, and the screen no longer displays one image at a time, but several.

   In spite of the rhythmical slowness of the floating concentric rectangles, it is sometimes confusing to distinguish between them as if this virtual multiplicity of time folding images *indexes* in intangible ways the constant confusion and dizziness of the protagonist of the film, Scottie (James Stewart) – and the viewer – who both are sometimes unable to distinguish between the different women (the woman remembered and the woman seen) as played by Kim Novak. Biermann's hypnotic repetition and manipulation of the characteristic soundtrack together with the "floating" iconography of the film highlights the entire repertoire of genres at play in VERTIGO, which itself floats in between a detective mystery thriller, a romantic melodrama and a horror movie. Most of the shots are of Scottie as he is observing or thinking; he hardly moves during these sequences. The images have a stuttering and discontinuous logic that arrests and focuses on perceptual phenomena, which slips away when we view the film. Biermann opens these intervals of the imperceptible, enlarges them and turns them into an art form of their own. It is as if he is using the technologically enhanced quality of the images to explore the optical unconscious in a way never envisioned by Walter Benjamin.

Fig. 3. Still from Gregg Biermann's SPHERICAL COORDINATES *(2005)*

This feature of the unconscious is taken to a different vein in SPHERICAL COOR-DINATES (2005), which remakes a short scene from Hitchcock's PSYCHO. Here, we concentrate on Janet Leigh who is driving. The image twists, bends, folds and turns around (sometimes still, sometimes moving) as she steers the wheel (fig. 3). "The camera moves in a variety of ways, examining the inside of a 3D animated sphere on the inside of which a scene from PSYCHO is wrapped", explains Biermann.[22] It is as if a camera is analyzing the manipulation of the image itself. SPHERICAL COORDINATES and LABYRINTHINE foreground the digital imaging tools in ways that turn the films into sensitive systems. He manipulates well-known found footage, that is, he intervenes in our memory, a collective system where images have become "emoticons" of sorts, and alters the very threads of this system. The exploration of abnormal movements between the still and the moving image create a system of post-cinematic "emoticons" mapping and altering the coordinates of a sensitive system which is collective or more than human.

The Time of Technology

These new spatio-temporal explorations seem to reveal a new potential for the visual. We need to question the relationship between images and the body, between the inhuman and the human in new ways. I will show how Mark B.N. Hansen does this with regards to the digital image, but first, Rodowick's critique of the digital image. He laments the inability of the digital image to convey an experience of time passing, and he continues:

> It might be clarifying at this point to insist on the rather radical point that in the digital universe there is no cinema, no photography, no images, and no sounds. The cosmogony of computers only recognizes symbolic notation and algorithmic operations, and is totally agnostic as to outputs. We are used to thinking of images on the model of painting or photography, as limited extensions of space present to us as a whole, and we want to think of digital or electronic "images" in this familiar way. But an electronic image is not "one" – it is never wholly present to us because screens are being constantly refreshed and rewritten. And again, the code writing this output to the screen can just as easily take the form of text, a sound, or an abstract symbolic notation. This is why I say in *The Virtual Life of Film* that the reconstitution of an image from digital information is something like making a very detailed painting from the information given in a very precise description. Or, to refer to a wonderful early text by Roland Barthes, digital "photography" cannot be considered as a "message without a code" – it is only code and nothing else.[23]

Rodowick poses a radical opposition between the analog and the digital image. He asserts that the radical otherness of the digital image creates a "naming crisis". We need a new name for the image, or for the no-longer-an-image-as-we-used-to-know-it. In *The Virtual Life of Film*, Rodowick argues that the specific quality of the analog image resides in the fact that it conveys a unique impression of time passing due to the fact that there is a causal relationship between input (the time of shooting) and output (projection). The digital image essentially lacks this causal relationship. Its multiplicity resides in its discontinuity between input and output. Furthermore, Rodowick establishes a causal relationship between the technical quality of the image and a certain mode of experience. One image conveys a certain experience of time, another does not. Significantly, Hansen establishes a similar causal relationship between technology and experience, but he reaches the opposite conclusion.

> As I see it, digitization requires us to reconceive the correlation between the user's body and the image in an even more profound manner. It is not simply that the image provides a tool for the user to control the "infoscape" of contemporary material culture, as Manovich [and Rodowick] suggests, but rather that the "image" has itself become a process, and, as such, has become irreducibly bound up with the body.[24]

Hansen's new embodied understanding of the digital image relies on a concept of affectivity, which he describes as "the capacity of the body to experience itself as 'more than itself' and thus to deploy its sensory-motor power to create the unpredictable, the experimental, the new" (7). Both Hansen and Rodowick use a modern phenomenology to posit their argument, but their phenomenology seems to be based on two different conceptions of technology and the self. To Rodowick, the analog image becomes a time traveler negotiating between two experiences of time, but the digital image is unable to capture this experience of duration because it is never "wholly present to us"; it is merely a contingent configuration of numerical values where an indexical basis is replaced by a continual scanning or updating, he would assert. Hansen, on the other hand, seeks to implicate the process of image making itself as a certain time of technology where information is "made perceivable through embodied experience" in new ways.[25]

Upon viewing Biermann's LABYRINTHINE, both Hansen and Rodowick offer significant insights into the analysis of the experience. On the one hand, Hitchcock's VERTIGO is replaced by a new "feel" of the image. The film no longer carries the same kind of aura as we experienced in the original theatrical release. However, the ground of this aura (its originary memory impact, so to speak) is addressed as a malleable nervous system (both emotional and visual). Rather than a photochemical "index", the experience of computer-generated image processing opens up the potential for a new experience of the film as a way of *indexing* the changing vocation of the life of the new media image itself. This new opening relates less (or not at all, as Rodowick would perhaps contend) to the kind of time or duration at play in an analog image, but it foregrounds a new technicity of the image which exposes time as a non-human nervous system or a becoming. In other words, the loss of a certain "feeling" of "human" time (Rodowick) may be the necessary condition for the new image to produce the mode of affective experience addressed by Hansen.

Kaleidoscope

The multiplicity of the digital image can be studied even more dramatically in the work by new media artists such as Mario "Quasimodo" Klingemann. He experiments with new algorithms and software on his website, which can be downloaded or simply interacted with. Some, like his piece *Kaleidoscope*, are pieces of software that can accept a painting or a still photograph as an input and a moving or an interactive image as an output. As soon as one engages with *Kaleidoscope*, the website takes complete control of the user's mouse and keyboard. Each key instantiates an algorithm, which alters the image. The old film/photo divide is deconstructed and integrated into a playful structure of interactivity. The viewer becomes a player interacting or infecting the image itself with movement. When the Web site is opened, *Kaleidoscope* presents a stilled wheel with images of a woman. The image is based on J.H. Lynch's drawing "Autumn Leaves". Once you click on the image, the keyboard is activated and "she" begins to move according to the following parameters:

[1] – start/stop rotation 1
[2] – start/stop rotation 2
[3] – start/stop rotation 3
[4] – toggle flip tiles
[+]/[-] – more/less tiles
[q]/[w] – rotation 1 speed
[a]/[s] – rotation 2 speed
[y]/[x] – rotation 3 speed
[e] – reset rotation 1 speed
[d] – reset rotation 2 speed
[c] – reset rotation 3 speed
[UP]/[DOWN] – zoom in/out
[m]/[n] – spiral offset
[o] – reset spiral offset
[5]/[6] – shearing 1
[7]/[8] – shearing 2.[26]

The process of interacting with the image is inseparable from what Hansen calls affectivity. This is an experimental becoming where the body of the player deploys "its sensory-motor power to create the unpredictable, the experimental, the new".[27] We don't view the image, we play with it, and each action activates an algorithm which instantiates a certain move and a certain speed of the image, as well as simulated camera moves. However, the algorithms also reveal themselves in the transitions between arrest and motion and in between different motions, etc. This kind of interaction with what looks like a still image is a feature of many of Klingemann's web installations, such as several of his so-called *Incubator* sketches, like *Rubber Screen*.

Klingemann's generative art work *Flickeur* is a software-based "machine" which intervenes or interacts with the database Flickr.com. Once the user/viewer presses play, *Flickeur* will randomly begin to retrieve images from Flickr.com and create an infinite "film" with a style that can vary between stream-of-consciousness, documentary or video clip. All the blends, motions, zooms or time leaps are completely random. *Flickeur* works, according to Klingemann, "like a looped magnetic tape where incoming images from Flickr.com will merge with older materials and be influenced by the older recordings' magnetic memory. The virtual tape will also play and record forward and backward to create another layer of randomness."[28] Klingemann actually programs a series of random errors and glitches to simulate the appearance of the wear and tear of a filmstrip or a magnetic band being over-written.[29] These marks and the nerve-wracking soundtrack sometimes turn the material into a very suggestive horror story. Here, www.flickr.com, which is one of the largest user-based digital photo archives in the world, is transformed into a thriller.

One could argue that the examples in this article are not representative of what we call the digital image. I think we need to go beyond many of the most popular theories about the digital image, such as Bolter's and Grusin's notion that new media basically remediates older media.[30] This is, as I have shown, insufficient. Rodowick, Hansen and Manovich's approaches (despite their internal disagreements) seem more promising. If we take into account that the characteristics of the digital image essentially reside in its processual aspects rather than in its product aspects, the examples in this chapter are exemplary. New media tools can be used to analyze old media in the fashion preferred by Laura Mulvey, but ultimately the digital image as envisioned by Hansen and Rodowick, and demonstrated by Müller-Pohle, Jacobs, Biermann and Klingemann, speak of a different image. It is connected to a new technical matrix, an algorithmic culture, which interrupts the image not to analyze it in its unique singularity, but to give birth to a potential multiplicity which is always more than one – and ready to change.

Thank you to Harald Østgaard Lund, Arthur Tennøe, Matthias Bruhn and James Elkins for useful comments.

Notes

1. See D.N Rodowick, *The Virtual Life of Film* (Cambridge, MA: Harvard University Press, 2007).
2. Stanley Cavell, *The World Viewed* enlarged ed. (Cambridge, MA: Harvard University Press, 1979), ix.
3. Laura Mulvey, *Death 24x a Second: Stillness and the Moving Image* (London: Reaktion Books, 2006), 7.
4. Ibid., 146.
5. See, for example, the works of Henry Jenkins, Thomas Elsaesser and David Bordwell, who basically agree on the fact that Hollywood's way of narrating stays the same, but more significantly, they agree that Hollywood can narrate films with greater complexity and oddness due to computer-generated imaging and further, they can expand their narratives through what Jenkins calls the business of "transmedia". See Jenkins, *Convergence Culture: Where Old and New Media Collide* (New York: New York University Press, 2006) and Thomas Elsaesser, "The Digital Paradox", unpublished lecture, 2010.
6. Manovich, *The Language of New Media* (Cambridge, MA: MIT Press, 2001).
7. As Les Goldschlager and Andrew Lister write in their classic textbook on computer science: The algorithm "is the unifying concept for all the activities which computer scientists engage in" (Goldschlager and Lister, *Computer Science: A Modern Introduction* (New York: Prentice Hall, 1988), 1.
8. Manovich, *Software Takes Command*. Available at http://www.manovich.net/ (accessed July 12, 2010).
9. D.N. Rodowick, *The Virtual Life of Film* (Cambridge, MA: Harvard University Press, 2007) 110.
10. Ibid.,130.
11. William Uricchio: "The Algorithmic Turn: Photosynth, Augmented Reality and the Changing Implications of the Image" (unpublished manuscript).
12. See Alexander Galloway, *Gaming: Essays on Algorithmic Culture* (Minneapolis: University of Minnesota Press, 2006).
13. Galloway, *Gaming*, 6.
14. Ibid., 14.
15. Alexander Galloway. "What You Get Is What You See" in *The Archive in Motion. New Conceptions of the Archive in Contemporary Thought and New Media Practices.* Nota bene: Studies from the National Library of Norway, E. Røssaak (ed.) (Oslo: Novus, 2010).
16. Geoffrey Batchen, *Each Wild Idea: Writing, Photography, History* (Cambridge, MA: MIT Press, 2002) 177.
17. Margaret Dikovitskaya, "An interview with Laura U. Marks". In Margaret Dikovitskaya, *Visual Culture: A Study of the Visual After the Cultural Turn.* (Cambridge, MA: MIT Press, 2005), p. 215-216.
18. Batchen, *Each Wild Idea*, 179.
19. Friedrich Kittler, "Computeranalphabetismus" in F. Kittler, *Short Cuts* (Frankfurt am Main: Zweitausendeins, 2002), 109-133.

20. I play here upon Jean-Luc Nancy's *The Ground of the Image* (New York: Fordham University Press, 2005). He talks about the ground (*fond*) of the image as that which "appears as what it is by disappearing" (p. 7). In the algorithmic culture, the ground of the image must be rethought, because the ground no longer "passes entirely into the image" as Nancy asserts. An important philosophical inspiration for me has been Gille Deleuze's idea about multiplicity as a complex structure that does not refer to a prior unity, but rather *is* a becoming. The digital image and even more so, the generative art image, is exemplary as a "sensory becoming": "sensory becoming is otherness caught in a matter of expression" (Deleuze and Guattari, *What is Philosophy?* (London: Verso, 1994), 177).

21. This is analyzed more fully in E. Røssaak: *The Still/Moving Image: Cinema and the Arts* (Saarbrücken: Lambert Academic Press, 2010).

22. Biermann quoted from his website, http://www.greggbiermann.com/spherical.htm (last accessed September 10, 2010).

23. Rodowick. "Thinking Virtual", lecture at University of Chicago, April 6, 2010.

24. Hansen, *New Philosophy for New Media* (Cambridge, MA: MIT Press) 10.

25. Ibid.

26. Listed on the website: http://www.quasimondo.com/archives/000579.php (last accessed October 10, 2010).

27. Hansen, p. 7.

28. Klingemann on http://www.quasimondo.com/archives/000579.php (last accessed October 10, 2010).

29. "I use the term 'Magnetic' more as a Metaphor to describe what a theoretical machine would work like if I'd be able to rebuild the software engine behind flickeur as a physical real-world model.... The equivalent of the 'magnetic tape' inside my program is just an area in the computer's memory (RAM). And since computers are unfortunately mostly perfect when it comes to reading and writing to memory I have to introduce the glitches and errors myself that happen when old data is merged with new data (image data in this case). For that purpose I have written a library of bitmap manipulation algorithms that try to create a big variety of visual effects. What was very important for me here is that I want the computer to be able to surprise me with unexpected visual output. Also there is the issue that computers cannot generate true randomness by themselves – there are random number generators but those are still all based on mathematical formulas which will create the same sequence of numbers for a given seed number. So the true randomness in this case comes from the outside in the form of the images. An image in a computer is just a big list of numbers and even though in a normal picture those numbers have a certain order they still can be considered as 'random' since looking at just a single pixel or number in an image it would be impossible to say what the next number will be." Klingemann in an email to the author, October 22, 2010.

30. Bolter and Grusin, *Remediation: Understanding New Media* (Cambridge, MA: MIT Press, 1999).

Archives in Between

"The Archives of the Planet" and Montage: The Movement of the Crowd and "the Rhythm of Life"

Trond Lundemo

The French-Jewish banker Albert Kahn (1860-1940) created his *"les Archives de la planète"* in the period 1908 to 1931 using color photography, film and, to a lesser extent, black-and-white photography and stereography. This means that this archive, conceptually as well as its physical holdings, depends on connections and divisions between still and moving images. The intersections between the still and the moving depict a constituting heterogeneity in the archive after the introduction of time-based media. These changes towards the storage of movement in the media architecture of the archive accommodate and coincide with the entrance of the anonymous and the everyday into the visible. The entrance of the masses into the "archives of the planet" is conditioned by the very same techniques as those that will eventually make the modes of everyday life stored there disappear. In this text, I propose that these constellations of media could lead to a different understanding of montage in an age of the archive; one based on gaps and dissociations between images and media as well as their intersections. This can perhaps be seen as a "montage at a distance", or a "soft montage":[1] one that is present as a possibility in the future and still to be concluded. It offers the material conditions for montage without its execution, and is consequently always a "montage to come". The configuration of visual media in the Albert Kahn archive is designed, as in any archive, with a future use in mind. The archival image becomes the object of future connections between images, instead of being restricted to playing a role in a single, fixed work. This, in turn, has consequences for how one thinks about the position of the moving image in archival constructions and its relation to history.

Albert Kahn was one of Europe's richest men as a consequence of his investments in diamond mines in South Africa and in Japan's emerging economy at the turn of the 20th century.[2] His philanthropic interests were formed by the colonialism and pacifism of his time: he was part of the intellectual life of France and a close friend of Henri Bergson. *"Les Archives de la planète"* was begun in late 1908 when Albert Kahn made a trip around the world. While visiting the United States, Japan and China, he had his chauffeur take photographs and films of the trip. This material is included in the archive, and, for this reason, marks the inception of 'les archives de la planète' by shaping its conceptualization. After this trip, Kahn decided to create an archive of the planet as an "inventory of the surface of the globe inhabited and developed by man as it presents itself at the start of the 20th century in order to fix once and for all the practices, the aspects and the modes of human activity, whose fatal disappearance is only a question of time" (my emphasis).[3] He appointed Jean Brunhes, an important researcher in the developing discipline of cultural geography, as the director of the archive, and between 1912 and 1931, Kahn financed cameramen who travelled to more than 50 countries around the world to make this inventory.[4] When the collection process finally came to an end 1932, due to Albert Kahn's bankruptcy in the wake of the stock market crash, it comprised 72,000 autochromes (a new color photography process on glass plates invented by Louis Lumière in 1907), 183,000 meters of film (over 100 hours of projection) and 4000 stereographs.[5] There are also some 4000 black-and-white photographs, but their role in the archive appears to be secondary in comparison to the other technologies used. A small part of the film footage was acquired from newsreel companies, and was not shot by the Kahn cameramen. The archive was kept intact after Kahn's bankruptcy and even survived the occupation of France shortly after Kahn's death in 1940, probably because it was considered to be of little or no financial value. Almost all of the film material is stored as unedited shots, as it was never exploited commercially, and only small parts of the material were ever spliced together for use in Jean Brunhes' courses at the Collège de France.

As to the question of who was the "director" of these films and photographs, we have to think in terms other than the traditional hierarchies of director, producer and cameraman in the film industry. Kahn was only present at the shooting during his trip around the world and on the shots that took place in his mansion and his garden in Boulogne on the outskirts of Paris. He did, however, appoint Jean Brunhes as director because he understood the project as connected to the emerging discipline of cultural geography. Kahn maintained an important role in the decision-making process regarding whom to hire as cameramen and he had the final say in where to send them. Kahn's role clearly exceeded that of instigator and financial backer of the enterprise. The many dignitaries invited to Kahn's home were filmed and photographed, and it seems that the decisions about which people and which geographical places should be included in the archive were largely his. There is little evidence of what orders were given to the cameramen and by whom, but it remains clear that the images from different places look stylistically coherent and similar in framing, distance, etc. These decisions were probably made in collaborations between Kahn, Brunhes and the experienced cameramen they hired, and the stylistic unity of the material makes it evident that there were directions given to the cameramen to secure a certain homogeneity in the framing, camera movements and the distance to people in the films as well as in the color photographs. Part of the explicit ideological background of the archive was to show the universality of mankind within the disparate cultures documented by the new technologies.[6]

Much of the research on this archive has been concerned with its role as a source of history, and has been devoted to identifying the events, people and places documented. Film scholars like Tom Gunning, Paula Amad, François de la Breteque and Teresa Castro have analyzed its film archive and its position within film history, particularly in relation to the documentary tradition. Tom Gunning has identified the footage as largely belonging to a pre-documentary "view" aesthetic, whereas Paula Amad refers to it as an anthology of film styles.[7] Teresa Castro has sought to save the material from 'the primitive mode' by inferring a mental montage already anticipated in the shots while de la Bretèque relates it to various movements in non-fiction cinema, like the films of Lumière as well as those of Vertov and the European avant-garde.[8] Amad has approached the archive from the perspective of its representation of transient, everyday events, claiming it to be a "counter-archive" because of the privilege it accords to the anonymous and the everyday.[9] In her outstanding recent monograph on the archive, she situates the "counter-archival" in a Bergsonist reading of cinematic memory.[10]

The tendency of the research on this archive has been to focus on single events or on one medium, and few scholars, with the notable exception of Paula Amad, have approached the theoretical questions emerging from the use of multi-media. This discussion will focus on the configuration of the media in the archive. Kahn's project is interesting from an analytical point of view regarding the "connections" between the moving image and other media in this physical archive as well as in the "archive" as a theoretical concept. The role of the moving image within larger media environments can also be approached in a contemporary context through Kahn's archive, as it is currently being digitized and made available as a database called FAKIR (Fonds Albert-Kahn Informatisée pour la Recherche).

There are three properties of the Archives of the Planet that makes it of particular interest to questions of media configurations in the archive:
- Firstly, it is not a collection of existing films and photographs, even if Kahn at some points augmented his collection by acquiring existing newsreel footage from Pathé or other newsreel companies. It differs, in this respect, from many of the discussions of the day about archiving existing films as historical sources. Kahn's archive is not a collection of existing films and photographs as a source of knowledge, but seeks to acquire knowledge through the act of shooting. Film is a *means* to make "an inventory of the surface of the globe", and not the object of collection itself. This idea of the recording of

a culture poses stylistic questions about distance, angles, framing, movement etc., but also about how the relations *between* the media are designed and conceived.

— Secondly, the film material was (with few exceptions) never edited together. This means that it was not given a narrative or a persuasive force through editing, but remained as raw shots, 'rushes', with the whole of the shots length intact. The montage of shots and intersections of media remained to be decided, as possible connections, and consequently open to future re-arrangements. This aspect of the Kahn films clearly sets them apart from the newsreel tradition that emerged during that period (*Pathé Journal* in 1908 and *Gaumont Actualités* in 1910).

— Thirdly, Kahn's archival impulse was formed by the anticipation of an approaching catastrophe, or at least of the disappearance of the cultures and social life, the signs of which he was collecting. Kahn made an archive for the time to come, after many of the cultures and modes of social life documented had ceased to exist. It was only then that this raw material could receive a reading, a montage.[11]

Throughout the 20 years the material was collected, Kahn remained with the multiple media model of films and autochromes. In addition, about 4000 stereoscopic plates were collected in the early years, and according to the Albert Kahn Museum exhibition, a phonograph was brought along for Kahn's first trip, but was never replaced after it was broken during the first part of the journey. Why did the archive keep with this media architecture? If these media were understood as true slices of reality, wouldn't the autochromes be sufficient? Or just the films? The media used in the archive demonstrates that none of them could give a full and accurate account of any one event. Kahn equipped his photographers and cinematographers with both still and moving image cameras because they complement each other. The visual modes of these techniques store different things, and are consequently techniques for the selection of information: color photography lacks movement, films lack not only color (except for the color film footage shot in the late 1920s) but also that frozen moment in time. Films were an essential part of the archive, however. In the phrasing of Jean Brunhes, the director of the archive, "the precious discovery of cinema adds to the form the expression of movement itself, that is the rhythm of life".[12]

This points to an important factor in the discussion of cinema as well as of the role of the image in the archive at the time. If Boleslas Matuszewski was already in 1898 arguing that films were "a new source of history",[13] the post-Gutenberg Galaxy archive, where sound is stored as sound and visual events as moving images, produces an awareness that what is seen is different from what is said, that texts tell other stories than images. The heterogeneity of the archive is a key feature of the *Aufschreibesysteme* of 1900, as analyzed by Friedrich Kittler in *Grammophon, Film, Typewriter*.[14] It is an archive of gaps, cracks and contradictions, where knowledge is produced by putting fragments together. In a very valuable discussion of Kahn's project from the perspective of the history of archive theory, Paula Amad asserts that the Kahn archive used film and photography in a synthesizing approach, and she refers to Ricciotto Canudo's view of cinema as a synthesis of the other arts ("the Sixth Art" (1911)) as a theoretical program for the collection.[15] However, the role of film in Kahn's project is a different one. Various media were used because they have different qualities, and consequently also different shortcomings. Film is not the synthesis of the other arts in this collection of media, since the moving image would have sufficed by itself.

It would be logical if film and photography were used for different purposes in the archive, for different kinds of events. However, this doesn't seem to be the case. At least, what one would expect a division by media – for instance, that photography would be for portraits, individuals, landscapes and things with less movement, while film would be used for fast or steadily moving objects – but this expectation was soon proven to be wrong. The Archives of the Planet often used film to make portraits of people and it used autochromes to show parades and moving objects, with the result being blurred images due to slow exposure speeds in the color process. It is striking how often the two media show the same things from a similar viewpoint. A city scene or a person in a given setting are often "recorded" twice; once in color and once in movement. The fact that the same events are photographed twice results in a division between film and photography, demonstrating that Kahn, Jean Brunhes and their cameramen didn't suffer from the illusion that cinema was the complete or "total medium".

Crowds

Kahn wanted to make an "inventory of the surface of the globe inhabited and developed by man…" This surface of the globe had only become visible with the emergence of photography, with a new kind of description in the literature of Flaubert and Balzac, and only came fully into view with the moving image. The movement of the crowd into light is accompanied by cinema, since it captures "the rhythm of life", as Brunhes claimed. The introduction of the moving image is closely linked to the entrance of the anonymous population into the visible, as it became possible to include visual events in the archive. Of course, Michel Foucault's account of the penal and medical discourses describes this movement into the visible as occurring somewhere *early* in the 19th century.[16] However, with the moving image as an object of storage and repetition, this "entrance of the population into light" takes on a new dimension, as is amply demonstrated by the films in the Archives of the Planet. As I will shortly return to, it may also simultaneously anticipate the reversal of this very movement, towards a retreat from visibility.

When Siegfried Kracauer in his 1960 *Theory of Film* discusses cinema as "the Establishment of Physical Existence", he interestingly devotes much attention to "the big" among "things normally unseen".[17] The crowd, or in his phrasing, 'The Masses', is such a large phenomenon that it demands a new optic to properly capture it:

> At the time of its emergence, the mass, this giant animal, was a new and upsetting experience. As might be expected, the traditional arts proved unable to encompass and render it. Where they failed, photography easily succeeded; it was technically equipped to portray crowds as the accidental agglomerations they are. Yet only film, the fulfillment of photography in a sense, was equal to the task of capturing them in motion. In this case, the instrument of reproduction came into being almost simultaneously with one of its main subjects. Hence the attraction which masses exerted on still and motion picture cameras from the outset.[18]

Kracauer goes on to mention the films of Lumière, early Italian cinema, D.W. Griffith and "the Russians", and then turns to the question of montage. Kracauer's account of the history of media is worth further attention here: Firstly, cinema supplies still photography with motion, with the "rhythm of life", to use Jean Brunhes's words. The movement of the mass is portrayed as a supplement to photography, a redemption of the movement of physical reality. This results in an account of media constellations as fluent transitions from one level to the next in a progression of technologies. If Kracauer places the emergence of photography and film more or less at the same time – "they came into being almost simultaneously with" the crowd – it is probably because early photography didn't have the capacity to "capture" the movement of the crowd. The images would become blurred, just as in the autochrome process. Instantaneous photography wasn't technically available until later in the century. With the higher levels of light sensitivity that allow for shorter exposure times, we are already on the way towards chronophotography, so often portrayed as something that smoothly led to the movement of film in traditional cinema histories. This is probably the background for Kracauer's conflation between the time of the "coming into being" of photography and film.

This account of matters, besides the obvious problems connected with teleological historical narratives, conflates what is so interesting in the composition of media divisions in the Kahn archive: the differences between the still and the moving. Kracauer, towards the end of his book, continues: "Where photography ends, film, much more inclusive, takes over".[19] Jean Brunhes's view, "the precious discovery of cinema adds to the form the expression of movement itself, that is the rhythm of life", also portrays media differences as a simple addition, securing a seemingly fluent transition from the still to the moving in the archive. Just as the accounts of the famous Lumière screening at Grand Café in 1895 tell us that it started with the projection of a still image that suddenly burst into motion, redeeming the movement of the masses leaving the Lumière factory, it proposes a media genealogy that obliterates the coexistence and, hence, the differences between the still and the time-based image in the archive. In practice, however, the Kahn archive displays the gaps and tensions that exist between still photography and the moving image in the archive.

Another property of Kracauer's account is that it sees in cinema technology the very condition for its subject – the masses. At least, the "instrument of reproduction came into being simultaneously with one of its main subjects". If Kracauer here makes a connection between social life and technology, he doesn't establish a causal relationship. However, as is made clear by Walter Benjamin and other Frankfurt School theorists, the masses, as a part of the social technologies of industrialization and urbanization, were constituted well before the introduction of cinematography. This is exactly the reason why filmmakers Jean-Luc Godard and Harun Farocki suggest that cinema "came too late" to have any influence on the formation of the political life of high capitalism. When cinema was introduced at the end of the 19th century, the political, social and economic structures of Fordist capitalism was already established and implemented.

Jacques Rancière gives another account of the genealogy of the visible crowd, when he claims that it was literature, and not cinema, that shed light on the masses. It was the attention to the infinitely small detail, the grain of dust, the anonymous people and the everyday routine in the works of Flaubert, Balzac, Dostoyevsky and Zola that made the masses visible. Rancière goes even further to say that it was this turn in literature that made photography and especially cinema accepted as an art form, and not only as a technique.[20] Cinema only gives a physical image to a visibility that has already been established through literary description, and consequently he has no reason to lament cinema's belated arrival on the scene of the masses.

The consequences of Rancière's assessment regarding the issue of technicity are huge. It would, for instance, imply that the rupture in the archive from a place that stores texts to one that also encompasses time-based media is diminished. The 19th-century novel and cinema describe different kinds of movement, however. These differences could be investigated through various perspectives, as that of montage, of psychotechnics or intermedial configurations.

Cinema is connected to other media in different ways than the literature that came before it, or the digital that came after. Also on a very basic material level, the movement of the crowd in literature is of a different kind than in cinema. The intermittent movement of the film strip through the camera and the projector belongs to a different logic of time and space than literary description. Giorgio Agamben has observed how gestures are submitted to an intermittent, jerky logic at the end of the 19th century, and that cinema offers a new gestural regime.[21] This is what makes cinema ethical and political besides its aesthetical dimensions, according to Agamben. Rancière, instead, sees the movement of the masses abstracted from technology. This indistinction between modes of movement in different technical media is also a common shortcoming in today's analysis of the conversion from cinematic movement to digital video compression, where many consider digital technology only as a means of access to a 'content'. We should instead speak of different 'rhythms of life' in these cases.

In order to examine the issue of media configuration further, it is interesting to note how the Kahn archive was seen as an undertaking that depended on the new technologies of color photography and cinema in order to *fix* the modes of human activity. The *dispositifs* are clearly seen as the condition for the subjects of the archive, the crowd and everyday life, but they are also the agents of this "disappearance, which is only a matter of time". The technologies that make the crowd and everyday life visible are also the tools of globalization. It is well known how the Lumière brothers, in particular but also their various competitors, sent cameramen to many countries around the world in the months following the introduction of the Cinematograph to shoot material in these places. They also organized screenings of material from other places while they were there. Cinema and sound recordings are part of a powerful globalization movement at the turn of the 20th century.

Kahn's archive does not only use the technologies that make the crowd visible, but also the ones that homogenize it. Cinema and photography are part of a larger network of world-encompassing techniques of control that regulated the local as part of a global system. Kahn's inventory of the cultures of the world cooperates with the standardization of time, telephone networks, world fairs and new means of travel to allow the local modes of life to adapt to a worldwide system of representation. The tools for capturing the modes of human activity are simultaneously the tools that make them disappear through economic, technological and social change. This is the disappearance that Kahn himself is stating as the reason for creating the archive. There is clearly a sense of loss in Kahn's archival impulse, as the disappearance of the modes of life are only a question of time, but there are no real signs of nostalgia on Kahn's part. His various philanthropic projects strove to create a better world of universal understanding and cooperation.

By fixing the existing modes of human life for the future, one also brings them to an end; such is the paradoxical logic of the archive. This is consistent with the archival function of selecting what to include as the past: This selection inevitably turns the present into the past. The double temporality of Kahn's, and probably any, archive, is that by collecting and storing material, it prepares for the end of what it stores. Its end is the only reason for archiving it. To fix an image of an event or a place is, ultimately, to make it disappear. These properties of the archive become especially acute and interesting in the multiple media model of Kahn's project, since it is constructed on the separation between movement and stillness. The time-based image continually supplements, contradicts and refers to the still image, thus accenting the heterogeneity of the post-Gutenberg archive. The ephemeral moment of film is contrasted with the immobile, and "the rhythm of life" is stilled in the encapsulated moment of the autochromes. Both modes of inscription fix a time lost, but based on different temporalities.

The end of the various modes of life in the face of globalizing modernity is not identical to the decline of the masses, however.[22] In the process of industrialization of non-Western societies, life has become increasingly regulated according to new structures of working time and leisure, housing principles are reconstructed, etc., while the crowd remains the dominant figure of social life. The masses become described, measured and visualized in photography, sound recordings and cinema. The masses survive this first wave of globalization, as documented and thereby accelerated in the creation of the Archives of the Planet. As I will note later, a gradual process of dispersal of the masses began after the Second World War. In the move away from the enclosing institutions of what Foucault described as a disciplinary society, represented by the agglomeration of people in schools, hospitals, factories and prisons, towards a 'society of control', processes of individuation are transformed at a range of levels.[23] In short, globalization in 1900 propelled the masses into the visible, whereas the 2000 version disperses these same masses into individual reception and representation, as epitomized by television, the personal computer and the Internet.

Modernity makes the end of the existing modes of life only a matter of time. The global transformation of the local is the driving force of the archive, as it anticipates the end of these life forms. Kahn's archival impulse lies with the approaching end, an invisible and unspoken element that nonetheless conditions what is stored. This is an invisible element of the archive that is apprehended and anticipated through the phantom of the crowd in the autochromes. The long exposure time of the color process blurs the masses in motion, rendering the fleeting presence of people as transparent spots in the image. This encapsulates the "media theory" of the Archives of the Planet. Film and photography are not a full record of any event or any form of life, but rather a temporal lack, producing specters of what once was. This is an archive for a future still to come, where these cultures and modes of social life would have been irretrievably lost. This apprehension of an unknown future invests the archive with a complex temporality.

The Image and History

The temporal figures of the Archives of the Planet lead us to the issue of the philosophy of history at work in this archival theory. The survival of these images into a time when these modes of human life have disappeared depends on their montage being open to future connections. These images are not – or not *solely* – images with a stable signification of pastness within a secure historical continuum because their temporality is split between the media of the archive – the still and the moving – and the fixation of a time lost. Since the film shots and stills were not edited together or organized for exhibition, the material establishes virtual connecting points between the images. This is a potential for a montage still to be executed. Film editing and photographic displays are archival work in that it entails the selection of the material to be included, and the discarding of things not considered part of the work or the exhibition. The Archives of the Planet is a special case, since this selection process never happened. All of the material has been kept independent of these selections, and without being edited into any defined context. These images surprise us with an unfamiliar look and freshness due to their unusual color and the primacy they give everyday life. However, just as striking is their unfinished character due to the fact that they were never edited. They were, and remain to this day, images for an unknown future.

Walter Benjamin, in his *Theses on History* understood the historical articulation of the past as "to take control of a memory, as it flashes in a moment of danger".[24] This image is an alluring one for the description of the relation of the past to the present in the Archives of the Planet. It would be tempting to see the ghost-like appearances of the autochromes of parades and passing people on the streets as the memory "as it flashes in a moment of danger". It is an emblematic image of the masses slowly becoming visible. The crowd also leaves the regime of the visible, as they have passed only as a flash at a certain moment that is shorter than the time of exposure of the image. It presents the entrance of the anonymous crowd into the visible followed by their subsequent dispersal into individual users and customers in the media sphere of the post-Fordist society. The ghostly figures of the image are "a monstrous abbreviation" ("*einer ungeheueren Abbreviatur*"), of these two historical regimes of visibility.[25]

By introducing such a split temporality in the image itself, the ghostly shad-ows shatter the continuum of history. The image is no longer a preserved mo-ment of past time. Technology instead inscribes itself to demonstrate how it conditions the representation of the past and the writing of history. These auto-chromes are images of the ephemerality of history itself. The stability of the im-print is broken as it introduces movement into the still image, resulting in an unidentifiable presence of invisible people in the image. This ephemerality is at the core of Benjamin's materialist approach to the concept of history. The auto-chromes provide the evanescence of the flash of lightning, as the people they depict have already passed. Their passage is abbreviated in a ghostly moment. They have, literally, left the picture. These images are haunting pictures of war. The parading soldiers have passed and gone, impossible to discern as indivi-duals in the image. They are the ghostly shadows of the sort that Maxim Gorky had already identified in the moving image upon his visit to the Cinematograph in 1896,[26] thus eluding a fixed historical signification or an indexical presence in the image alone.

However, Benjamin's famous expression of "memory, as it flashes in a mo-ment of danger" cannot be reduced to the stable, moving images of Kahn's films alone. Neither is this dimension to be found in the still photography in the ar-chive, since these images remain before us at any time, and not only at a mo-ment of danger. The flash of memory is a matter of montage. As the images of the Archives of the Planet were not edited together for screening, the archive is the site of future connections and virtual montage. However, it would, in this case, be insufficient to understand montage only as the editing of film shots or the arrangements of still photos. Instead, the historical articulation of the past depends on the configurations and intersections of media. The role of photogra-phy and the moving image in Kahn's archival project is to establish connecting points with other technologies, media, visibilities and utterances. The centrality of the media interconnections and gaps is commented upon by Samuel Weber in relation to Benjamin's concepts of allegory and aura:

> What this meteoric event [of the allegorical that exceeds or eludes signification] leaves
> behind in its wake is what I would be tempted to call – if a neologism can be allowed
> – the *mediauric*: auratic flashes and shadows that are not just produced and repro-
> duced by the media but which *are* themselves the media, since they come to pass in
> places that are literally inter-mediary, in the interstices of a process of reproduction
> and of recording – *Aufnahme* – that is above all a mass movement of collection and
> dispersion, of banding together and of disbanding.[27]

The rupture of the continuum of historical time and the presence of the past in monstrous abbreviation in the present makes these autochromes of ghostly pro-cessions in Kahn's archive into *seductive* images indeed. The historical articulation of the past depends not on the single image, however, but on virtual montage and future connections: these flashes occur in 'inter-mediary' places. They occur in the spaces between the media. It is too simple to assign to these images a Benjaminian materialist historicity in their own right. The image as a flash is what one cannot see in one image alone. Even if these images are invested with a split temporality, and they could be said to display movement at the same time as they are still, the flashes that *are* the media exist in the virtual connections between the still image and the moving.

This virtual montage is already suggested in the heterogeneity of the temporal modes of the images of the archive: the phantoms of the still color photographs relate to the film shots of the same subjects and places at the same time. These images establish distant points of connection to each other, as well as to other images of this and other archives. Instead of illustrating Benjamin's flash of memory in a moment of danger, the autochromes demonstrate how any archival medium remains incomplete and fragmented. It produces distant connections, intermedial spaces, gaps and ruptures. The connecting points between the stills and the editing of one image after another are absent in this archive. This is a "soft montage", as the connections are only fleeting and temporary. It is a montage at a distance, in the sense that its elements are physically separated and only associated in thought. If we see these virtual connections in the Kahn archive as a form of montage, it could be one that oscillates between the still and the moving in similar ways as Benjamin's theses on history, between an image to be retained and the evanescence of a flash. It is a montage made of the memory of images, suddenly and momentarily associated and disconnected at the same moment. The montage, consequently, always remains in the future, in new situations and intermediary configurations.

"Memory, as it flashes in a moment of danger" is for Benjamin an *Erlösung* of the past: This redemption of physical reality is what Kracauer found in cinema.[28] The redemption is, however, not in the single image itself but in montage. French art theorist Georges Didi-Huberman discussed the relevance of montage in an attempt to understand the role of the image in the archive.[29] The issue is whether the archive image tells us anything about the horrors of war. Didi-Huberman argues that even if the image doesn't tell us everything, even if it is not *all* of an event, it is still an essential part in the process where one constructs a knowledge about an event. Didi-Huberman evokes Godard's claim in *Histoire(s) du cinéma* that there are no images of the Nazi extermination camps in cinema, and that this is where cinema failed to fulfill its mission: To make the Third Reich extermination camps known and understood.[30] This is the field where the questions raised in relation to the Kahn archive become essential.

Of course, there are many documentary images of the camps, of the mass graves and of the horrors of the genocides. What Godard is implying with his claim is that the montage of images that could produce a way of thinking about these events were missing at the time. An image is never *one* in Godard's theory of cinema, it is always a juxtaposition. The image of the Shoah is not the image that captures the gas chambers, but on the contrary one that shows what one cannot see. The montage, as "a form that thinks" according to Godard in part *3a: La monnaie de l'absolue* of *Histoire(s) du cinéma*, relies on putting images, sounds and texts of various sorts together, and its exemplary experimental field is in many ways *Histoire(s) du cinéma*. The work in the archive is exactly this; to juxtapose media and fragments of different sorts to construct a dimension that is not in the archival document alone. These gaps and fissures between the archival parts take on a new dimension with the introduction of the time-based media in the archive. As its images largely remained unedited, it is clear that the Archives of the Planet is not this type of montage construction. But exactly *because* it was not edited for exploitation, because it was kept as raw footage almost as a time capsule, it still maintained a virtual dimension for eventual connections and juxtapositions. Because these images were made for a time to come, after the end of the existence of the modes of social life portrayed in the images, the connecting points between the events and places depicted were still not resolved. The miraculous survival of the images of the Kahn archive even during the Vichy regime – one would expect that an archive established by an international Jewish banker would have been seen as politically suspect and economically valuable – constitute a rare case where the images of the 20th century have not yet received a reading through established connecting points.

The Digital Return

We are moving from the analog to the digital. The conversion of *"les Archives de la planète* into the FAKIR (Fonds Albert-Kahn Informatisée pour la Recherche) database is part of a development that often – maybe far too often – leads to discussions of the role of the indexical and the loss of the link to physical reality. This version of digitization is grossly simplified. Digitization doesn't mean that film preservation becomes obsolete, and the unedited films of *les Archives de la planète* remain intact. Despite many of the programmatic statements typical of our current period of transition, the conversion to digital files doesn't mean the end of the film base, which remains unchallenged as the superior storage medium for moving images. FAKIR does not eliminate all of the material links with the events and cultures in the archive. What we are moving into is an age of "compound" archives, where film-base and digital files of the same material co-exist and are connected in specific ways. The task of contemporary archive theory is to think about the various ways that these connections are constructed, and how the relations between film and bits are coded.

In the age of the digitization of analog materials, there is a demand that archives make their holdings "accessible" online, or at least on the computers at the archive itself. The access imperative is a prerequisite for public funding, and implies an economy of the "content". The question how the "content" of an archive, a museum or a collection can be made "accessible" varies according to the media of their holdings. Nobody supposes that the digital representations of the ancient objects of a historical museum is access to the actual "content" of the museum, but this confusion is quite often the case involving film and photographic archives. This relationship between the analog and the digital makes the Archives of the Planet a very important case in the discussion of montage in an age of online access. This entails the reconsideration of many key concepts of film theory, from the notion of "the work" to the idea of montage itself. My argument has, perhaps paradoxically, exalted the montage dimension of the Archives of the Planet because its films are not edited together. This leaves space for temporary intersections and provisional montage, for future juxtapositions and virtual connections. According to the general idea of what was once called "new media", the interactivity and navigation supplied by computer interfaces in an age of online access seem to promise exactly these properties of the archive. In a database structure, momentary connections between images and "soft montage" seem to be the governing principles. There are, however, at least two reasons why this is not the case.

On a general level, any database is designed, programmed and indexed according to certain structures. The algorithms of the database may hide themselves, but they are the regulating force of the use of the material. The montage made by the user of the database may often be the most conventional known, as it tends to retrace the habitual paths of navigation of our culture. In the FAKIR database, which became accessible in the spring of 2010 online at <www.albert-kahn.fr>, the unedited shots of the films are suddenly linked in various but specific ways. If they are not edited together, they are linked by new cues; geographical, topical, thematic and material. The database architecture is designed for navigation according to a world map, where one narrows in by choosing continents, countries and sometimes cities. The links of the database already programs the paths of navigation and there is nothing that implies that the unexpected, sudden connection is facilitated by the new interface. The pathways of navigation in the database are, at present at least, as established and disciplining as those in the adjoining gardens from different parts of the world outside the Albert Kahn museum in Boulogne on the outskirts of Paris.

The only access to the Archives of the Planet for the ordinary user is in the edited mode. The films in the FAKIR database are edited together to represent a place or an event, either produced for earlier TV productions or special screenings. Sometimes, the shots by the Kahn cameramen are intercut with other kinds of archival and stock footage. The autochromes are linked in succession, almost in PowerPoint mode, according to place or event. The user is also presented with a narrative in the Kahn Museum in Boulogne, where geographical unity of the stills and the occasional film montage is the structuring principle (recent topics being the Maghreb, "Infinitely India" and Japan). The BBC series *Edwardians in Colour: The Wonderful World of Albert Kahn* makes use of parts of the material intercut with new shots and other archival materials as well as with explanatory interviews to tell the stories of events and places. This is the only access to the archive made possible for the public. The raw shot quality of the archive, which makes it stand out from all other film collections and archives, where the beginning and end of each shot is still intact, is only accessible to the researcher of the analog material. The image alone, without a commentary, the shot without an adjoining shot, is a horror for archive culture. It is seen as devoid of public interest by archives, meaningless by the public and a disturbance of database design. The image always seems to come supplied with a nametag, a place and date of birth, to make it possible to embed in a historical narrative and in an educational and political project.

The computer media environments provide a setting determined by another logic than the globalization movement of the film and the photographs of the archive. The digital database provides a mode of media connectivity "after" the heterogeneity of the 1900 paradigm of the archive, where the gaps and conflicts resulting from the juxtaposition of the temporal image and the still are no longer present. In the digital database, the local and communal modes of human activity of which Kahn set out to make an inventory have disappeared. The globalized image of the mass in film and photography has dispersed into individual units with a user name, a password and a customer profile. Addressing the forms of globalization pertaining to the digital code of the control society depends on understanding how media form our life environments. The media ecology of "universal machines" condition other kinds of media interrelations than those of the age where the crowd remained visible. While the masses entered into the visible through the medium of the moving image, as discussed in different ways by Kahn and Kracauer, the media environments of the computer age are accompanied by a dispersal of the masses. Post-Fordist production no longer requires workers in a factory, but relies on individualized work patterns in front of screens and computers.

This is an age of the archive where the analog exists with a digital "alias", where everything returns twice. The photographic and filmic are superimposed with the digital files of the same events. The communities and people at the center of Kahn's archival project were on the brink of disappearance. The fleeting moments inscribed in the archive's films and autochromes were inhabited by ghosts and specters of a lost time. When these images return in digital code, it is not the return of the same temporality and social technologies as the one designed by Kahn for his archive. When this haunted archive returns in digital mode, it is a return of ghosts of ghosts. As a result of this conversion from a media set-up of the first wave of globalization to the current second globalization, the "rhythm of life" has been altered and the montage between the images is a different one. In this change of pace and mobility, in this reconfigured temporality, intermediary spaces open up. These spaces are the field for an analysis of image connectivity and modes of montage in the digital age.

Notes

1. The Armenian filmmaker Artavazd Peleshian has developed the concept of "Distance Montage" in a different sense, as it still depends on the material cuts of the film: Peleshian, "Distance Montage, or The Theory of Distance", in *Documentary Films of the Armenian Soviet Republic; A Retrospective*, Moritz de Hadeln, Hans-Joachim Schlegel (eds.), (Berlin 1989), 79-102. Harun Farocki develops the concept of "soft montage" as the comparison of images through multi-channel moving image installations in: Harun Farocki, "Cross Influence/Soft Montage", in *Harun Farocki. Against What? Against Whom?*, Antje Ehmann and Kodwo Eshun (eds.) (London: Koenig Books, 2009), 69-74. See also: Kaja Silverman and Harun Farocki, *Speaking about Godard* (New York: New York University Press, 1998), 142. I here draw on these concepts in a different sense.

2. These biographical details are from: Paula Amad, "Cinema's 'Sanctuary': From Pre-documentary to Documentary Film in Albert Kahn's *Archives de la Planète* (1908-1931)", *Film History*, vol. 13, no. 2 (2001): 140-143.

3. Albert Kahn quoted in: ibid., 144.

4. Before this grand-scale mapping, Kahn visited Norway in 1910 where he collaborated with the famous Norwegian photographer Anders Beer Wilse. An exhibition of these images from Norway will take place at the Norwegian Museum of Cultural History (Norsk Folkemuseum) in 2011.

5. Ibid., 139.

6. For a good discussion of the implications of the "universality" in this archive, see: Jakob Nilsson, "The Ambivalence of Universalization in "Albert Kahn's Archive of the Planet", *Site* no. 28 (2009), 18-23.

7. Tom Gunning, "Before Documentary; Early Nonfiction Films and the 'View' Aesthetic", in *Uncharted Territory; essays on early nonfiction film*, Daan Hertogs and Nico de Klerk (eds.) (Amsterdam: Stichting Nederlands Filmmuseum), 1997, 19-20. Paula Amad, "Cinema's 'Sanctuary': From pre-documentary to documentary film in Albert Kahn's *Archives de la Planète* (1908-1931)", 138-159.

8. Teresa Castro, "*Les Archives de la Planète*; A Cinematographic Atlas", *Jump Cut*, no. 48, (winter 2006).

Francois de la Breteque, "Les films des Archives de la planète d'Albert Kahn, d'un certain regard sur le monde et sa place dans l'histoire", *Le cinéma d'Albert Kahn: quelle place dans l'histoire?; Les Cahiers de la Cinémathèque* no. 74 (Dec. 2002), 137-146.

9.   Paula Amad, "Les Archives de la planète d'Albert Kahn (1908-1931): Archives ou contre-archives de l'histoire?", *Le cinéma d'Albert Kahn: quelle place dans l'histoire?; Les Cahiers de la Cinémathèque* no. 74 (Dec. 2002), 19-31.

10. Paula Amad, *Counter-Archive: Film, the Everyday, and Albert Kahn's Archives de la Planète* (New York: Columbia University Press 2010), 122-128.

11. Perhaps this is not an altogether positive aspect of the project; in the 2007 nine-part BBC production *Edwardians in Colour: The Wonderful World of Albert Kahn* made from the documents of the Kahn archive, not a single image is allowed to remain still, and every shot zooms in and out of the still images. In addition, we are often subjected to an English commentary with a phony French accent, narrativizing the material into banality.

12. *"La précieuse découverte du cinéma ajoute à la forme l'expression même du mouvement, c'est-à-dire le rythme de la vie"*, J. Brunhes quoted in: F. de la Bretèque, 139.

13. Boleslas Matuszewski, "A New Source of History" ["Une nouvelle source de l'histoire", 1898], *Film History* vol. 7, no. 4 (1995), 322-324.

14. Friedrich Kittler, "Einleitung", in *Grammophon, Film, Typewriter* (Berlin: Brinckmann & Bose, 1986), 7-33. See also: Kittler, "Untranslatability and the Transposition of Media", in *Discourse Networks 1800/1900*, [1985] (Stanford: Stanford University Press, 1990), 265-273.

15. Paula Amad, "Les Archives de la planète d'Albert Kahn (1908-1931): Archives ou contre-archives de l'histoire?", 22. Ricciotto Canudo, "La naissance d'un sixième art; essai sur le cinématographe" [1911], in *L'usine aux images* (Paris: Séguier, 1995), 32-40.

16. Michel Foucault, *L'archéologie du savoir* (Paris: Gallimard, 1969), 214. See also Gilles Deleuze, *Foucault* (Paris: Minuit, 1986), 40.

17. Siegfried Kracauer, *Theory of Film; The Redemption of Physical Reality* (London: Oxford University Press, 1960), 50-52.

18. Ibid., 50-51.

19. Ibid., 299.

20. Jacques Rancière, *La partage du sensible; esthétique et politique* (Paris: La Fabrique, 2000), 46-48.

21. Giorgio Agamben, "Notes sur le geste", *Trafic* no. 1 (1992). There is, however, an affinity with Rancière's position when Agamben finds in Balzac a precursor to this cinematic regime of movement.

22. I am indebted to Professor Tom Gunning, University of Chicago, for his lucid comments on this part of my argument.

23. Gilles Deleuze, "Post-scriptum sur les sociétés de contrôle", *Pourparlers* (Paris: Minuit, 1990), 240-247.

24. "[S]ich eine Erinnerung bemächtigen, wie sie im Augenblick einer Gefahr aufblitzt", Walter Benjamin. "Über den Begriff der Geschichte", *Gesammelten Schriften I:2* (Frankfurt am Main: Suhrkamp, 1974), 695. English translation: www.efn.org/~dredmond/Theses_on_History.PDF.

25. Ibid., 703.

26. Maxim Gorky, "The Lumière Cinematograph" [1896] in *The Film Factory; Russian and Soviet Cinema in Documents 1896-1939*, Richard Taylor and Ian Christie (eds.) (London: Routledge, 1988), 25-26.

27. Samuel Weber, "Mass Mediauras, or: Art, Aura and Media in the Work of Walter Benjamin", in *Mass Mediauras; Form, Technics, Media* (Stanford: Stanford University Press, 1996), 107.

28. This is the subtitle of Kracauer's film theory book: Siegfried Kracauer, *Theory of Film; The Redemption of Physical Reality.*

29. Georges Didi-Huberman, *Images malgré tout* (Paris: Minuit, 2003), 151-193.

30. Ibid., 175-187.

General Bibliography

This bibliography is not exhaustive. It is general in the sense that it is not limited to studies on stillness and motion in cinema, photography and new media, bringing together references from various disciplines and research areas. Partly a selection of the references cited by the different contributors, it cites entries relevant for the contextualization and theory formation of the subject.

Adorno, Theodore. *In Search of Wagner*. London: NLB, 1981.

Agamben, Giorgio. "Notes sur le geste." *Trafic* 1, 1992.

Albera, François and Maria Tortajada. *Cinema before Film: Media Epistemology in the Modern Era*. Amsterdam, Amsterdam University Press, 2010.

Altman, Rick. *Sound Theory, Sound Practice*. New York: Routledge, 1992.

Amad, Paula. "Cinema's 'Sanctuary': From Pre-documentary to Documentary Film in Albert Kahn's *Archives de la Planète* (1908-1931)." *Film History* 13.2, 2001.

Amad, Paula, "Les Archives de la planète d'Albert Kahn (1908-1931): Archives ou contre-archives de l'histoire?" *Le cinéma d'Albert Kahn: quelle place dans l'histoire?; Les Cahiers de la Cinémathèque* 74, Dec., 2002.

Anderson, Joseph &Barbara Fisher. "The Myth of Persistence of Vision." *Journal of the University Film Association* 4 (Fall 1978): 3-8.

Aristotle. *Poetics*. Trans. Richard Janko.Indianapolis, Indiana: Hackett Publishing Company, 1987. Originally written about 335 BC.

Aumont, Jacques. *The Image*. Trans. Claire Pajackowska. London: BFI Publishing, 1997 [1980].

Baker, George. "Photography's Expanded Field." *Still Moving: Between Cinema and Photography*. Eds. Karen Beckman and Jean Ma. Durham: Duke University Press, 2008.

Barthes, Roland. "The Third Meaning. Research Notes on Some Eisenstein Stills." *Image, Music, Text*. Trans. Stephen Heath. New York: Hill and Wang, 1977.

Barthes, Roland. Camera Lucida: Reflections on Photography. London: Fontana Paperbacks, 1993 [1980].

Barthes, Roland. La Chambre claire. Notes sur la photographie. Œuvres complètes. Livres, textes, entetiens. 1977-1980. Paris: Seul, 1995: 785-894.

Bazin, André. "The Ontology of the Photographic Image." *What is Cinema?* Vol. 1. Trans. Hugh Gray. Berkeley, CA: UC Press, 1967 [1947].

Beckman, Karen and Jean Ma. Eds. *Still Moving: Between Cinema and Photography*. Durham: Duke University Press, 2008

Bellour, Raymond. "Le spectateur pensif." *L'Entre-Images. Cinema, Photo, Cinéma, Vidéo*. Paris: Edition de la Différence, 1990 [1984]: 75-80. English translation: "The Pensive Spectator." *Wide Angle* 9.1, 1987: 6-10.

Bellour, Raymond. "L'interruption, l'instant." *L'Entre-Images. Cinema, Photo, Cinéma, Vidéo*. Paris: Edition de la Différence, 1990 [1987]: 109-133. English translation: "The Film Stilled." *Camera Obscura* 24, 1990: 99-123.

Bellour, Raymond. *L'Entre-Images 2. Mots, Images*. Paris: P. O. L. Trafic, 1999.

Bellour, Raymond. "L'effet Daney ou l'arrêt de vie et de mort." *Trafic* 37, Spring 2001: 75-86.

Bellour, Raymond. *L'Entre-Images. Photo, Cinéma, Video. Nouvelle édition revue et corrigée*. Paris: Éditions de la Différence, 2002.

Bellour, Raymond. "The Double Helix." *Electronic Culture. Technology and Visual Culture*. Ed. Timothy Druckrey, Trans. J. Eddy. New York: Aperture, 1996: 173-199.

Benjamin, Walter. "The Work of Art in the Age of Mechanical Reproduction." *Illuminations*. London: Fontana, 1973: 211-244 .

Benjamin, Walter. "Über den Begriff der Geschichte." *Gesammelten Schriften I:2*. Frankfurt am Main: Suhrkamp, 1974.

Benjamin, Walter. "Das Kunstwerk im Zeitalter seiner technischen Reproduzierbarkeit [2. fassung]." *Walter Benjamin. Ein Lesebuch*, Frankfurt am Main: Suhrkamp, 1996 [1935/36]: 313-350.

Bergson, Henri. *Time and Free Will. An Essay on the Immediate Data of Consciousness*. Trans. F. L. Pogson. New York: Harper &Row. 1960 [1889].

Bergson, Henri. *Matter and Memory*. Trans. N.M. Paul and W.S. Palmer. New York: Zone Books, 1991 [1896].

Bissell, David and Gillian Fuller. Eds. *Stillness in a Mobile World*. London: Routledge, 2011.

Bohrer, Karlheinz. *Plötzlichkeit. Zum Augenblick des ästhetischen Scheins*. Frankfurt/M.: Suhrkamp, 1981. English translation: *Suddenness: On the Moment of Aesthetic Appearance*. New York: Columbia University Press, 1994.

Bolter, Jay David and Grusin, Richard. *Remediation: Understanding New Media*. Cambridge, Massachusetts: The MIT Press, 1999.

Bourriaud, Nicolas. *Postproduction: Culture as Screenplay: How Art Reprograms the World*. New York: Lukas &Sternberg, 2002.

Braun, Marta. *Picturing Time: The Work of Etienne-Jules Marey (1830-1904)*. Chicago: University of Chicago Press, 1992.

Brooks, Peter. *Reading for the Plot: Design and Intention in Narrative*. Oxford: Clarendon Press, 1984.

Brunette, Peter and David Wills. *SCREEN/PLAY. Derrida and Film Theory*. Princeton, N.J., Princeton University Press, 1989.

Burch, Noël. *Life to those Shadows*. Trans. B. Brewster. London: BFI Publishing, 1990.

Burch, Noël. "Primitivism and the Avant-gardes: a Dialectical Approach." *In and Out of Synch. The Awakening of a Cine-Dreamer*. Aldershot: Scolar Press, 1991: 157-186.

Campany, David. "Introduction. When to be Fast? When to be Slow?" *The Cinematic*. Ed. D. Campany. London: Whitechapel, 2007: 10-17.

Canudo, Ricciotto. "La naissance d'un sixième art; essai sur le cinématographe." *L'usine aux images*. Paris: Séguier, 1995 [1911].

Carroll, Noël. "Towards an Ontology of the Moving Image." *Philosophy and Film*. Eds. Cynthia A. Freeland and Thomas E. Wartenberg. London, N.Y.: Routledge, 1995: 68-85.

Castro, Teresa. "*Les Archives de la Planète*; A Cinematographic Atlas." *Jump Cut* 48, winter 2006.

Ceram, C. W. *Archeology of the Cinema*. London: Thames and Hudson, 1965.

Chion, Michel. *Audio-Vision: Sound on screen*. New York: Columbia University Press, 1994. First published in 1990.

Chun, Wendy Hui Kyong and Thomas Keenan. Eds. *New Media Old Media. A History and Theory Reader*. New York and London: Routledge, 2006.

Cortade, Ludovic. *Le cinéma de l'immobilité: style, politique, reception*. Paris: Publications de la Sorbonne, 2008.

Crary, Jonathan. *Techniques of the Observer: On Vision and Modernity in the Nineteenth Century*. Cambridge: MIT Press, 1990.

Crimp, Douglas. "Pictures." *Art after Modernism: Rethinking Representation*. Eds. Brian Wallis. New York: New Museum of Contemporary Art, 1984: 175-188. Originally in *October*, 8 (Spring): 75-88.

Daney, Serge. "From Movies to Moving." *Art and the Moving Image: A Critical Reader*. Ed. Tanya Leighton. London: Tatepublishing &Afterall, 2008 [1989]: 334-349.

Daney, Serge. "Réponse à l'enquête 'Cinéma et Photographie." *Photogénies* 5.

Daney, Serge. "Du défilement au defile." *La recherche photographique* 7, 1989: 49-51

Daney, Serge. "La dernière image." *Passages de l'image*. Eds. R. Bellour, C. David, C. Van Assche. Paris: Editions du Centre Pompidou, 1989: 57-59.

de la Breteque, Francois. "Les films des Archives de la planète d'Albert Kahn, d'un certain regard sur le monde et sa place dans l'histoire." *Le cinéma d'Albert Kahn: quelle place dans l'histoire?; Les Cahiers de la Cinémathèque* 74, Dec. 2002.

Deleuze, Gilles. *Cinema I: The Movement-Image*. Trans. Hugh Tomlinson and Barbara Habberjam. Minneapolis: University of Minnesota Press, 1986.

Deleuze, Gilles. *Cinema-2. The Time-Image*. Trans. Hugh Tomlinson and Barbara Habberjam. London: The Athlone Press, 1989 [1985].

Deleuze, Gilles. *Foucault*. Paris: Minuit, 1986.

Deleuze, Gilles. "Post-scriptum sur les sociétés de contrôle." *Pourparlers*. Paris: Minuit, 1990.

Deleuze, Gilles. *Francis Bacon: The Logics of Sensation*. Trans. D. W. Smith. London: Continuum, 2003 [1981].

Deslandes, Jacques. *Histoire comparitif du cinema* Vol. 1 Paris: Casterman, 1966.

Dickinson, Thorold. *A Discovery of Cinema*. Oxford: Oxford University Press, 1971.

Didi-Huberman, Georges. *Images malgré tout*. Paris: Minuit, 2003.

Didi-Huberman, Georges. "*La Danse de Toute Chose*." *Mouvements de l'Air: Etienne-Jules Marey, Photographe des Fluides*. Paris: Editions Gallimard, 2004.

Diekmann, Stefanie and Winfried Gerling. Eds. *Freeze Frames: Zum Verhältnis von Fotografie und Film*. Bielefeld: Transcript, 2010.

Dikovitskaya, Margaret. "An interview with Laura U. Marks." *Visual Culture: A Study of the Visual After the Cultural Turn*. Cambridge, MA: The MIT Press, 2005.

Doane, Mary Ann. *The Emergence of Cinematic Time. Modernity, Contingency, the Archive*. Cambridge, Massachusetts: Harvard University Press, 2002.

Doane, Mary-Ann. "The Close Up: Scale and Detail in the Cinema." *Differences: a Journal of Feminist Cultural Studies* 14.3, Fall 2003.

Doane, Mary Ann. "Movement and Scale: Vom Daumenkino zur Filmprojektion." *Apparaturen bewegter Bilder, Kulture und Technik,* vol. 2. Ed. Daniel Gethmann. Munster: Lit, 2006.

Dubois, Philippe. "Photography Mise-en-Film. Autobiographical (Hi)stories and Psychic Apparatuses." *Fugitive Images, From Photography to Video.* Ed. Patrice Petro. Bloomington: Indiana University Press, 1995.

Dubois, Philippe. *L'Effet film, figures, matières et formes du cinéma en photographie.* Lyon: Galérie le Réverbère, 1999.

Eisenstein, Sergei. "Word and Image." *The Film Sense.* Ed. and trans. Jay Leyda. London: Faber and Faber, 1986.

Eisenstein, Sergei. "Laocoön." *Selected Works. Vol. 2. Towards a Theory of Montage.* Eds. M. Glenny and R. Taylor. Trans. Michael Glenny. London: BFI Publishing, 1991: 109-202.

Elsaesser, Thomas. "General Introduction. Early Cinema: From Linear History to Mass Media Archaeology." *Early Cinema: Space, Frame, Narrative.* Eds. Thomas Elsaesser and Adam Barker. London: BFI, 1990: 1-10.

Elsaesser, Thomas. *Rainer Werner Fassbinder.* Berlin: Bertz, 2001. English translation: *Fassbinder's Germany. History, identity, subject.* Amsterdam: Amsterdam University Press, 1996.

Elsaesser, Thomas. "Early Film History and Multi-Media: An Archaeology of Possible Futures?" *New Media Old Media. A History and Theory Reader.* Eds. Wendy Hui Kyong Chun and Thomas Keenan. New York and London: Routledge, 2006: 13-25.

Epstein, Jean. "L'intelligence d'une machine." Vol. 1. *Ecrits sur le cinéma, 1921-1953.* Paris: Seghers, 1974 [1946].

Farocki, Harun. "Cross Influence/Soft Montage." *Harun Farocki. Against What? Against Whom?* Eds. Antje Ehmann and Kodwo Eshun. London: Koenig Books, 2009.

Fidler, Tristan. *Music Video Auteurs: The Directors Label DVDs and the Music Videos of Chris Cunningham, Michel Gondry and Spike Jonze.* Thesis for the degree of Doctor of Philosophy. University of Western Australia, 2008.

Foucault, Michel. *L'archéologie du savoir.* Paris: Gallimard, 1969.

Frampton, Hollis. "For a Metahistory of Film: Commonplace Notes and Hypotheses." *On the Camera Arts and Consecutive Matters: The Writings of Hollis Frampton.* Ed. B. Jenkins. Cambridge: MIT Press, 2009.

Fried, Michael. *Absorption and Theatricality: Painting and Beholder in the Age of Diderot.* Chicago: University of Chicago Press, 1980.

Galloway, Alexander R. *Gaming: Essays on Algorithmic Culture.* Minneapolis: University of Minnesota Press, 2006.

Galloway, Alexander R. "What You See Is What You Get?" In *The Archive in Motion: New Conceptions of the Archive in Contemporary Thought and New Media Practices,* ed. Eivind Røssaak Oslo: Studies from the National Library of Norway, 2010.

Gaudreault, André and Tom Gunning. "Early Cinema as a Challenge to Film History." *The Cinema of Attraction Reloaded.* Ed. W. Strauven. Amsterdam: Amsterdam University Press, 2006 [1986]: 365-388.

Gibson, J.J. *The Ecological Approach to Visual Perception.* New York: Taylor &Francis Group, 1986.

Gorky, Maxim. "The Lumière Cinematograph." *The Film Factory; Russian and Soviet Cinema in Documents 1896-1939.* Eds. Richard Taylor and Ian Christie. London: Routledge, 1988 [1896].

Green, David and Joanna Lowry. Eds. *Stillness and Time: Photography and the Moving Image*, Brighton: Photoworks, 2006.

Gregory, R. L. *Eye and Brain:The Psychology of Seeing*. London: World University Library, 1997.

Groys, Boris. "Iconoclasm as an Artistic Device. Iconoclastic Strategies in Film." *Iconoclash: Beyond the Image Wars in Science, Religion, and Art*. Eds. Bruno Latour and Peter Wibel, Trans. M. Partridge. Cambridge, Mass.: The MIT Press, 2002: 282-295.

Groys, Boris. "Medienkunst im Museum." *Topologie der Kunst*. München: Carl Hanser Verlag, 2003: 59-76.

Gunning, Tom. "The Cinema of Attractions: Early Film, Its Spectator and the Avant-Garde." *Early Cinema: Space, Frame, Narrative*. Eds. Thomas Elsaesser and Adam Barker. London: BFI: 56-62, 1990 [1986].

Gunning, Tom. "Before Documentary; Early Nonfiction Films and the 'View' Aesthetic." *Uncharted Territory; essays on early nonfiction film*. Eds. Daan Hertogs and Nico de Klerk. Amsterdam: Stichting Nederlands Filmmuseum, 1997.

Gunning, Tom. "An Aesthetic of Astonishment: Early Film and the (In)Credulous Spectator." *Film Theory and Criticism*. Eds. Leo Braudy and M. Cohen. Oxford: Oxford University Press, 1999 [1989]: 818-832.

Gunning, Tom. "Never Seen This Picture Before. Muybridge in Multiplicity." *Time Stands Still: Muybridge and the Instantaneous Photography Movement*. Ed. Phillip Prodger. New York and Stanford: Oxford University Press, 2003: 222-272.

Gunning, Tom. "Re-Newing Old Technologies: Astonishment, Second Nature, and the Uncanny in Technology from the Previous Turn-of-the-Century." *Rethinking Media Change: The Aesthetics of Transition*. Eds. David Thorburn and Henry Jenkins. Cambridge, MA: MIT Press, 2003.

Gunning, Tom. "Attractions: How They Came into the World." In *The Cinema of Attraction Reloaded*. Ed. W. Strauven. Amsterdam: Amsterdam University Press, 2006: 31-40.

Gunning, Tom. "Moving Away from the Index: Cinema and the Impression of Reality." *differences: A Journal of Feminist Cultural Studies* 18.1, 2007: 29-52.

Gunning, Tom &David Swartz. "Interview with Ken Jacobs. August 10 and 11, 1989." *Films That Tell Time: A Ken Jacobs Retrospective*. Ed. David Swartz. New York: American Museum of the Moving Image, 1989: 29-60.

Hámos, Gusztáv, Katja Pratschke and Thomas Tode. Eds. *Viva Fotofilm: Bewegt/unbewegt*. Marburg: Schüren Verlag, 2009.

Hansen, Mark B.N. *New Philosophy for New Media*. Cambridge: MIT Press, 2004.

Hansen, Mark B.N. *Bodies in Code: Interfaces with new media*. New York: Routledge, 2006.

Hausken, Liv. *Om det utidige. Medieanalytiske undersøkelser av fotografi, fortelling og stillbildefilm*. Doctoral Dissertation. Bergen: Universitetet i Bergen, 1998.

Herbert, Stephen. *A History of Pre-Cinema*. London: Routledge, 2002.

Herskovic, Marika. *American Abstract Expressionism of the 1950s: An Illustrated Survey: With Artists' Statements, Artwork and Biographies*. New York: New York School Press, 2003.

Hofmann, Hans. *Search for the Real and Other Essays*. Cambridge, Massachusetts: The MIT Press, 1948.

Hofmann, Hans. "On the Aims of Art". *Art in Theory: 1900-2000: An Anthology of Changing Ideas*. Eds. Charles Harrison and Paul Wood. Malden, Mass.: Blackwell, 2003 [1932]: 371-374.

Husserl, Edmund. *On the Phenomenology of the Consciousness of Internal Time (1893-1917)*. Trans. J. Brough. Dordrecht, The Netherlands: Kluwer Academic Publishers, 1991.

Irwin, William. Ed. The Matrix *and Philosophy. Welcome to the Desert of the Real.* Chicago: Open Court, 2002.

Jacobs, Frederika H. *The Living Image in Renaissance Art.* Cambridge: Cambridge University Press, 2005.

Jacobs, Ken. "Beating My Tom Tom." *Exploding. Special Issue* October 2000/ reedition 2002 (for the release of Ken Jacobs's *Tom, Tom, the Piper's Son* on VHS, Paris: Re:Voir), 2002: 5-18.

James, Henry. "The art of fiction." *Henry James: Selected Literary Criticism.* Ed. Morris Shapira. Harmondsworth: Penguin, 1963 [1884].

Katzenstein, Inés. "Sharon Lockhart, Ethnography Home." *Pine Flat.* Bilbao: Sala Rekalde, 2006.

Kessler, Frank."The Cinema of Attraction as *Dispositif." The Cinema of Attraction Reloaded.* Ed. W. Strauven. Amsterdam: Amsterdam University Press, 2006: 57-70.

Kittler, Friedrich. "Einleitung." *Grammophon, Film, Typewriter.* Berlin: Brinckmann &Bose, 1986.

Kittler, Friedrich. "Untranslatability and the Transposition of Media." *Discourse Networks 1800/1900.* Stanford: Stanford University Press, 1990 [1985].

Kittler, Friedrich. *Gramophone, Film, Typewriter.* Trans. G. Winthrop-Young and M. Wutz. Stanford: Stanford University Press, 1999 [1986].

Kolker, R. P. and J. Douglas Ousley. "A Phenomenology of Cinematic Time and Space." *The British Journal of Aesthetics* 13, 1973: 388-396.

Koningsberg, Ira. *The Complete Film Dictionary.* London: Bloomsbury, 1997.

Kracauer, Siegfried. *Theory of Film; The Redemption of Physical Reality.* London: Oxford University Press, 1960.

Krauss, Rosalind E. *The Optical Unconscious.* Cambridge, Mass.: The MIT Press, 1993.

Kuntzel, Thierry. "Le Défilement." *Cinéma: Théories, Lectures.* Ed. Dominique Noguez. Paris: Klincksieck, 1973: 97-110.

Latour, Bruno and Peter Weibel. Eds. *Iconoclash: Beyond the Image Wars in Science, Religion, and Art.* Cambridge, Mass.: The MIT Press, 2002.

Lazzarato, Maurizio. *Videophilosophie. Zeitwahrnähmung in Postfordismus.* Trans. Stephan Geene and Erik Stein. Berlin: b-books, 2002.

Lepecki, André. "Still: On the Vibratile Microscopy of Dance." *ReMembering the Body.* Eds. Gabriele Brandstetter and Hortensia Völckers. Ostfildern-Ruit: Hatje Cantz, 2000: 334-365.

Lepecki, André. *Exhausting Dance. Performance and the Politics of Movement.* London: Routledge, 2006.

Lessing, Gotthold Ephraim. *Laocoön: An Essay on the Limits of Painting and Poetry.* Trans. E. A. McCormock. Baltimore and London: The John Hopkins University Press, 1962 [1766].

Libet, Banjamin. *Mind Time: The Temporal Factor in Consciousness.* Cambridge: Harvard University Press, 2004.

Lundemo, Trond. *Bildets oppløsning. Filmens bevegelse i historisk og teoretisk perspektiv.* Oslo: Spartacus, 1996.

Lunenfeld, Peter. "Hollis Frampton: The Perfect Machine." *Snap to Grid.* Cambridge: MIT Press, 2000.

MacDonald, Scott. "Ken and Flo Jacobs". *A Critical Cinema 3. Interviews with Independent Filmmakers.* Berkely. University of California Press, 1998.

MacDonnell, Kevin. *Eadweard Muybridge. The Man who Invented the Moving Picture.* London: Weidenfeld and Nicolson, 1972.

Mangolte, Babette. "Afterword: A Matter of Time. Analog Versus Digital, the Perennial Question Shifting Technology and Its Implications for an Experimental Filmmaker's Odyssey." *Camera Obscura, Camera Lucida. Essays in Honor of Annette Michelson.* Eds. Richard Allen and Malcolm Turvey. Amsterdam: Amsterdam University Press, 2003: 261-274.

Manning, Erin. "Coloring the Virtual." *Configurations* 16.3, Fall 2008: 325-345.

Manning, Erin. *Relationscapes: Movement, Art, Philosophy.* Cambridge: MIT Press, 2009.

Mannoni, Laurent. *The Great Art of Light and Shadow, Archeology of the Cinema.* Exeter: University of Exeter Press, 2000.

Manovich, Lev. *The Language of New Media.* Cambridge, MA: MIT Press, 1999.

Manovich, Lev. "Image Future." *Animation.* London: Sage, 2006.

Martin, Timothy. "Documentary Theater." *Sharon Lockhart: Teatro Amazonas.* Rotterdam: Museum Boijmans Van Beuningen, 1999.

Massumi, Brian. "Strange Horizon." *Parables for the Virtual.* Durham: Duke University Press, 2002.

Massumi, Brian. "The Thinking-Feeling of What Happens." *Inflexions* 1.1, May 2008: 1-40.

Matuszewski, Boleslas. "A New Source of History" ["Une nouvelle source de l'histoire", 1898]. *Film History* 7.4, 1995.

Metz, Christian. "On the Impression of Reality in the Cinema." *Film Language: A Semiotics of the Cinema.* Trans. M. Taylor. Chicago: University of Chicago Press, 1974.

Metz, Christian. *Language and Cinema.* Trans. D. J. Umiker-Sebok. The Hague: Mouton, 1974.

Metz, Christian. *Film Language. A Semiotics of the Cinema.* Trans. M. Taylor. Chicago: The University of Chicago Press, 1974 [1968].

Metz, Christian."Photography and Fetish." *The Critical Image. Essays on Contemporary Photography.* Ed. Carol Squiers. Seattle: Bay Press, 1990: 155-164. First published in 1990.

Middleton, Richard. "Popular Music Analysis and Musicology: Bridging the Gap." *Reading pop: approaches to textual analysis in popular music.* London: Oxford University Press, 2000.

Mitchell, W.J.T. *The Reconfigured Eye. Visual Truth in the Post-Photographic Era.* Cambridge: The MIT Press, 1992.

Mitchell, W.J.T. *What Does Pictures Want? The Lives and Loves of Images.* Chicago: The University of Chicago Press, 2005.

Mozley, Anita Ventura. "Introduction to the Dover Edition." *Complete Human and Animal Locomotion. All 781 Plates from 1887. Volum 1.* Eadweard Muybridge. New York: Dover Publications, 1979.

Mulvey, Laura. "Visual Pleasure and Narrative Cinema" [1975] in Braudy and Cohen (eds.), *Film Theory and Criticism* (Oxford: Oxford U Press, 1999).

Mulvey, Laura. *Death 24x a Second. Stillness and the Moving Image.* London: Reaktion Books, 2006.

Musser, Charles. *History of the American Cinema. 1. The Emergence of Cinema. The American Screen to 1907*. New York: Charles Schreibner's Sons, 1990.

Muybridge, Eadweard. 1979. *Complete Human and Animal Locomotion. Vol. 1-3*. New York: Dover Publications, 1979 [1887].

Münsterberg, Hugo. *The Photoplay: A Psychological Study*. New York: Appleton and Company, 1916.

Münsterberg, Hugo. *The Photoplay: A Psychological Study. Hugo Münsterberg on Film*. Ed. A. Langdale. New York: Routledge, 2002.

Ndalianis, Angela. *Neo-Baroque Aesthetic and Contemporary Entertainment*. Cambridge, MN: The MIT Press, 2004.

Nilsson, Jakob. "The Ambivalence of Universalization in Albert Kahn's Archive of the Planet." *Site* (Stockholm) 28, 2009.

Païni, Dominique. *Le temps exposé: Le Cinéma de la salle au musée*. Paris: Cahiers du Cinema, 2002.

Panofsky, Erwin."Style and Medium in the Motion Picture." *Film Theory and Criticism*. Eds. Leo Braudy and M. Cohen. Oxford: Oxford University Press, 1999: 279-292.

Paris, John Ayrton. *Philosophy in Sport Made Science in Earnest. An attempt to illustrate the first principles of natural philosophy by the aid of popular toys and sports*. London: John Murray, 1849, fifth edition.

Pierson, Michele. *Special Effects. Still in Search for Wonder*. New York: Columbia University Press, 2002.

Prodger, Phillip. *Time Stands Still. Muybridge and the Instantaneous Photography Movement*. New York and Stanford: Oxford University Press, 2003.

Rancière, Jacques. *La partage du sensible; esthétique et politique*. Paris: La Fabrique, 2000.

Richter, Hans. *Film ist Rhythmus*. Eds. Ulrich Gregor, Jeanpaul Goergen, and Angelika Hoch. Berlin: Freunde d. Dt. Kinemathek, 2003.

Rimmon-Kenan, Shlomith. *Narrative Fiction: Contemporary Poetics*. London: Methuen, 1992. First published in 1983.

Rodowick, D. N. *The Virtual Life of Film*. Cambridge: Harvard University Press, 2007.

Røssaak, Eivind. "Figures of Sensation, Between Still and Moving Images." *The Cinema of Attraction Reloaded*. Ed. W. Strauven. Amsterdam: Amsterdam University Press, 2006: 321-336.

Røssaak, Eivind. *The Still/Moving Image: Cinema and the Arts*. Saarbrücken: Lambert Academic Publishing, 2010.

Salanskis, Jean-Michel. *Husserl*. Paris: Les Belles Lettres, 2004.

Schmidgen, Henning. "Mind, the Gap: The Discovery of Physiological Time." *Film 1900: Technology, Perception, Culture*. Eds. A. Ligensa and K. Kreimeier. England: John Libbey, 2009.

Seel, Martin. *Aesthetics of Appearing*. Trans. John Farrell. Stanford: Stanford University Press, 2005 [2000].

Shklovsky, Viktor. "Art as Technique." *Contemporary Literary Criticism. Literary and Cultural Studies*, third edition. Eds. R.C. Davis and R. Schleifer. New York and London: Longman, 1989.

Silverman, Kaja and Harun Farocki. *Speaking about Godard*. New York: New York University Press, 1998.

Sitney, P. Adams. "Structural Film." *Film Culture* 47 (summer), 1969: 1-10.

Sitney, P. Adams. *Visionary Film: The American Avant-Garde, 1943-2000.* Third Edition. Oxford/ New York: Oxford University Press, 2002.

Simon, Bill. "Talking About *Magellan*: An Interview with Hollis Frampton." *Millennium Film Journal* 14, 1981. Republished in *On the Camera Arts*.

Sjöberg, Patrik. *The World in Pieces: A Study in Compilation Film.* Stockholm: Aura Förlag, 2001.

Snyder, Joel. "Visualization and Visibility." *Picturing Science, Producing Art.* Eds. C. Jones and P. Galison. New York: Routledge, 1998.

Sobchack, Vivian. "'Cutting to the Quick': *Techne, Physis,* and *Poiesis* and the Attractions of Slow Motion." *The Cinema of Attraction Reloaded.* Ed. W. Strauven. Amsterdam: Amsterdam University Press, 2006: 337-354.

Stewart, Garrett. "Photogravure: Death, Photography and Film Narrative." *Wide Angle* 9.6, 1987: 11-31.

Stewart, Garrett. *Between Film and Screen: Modernism's Photosynthesis.* Chicago: Univ. of Chicago Press, 1999: 27-73.

Stiegler, Bernard. "The time of cinema." Trans. G. Collins. *Teknema. Journal of Philosophy and Technology,* 4/1998: 62-113.

Sæther, Susanne Østby. *The Aesthetics of Sampling: Engaging the Media in Recent Video Art.* Oslo: Department of Media and Communicaton, 2009.

Talbot, Frederick. *Moving Pictures: How They are Made and Worked.* London: J.B. Lippincott Co, 1912.

Vacche, Angela Dalle. *Cinema and Painting. How Art is used in Film.* London: Athlone, 1996.

Valery, Paul. "The Conquest of Ubiquity." *Aesthetics: The Collected Works of Paul Valery,* Volume XIII. Ed. Jackson Mathews. London: Routledge, 1964.

Vertov, Dziga. *The Writings of Dziga Vertov.* Ed. Annette Michelson, trans. Kevin O'Brien. Berkeley: University of California Press, 1984.

Viola, Bill. *Reasons for Knocking at an Empty House. Writings 1973-1994.* Cambridge, Mass.: The MIT Press, 1995.

Wade, Nicholas J. Ed. *A Natural History of Vision.* Cambridge: MIT Press, 1998.

Walsh, John. "Emotions in Extreme Time: Bill Viola's *Passions* project." *Bill Viola The Passions.* Ed. John Walsh. Los Angeles: Getty Publications, 2003: 25-64.

Weber, Samuel. "Mass Mediauras, or: Art, Aura and Media in the Work of Walter Benjamin." *Mass Mediauras; Form, Technics, Media.* Stanford: Stanford University Press, 1996.

Wees, William C. *Recycled Images. The Art and Politics of Found Footage Films.* New York: Anthology Archives, 1993.

Wik, Annika. *Förebild film. Panoreringer över den samtida konstscenen.* Stockholm: Aura förlag, 2001.

Zielinski, Siegfried. *Deep Time of the Media. Toward an Archaeology of Hearing and Seeing by Technical Means.* Trans. G. Custance. Cambridge, Massachusetts: The MIT Press, 2006 [2002].

Zielinski, Siegfried. *Audiovisions. Cinema and television as entr'actes in history.* Trans. G. Custance. Amsterdam: Amsterdam University Press, 1999 [1989].

Contributors

George Baker is Associate Professor of Art History at UCLA, where he has taught modern and contemporary art and theory since 2003. A New York and Paris-based critic for Artforum magazine throughout the 1990s, he also works as an editor of the journal October and its publishing imprint October Books. Baker is the author, most recently, of *The Artwork Caught by the Tail: Francis Picabia and Dada in Paris* (MIT Press, 2007), and several other books including *James Coleman: Drei Filmarbeiten* (Sprengel Museum, 2002), and *Gerard Byrne: Books, Magazines, and Newspapers* (Lukas & Sternberg, 2003). He has published essays on a variety of postmodern and contemporary artists including Robert Smithson, Robert Whitman, Anthony McCall, Paul Thek, Louise Lawler, Andrea Fraser, Christian Philipp Müller, Tom Burr, Rachel Harrison, Richard Hawkins, Paul Chan, and Knut Åsdam. Currently, he is working on disparate projects including a revisionist study of Picasso's modernism and a shorter book on the work of four women artists – Zoe Leonard, Tacita Dean, Moyra Davey and Sharon Lockhart – to be entitled *Lateness and Longing: On the Afterlife of Photography*. The latter is part of a larger project that Baker has termed "photography's expanded field," detailing the fate of photography and film works in contemporary cultural production.

Thomas Elsaesser has worked as Professor at the University of Amsterdam, and Chair of the Department of Film and Television Studies (1991-2001). His essays on film theory, film genre, film history and television have appeared in well over two hundred collections and anthologies, with essays translated into in French, German, Italian, Spanish, Portuguese, Danish, Dutch, Polish, Slovenian, Czech, Chinese, Japanese and Korean. His books as author include *New German Cinema: A History* (London: Macmillan and New Brunswick: Rutgers University Press, 1989, reprinted 1994) which received the Jay Leyda Prize (NYU) and the Kovacs Book Award (SCMS), *Fassbind's Germany: History Identity Subject* (Amsterdam: AUP, 1996), *Weimar Cinema and After* (London/ New York: Routledge, 2000 [winner of the Kovacs Book Award of SCMS]), *Metropolis* (London: BFI, 2000), (with W.Buckland) *Studying Contemporary American Film* (London/NY, 2002) and *Filmgeschichte und Frühes Kino* (Munich, 2002), *European Cinema: Face to Face with Hollywood* (Amsterdam: Amsterdam University Press, 2005), and edited *Early Cinema: Space Frame Narrative* (London: British Film Institute and Bloomington: Indiana University Press, 1990), *The Last Great Ameri-*

can Picture Show (Amsterdam: Amsterdam University Press, 2004), *Harun Farocki: Working on the Sight Lines* (Amsterdam: Amsterdam University Press,
2004).

Ina Blom is Professor at the Department of Philosophy, Classics, History of Art
and Ideas, University of Oslo. She is the author of *On The Style Site. Art Sociality
and Media Culture,* (Sternberg Press, 2007), *Joseph Beuys* (Gyldendal, 2001), *The
Postal Performance of Ray Johnson* (Kassel/Sittard 2003) and *The Cut Through
Time. A Version of the Dada/Neo-Dada Repetition,* (Acta Humaniora, 1999). Her
field of research is modernism/avant-garde studies and contemporary art with
a special emphasis on media aesthetics and the relationship between art, technology, media and politics. She is currently directing the research project *The
Archive in Motion* (2011-2013) and is also a regular contributor to *Artforum,
Frieze, Parkett* and *Texte zur Kunst.* A book on Raoul Hausmann and the avant-
gardes (edited with Timothy Benson and Hanne Bergius) is forthcoming from
Les presses du réel.

Christa Blümlinger is Professor in film studies at the University Vincennes-
Saint-Denis (Paris 8). Among her former teaching activities, assistant professor
at the University Sorbonne Nouvelle (Paris 3), assistant professor and guest professor at the Free University Berlin. Numerous curatorial and critical activities
in Vienna, Berlin and Paris. Her publications include the edition of writings of
Harun Farocki (in french) and of Serge Daney (in german) and books about
essay film, media art, avantgarde cinema and film aesthetics. Her recent publications in german include : *Kino aus Zweiter Hand. Zur Ästhetik materieller An-
eignung im Film und in der Medienkunst,* Berlin: Vorwerk 8, 2009 (about appropriation in cinema and media art), and in french, *Théâtres de la mémoire.
Mouvement des images,* co-ed. with Sylvie Lindeperg, Michèle Lagny *et alii,* Paris,
Presses Sorbonne Nouvelle, « Théorème 14 », 2011. In English, she published
numerous articles about film aesthetics and media art, such as "Harun Farocki,
the art of the possible" [2002], in Tanya Leighton (ed), *Art and the Moving Image,
A Critical Reader,* Tate Publishing, London, 2008, p. 273-282; "Remake, Ready-
Made, Reconfiguration: Film as Metahistory", in Hans D. Christ and Iris Dress-
ler (ed), *Stan Douglas, Past Imperfect,* Ostfildern, Hatje Cantz, 2007, p. 31-39; "Lumière, the Train and the Avant-Garde" in Wanda Strauven (ed.),*The Cinema of
Attractions Reloaded,* Amsterdam University Press, 2006, p. 245-265; "The imaginary of the documentary image. On Chris Marker's *Level Five*" (2000), in *Image
& Narrative,* Vol 11, No 1 (2010), http://ojs.arts.kuleuven.be/index.php/imagen-
arrative/issue/view/4; "Figures of Disgust", in Roy Grundmann (ed.), *A Companion to Michael Haneke,* Chichester: Wiley-Blackwell, 2010, p. 147-160.

Liv Hausken is Associate Professor at Department of Media and Communication, University of Oslo, and the leader of the research project "Media Aesthetics – Materiality, Practice, Experience" of which the seminar on Visual Culture: Images Between the Still and the Moving is part. Her doctoral dissertation, *Of the untimely. Media-analytic investigations of photography, narrative and slide-motion film* (in Norwegian 1998), focuses on the experience of temporality influenced by and connected to modern media and different forms of expression. Through critical readings and discussions of the figures of death in a phenomenological theory of photography (Barthes 1980) and in a psychoanalytical theory of narrative (Brooks, 1984), the temporalities of photography and narrative are put into play with the strange temporality of what she calls the slide-motion film, a concept developed in this dissertation. She is the co-editor, with Peter Larsen, of *Medievitenskap*, a four-volume textbook in Media Studies (1999), and has published numerous articles on narrative theory, film, television, photography, and medical imaging, most recently "The Aesthetics of X-ray Imaging" in Melberg, Arne (ed.) *Aesthetics at Work* (2007), and "Billedbehandling og troverdighet" (Photographic modification and credibility), in Skogerbø, Eli og Enli, Gunn (eds.) *Digitale Dilemma* (2008).

Tom Gunning is Professor at the Department of Art History, Committee on Cinema & Media Studies, University of Chicago. His published work (approximately one hundred publications) has concentrated on early cinema (from its origins to the WW I) as well as on the culture of modernity from which cinema arose (relating it to still photography, stage melodrama, magic lantern shows, as well as wider cultural concerns such as the tracking of criminals, the World Expositions, and Spiritualism). His concept of the "cinema of attractions" has tried to relate the development of cinema to other forces than storytelling, such as new experiences of space and time in modernity, and an emerging modern visual culture. His field specialities are international early and silent cinema; American avant-garde cinema; Hollywood film genres; film and narrative theory; classical film theory; film and still photography; Japanese cinema; early cinema and the experience of modernity; directors' styles (especially, Lang, Griffith, Von Strernberg, Hitchcock, Godard, Bresson, Borzage); film historiography; film exhibition and spectatorship; modernist cinema of the twenties (Soviet, French, and German). Among his publications we find *D.W. Griffith and the Origins of American Narrative Film: The Early Years at Biograph*. University of Illinois Press, 1991; "From Kaleidoscope to the X-Ray: Urban Spectatorship, Poe, Benjamin and Traffic is Souls (1913)" in *Wide Angle*, Vol. 19, no. 4, pp. 25-63; "Tracing the Individual Body AKA Photography, Detectives, Early Cinema and the Body of Modernity" in *Cinema and the Invention of Modern Life* ed. Vanessa R. Schwartz and Leo Charney (University of California Press, 1995); "The Horror of Opacity: The Melodrama of Sensation in the Plays of André de Lorde" in *Melodrama – Stage, Picture, Screen* BFI ed. J.S. Bratton, Jim Cook and Christine Gledhill, 1994; "An Aesthetic of Astonishment: Early Film and the [In]Credulous Spectator" in *Viewing Positions*, ed. Linda Williams (New Brunswick: Rutgers, 1995); and "The Cinema of Attractions: Early Film, Its Spectator and the Avant-Garde"; in *Early Film* ed. Thomas Elsaesser and Adam Barker (British Film Institute, 1989).

Mark B.N. Hansen is Professor of English and Cinema/Media Studies at Duke University. He is author of *Embodying Technesis: Technology Beyond Writing* (Michigan 2000), *New Philosophy for New Media* (MIT 2004), and *Bodies in Code* (Routledge 2006), as well as numerous essays on cultural theory, contemporary literature, and media. He has co-edited (with Taylor Carman) *The Cambridge Companion to Merleau-Ponty* and *Critical Terms for Media Studies* (with W.J.T. Mitchell) and *Neocybernetic Emergence* (with Bruce Clarke).

His current projects include: *The Politics of Presencing*, a study of embodied human agency in the context of realtime media and computing, Becoming-Human, an ethics of the posthuman, and *Fiction After Television*, a study of the novel in the age of digital convergence.

Arild Fetveit is Associate Professor, dr.art., in the Department of Media, Cognition, and Communication, University of Copenhagen, Denmark. He has published in the fields of reception studies, reality TV, and digitalization of film and photography, and has written a dissertation on the discursive possibilities between documentary and fiction film. He is now working on the digitalization of photography as part of the research project Media Aesthetics, located at the University of Oslo. He is also the director of the research network, Digital Art and Culture in the Age of Pervasive Computing (funded by the Danish Research Council in the period 2007-2009). His latest publication is a co-edited volume of Northern Lights on Digital Aesthetics and Communication (Intellect Press, 2007).

Trond Lundemo is Associate Professor at the Film Department, University of Stockholm. In 2002 and 2004/2005 he was visiting professor at Seijo University in Tokyo. His research interests are sentered around time technologies, aesthetics and intermediality with focus on the mnemotechniques of the digital archives, the film theory of Jean Epstein and Japanese film from the interwar period. His publications include amongst others *Bildets oppløsning; Filmens bevegelse i teoretisk og historisk perspektiv* (1996); *Jean Epstein: The Intelligence of a Machine* (2001) and two anthologies on the relation between film and other art forms (*Film/Konst*, Kairos vol. 9:1 og 9:2, 2004).

Eivind Røssaak is Associate Professor at the Department of Scholarship and Collections at the National Library of Oslo, The Film and Music Section. Visiting Associate Professor at Cinema and Media Studies, University of Chicago (2011). Visiting Scholar at the Cinema Department, New York University (2008). His publications include amongst others *The Still/Moving Image: Cinema and the Arts*, 2010; *The Archive in Motion* (editor), 2010; *Sic: Fra Litteraturens Randsoner*, 2001; *Selviakttakelse en tendens i kunst og litteratur*, 2005; *Kissing and fighting. Four chapters on film*, (in Norwegian with C. Refsum) 2004; "Acts of Delay: The Play Between Stillness and Motion in *Tom, Tom, the Piper's Son*" in *Optic Antics* ed. M. Pierson, P. Arthur and D. James (Oxford 2011), "The unseen of the real: Or, Evidential Efficacy from Muybridge to The Matrix" in *Witness. Memory, Representation, and the Media in Question.* Ed. Ulrik Ekman. Copenhagen, 2008; "Showteori. *Is that what you want?*" in Ove Solum og Ola Erstad (ed.): *Refleksjoner over film*, Oslo: Gyldendal Forlag, 2007; "Figures of Sensation. Between still and moving images." In *The Cinema of Attractions Reloaded* Ed. Wanda Strauen, Amsterdam. University of Amsterdam Press, 2006, and he has reviewed several of the *documenta*-exhibitions and *La Biennale di Venezia* in different media focusing on the moving image works.

Film Culture in Transition

General Editor: *Thomas Elsaesser*

Thomas Elsaesser, Robert Kievit and Jan Simons (eds.)
Double Trouble: Chiem van Houweninge on Writing and Filming, 1994
ISBN paperback 978 90 5356 025 9

Thomas Elsaesser, Jan Simons and Lucette Bronk (eds.)
Writing for the Medium: Television in Transition, 1994
ISBN paperback 978 90 5356 054 9

Karel Dibbets and Bert Hogenkamp (eds.)
Film and the First World War, 1994
ISBN paperback 978 90 5356 064 8

Warren Buckland (ed.)
The Film Spectator: From Sign to Mind, 1995
ISBN paperback 978 90 5356 131 7; ISBN hardcover 978 90 5356 170 6

Egil Törnqvist
Between Stage and Screen: Ingmar Bergman Directs, 1996
ISBN paperback 978 90 5356 137 9; ISBN hardcover 978 90 5356 171 3

Thomas Elsaesser (ed.)
A Second Life: German Cinema's First Decades, 1996
ISBN paperback 978 90 5356 172 0; ISBN hardcover 978 90 5356 183 6

Thomas Elsaesser
Fassbinder's Germany: History Identity Subject, 1996
ISBN paperback 978 90 5356 059 4; ISBN hardcover 978 90 5356 184 3

Thomas Elsaesser and Kay Hoffmann (eds.)
Cinema Futures: Cain, Abel or Cable? The Screen Arts in the Digital Age, 1998
ISBN paperback 978 90 5356 282 6; ISBN hardcover 978 90 5356 312 0

Siegfried Zielinski
Audiovisions: Cinema and Television as Entr'Actes in History, 1999
ISBN paperback 978 90 5356 313 7; ISBN hardcover 978 90 5356 303 8

Kees Bakker (ed.)
Joris Ivens and the Documentary Context, 1999
ISBN paperback 978 90 5356 389 2; ISBN hardcover 978 90 5356 425 7

Egil Törnqvist
Ibsen, Strindberg and the Intimate Theatre: Studies in TV Presentation, 1999
ISBN paperback 978 90 5356 350 2; ISBN hardcover 978 90 5356 371 7

Michael Temple and James S. Williams (eds.)
The Cinema Alone: Essays on the Work of Jean-Luc Godard 1985-2000, 2000
ISBN paperback 978 90 5356 455 4; ISBN hardcover 978 90 5356 456 1

Patricia Pisters and Catherine M. Lord (eds.)
Micropolitics of Media Culture: Reading the Rhizomes of Deleuze and Guattari, 2001
ISBN paperback 978 90 5356 472 1; ISBN hardcover 978 90 5356 473 8

William van der Heide
Malaysian Cinema, Asian Film: Border Crossings and National Cultures, 2002
ISBN paperback 978 90 5356 519 3; ISBN hardcover 978 90 5356 580 3

Bernadette Kester
Film Front Weimar: Representations of the First World War in German Films of the Weimar Period (1919-1933), 2002
ISBN *paperback 978 90 5356 597 1;* ISBN *hardcover 978 90 5356 598 8*

Richard Allen and Malcolm Turvey (eds.)
Camera Obscura, Camera Lucida: Essays in Honor of Annette Michelson, 2003
ISBN paperback 978 90 5356 494 3

Ivo Blom
Jean Desmet and the Early Dutch Film Trade, 2003
ISBN paperback 978 90 5356 463 9; ISBN hardcover 978 90 5356 570 4

Alastair Phillips
City of Darkness, City of Light: Émigré Filmmakers in Paris 1929-1939, 2003
ISBN paperback 978 90 5356 634 3; ISBN hardcover 978 90 5356 633 6

Thomas Elsaesser, Alexander Horwath and Noel King (eds.)
The Last Great American Picture Show: New Hollywood Cinema in the 1970s, 2004
ISBN paperback 978 90 5356 631 2; ISBN hardcover 978 905356 493 6

Thomas Elsaesser (ed.)
Harun Farocki: Working on the Sight-Lines, 2004
ISBN paperback 978 90 5356 635 0; ISBN hardcover 978 90 5356 636 7

Kristin Thompson
Herr Lubitsch Goes to Hollywood: German and American Film after World War I, 2005
ISBN paperback 978 90 5356 708 1; ISBN hardcover 978 90 5356 709 8

Marijke de Valck and Malte Hagener (eds.)
Cinephilia: Movies, Love and Memory, 2005
ISBN paperback 978 90 5356 768 5; ISBN hardcover 978 90 5356 769 2

Thomas Elsaesser
European Cinema: Face to Face with Hollywood, 2005
ISBN paperback 978 90 5356 594 0; ISBN hardcover 978 90 5356 602 2

Michael Walker
Hitchcock's Motifs, 2005
ISBN paperback 978 90 5356 772 2; ISBN hardcover 978 90 5356 773 9

Nanna Verhoeff
The West in Early Cinema: After the Beginning, 2006
ISBN paperback 978 90 5356 831 6; ISBN hardcover 978 90 5356 832 3

Anat Zanger
Film Remakes as Ritual and Disguise: From Carmen to Ripley, 2006
ISBN paperback 978 90 5356 784 5; ISBN hardcover 978 90 5356 785 2

Wanda Strauven
The Cinema of Attractions Reloaded, 2006
ISBN paperback 978 90 5356 944 3; ISBN hardcover 978 90 5356 945 0

Malte Hagener
*Moving Forward, Looking Back: The European Avant-garde and the Invention of Film
     Culture, 1919-1939,* 2007
ISBN paperback 978 90 5356 960 3; ISBN hardcover 978 90 5356 961 0

Tim Bergfelder, Sue Harris and Sarah Street
*Film Architecture and the Transnational Imagination: Set Design in 1930s European
     Cinema,* 2007
ISBN paperback 978 90 5356 984 9; ISBN hardcover 978 90 5356 980 1

Jan Simons
Playing the Waves: Lars von Trier's Game Cinema, 2007
ISBN paperback 978 90 5356 991 7; ISBN hardcover 978 90 5356 979 5

Marijke de Valck
Film Festivals: From European Geopolitics to Global Cinephilia, 2007
ISBN paperback 978 90 5356 192 8; ISBN hardcover 978 90 5356 216 1

Asbjørn Grønstad
Transfigurations: Violence, Death, and Masculinity in American Cinema, 2008
ISBN paperback 978 90 8964 010 9; ISBN hardcover 978 90 8964 030 7

Vinzenz Hediger and Patrick Vonderau (eds.)
Films that Work: Industrial Film and the Productivity of Media, 2009
ISBN paperback 978 90 8964 013 0; ISBN hardcover 978 90 8964 012 3

Pasi Väliaho
Mapping the Moving Image: Gesture, Thought and Cinema circa 1900, 2010
ISBN paperback 978 90 8964 140 3; ISBN hardcover 978 90 8964 141 0

Pietsie Feenstra
New Mythological Figures in Spanish Cinema: Dissident Bodies under Franco
ISBN paperback 978 90 8964 304 9; ISBN hardcover 978 90 8964 303 2